INSPIRALIZED
& BEYOND

INSPIRALIZED & BEYOND

SPIRALIZE / CHOP /
RICE & MASH
YOUR VEGETABLES
INTO CREATIVE,
CRAVEABLE MEALS

ALI MAFFUCCI

Clarkson Potter/Publishers
New York

Copyright © 2018 by Alissandra Maffucci
Photographs copyright © 2018 by Evan Sung

Published in the United States by Clarkson Potter/Publishers,
an imprint of the Crown Publishing Group, a division of
Penguin Random House LLC, New York.
crownpublishing.com
clarksonpotter.com

CLARKSON POTTER is a trademark and POTTER with colophon
is a registered trademark of Penguin Random House LLC.

Library of Congress Cataloging-in-Publication Data is available.

ISBN 978-1-5247-6268-1
Ebook ISBN 978-1-5247-6269-8

Printed in China

Book and cover design by Laura Palese
Cover photographs by Evan Sung

1 3 5 7 9 10 8 6 4 2

First Edition

TO MY BABY BOY,
LUCA LEO.
Everything from
this point on is for you.
Mommy loves you.

CONTENTS

INTRODUCTION

The question I get asked most is, "Do you only eat spiralized food?" I am the self-proclaimed biggest proponent and fan of spiralizing, so it's a completely warranted question.

But let me back up. If you're new to Inspiralized, allow me to introduce myself. (If you're already familiar with Inspiralized and you're flipping through this book wondering why you're seeing non-spiralized recipes, hang tight and I'll explain that, too.)

In 2013, I quit my corporate job to pursue a dream of building Inspiralized, a healthy brand and community dedicated to cooking with the spiralizer, a kitchen tool that transforms vegetables and fruits into noodles. Inspiralized started off as a food blog, but over these past few years, it's grown to much more than that, including the creation of my own branded spiralizer and the publishing of two cookbooks on the topic. Needless to say, I've been busy spiralizing for a while now!

I never get bored of spiralizing—not with so many fruits and vegetables that can be spiralized and so many ways to cook spiralized noodles. And I'm constantly discovering new produce to use. I recently did pineapple for the first time! But while, yes, I *do* spiralize almost every single day . . . I *don't* exclusively eat spiralized food. Cue the gasps!

What initially drew me to spiralizing was how it unleashed my creative side in the kitchen, where I had previously been in a rut. I felt inspired to transform all my food into something exciting. Every meal could be a magical, inventive piece of art—a masterful Bolognese over zucchini noodles or the perfect chicken and carrot noodle soup. I don't think I've made a boring meal since!

Most important, these recipes became integral to my own personal health journey. After launching Inspiralized, my spiralized recipes helped me lose thirty pounds. As someone who had struggled with portion control and weight yo-yoing in the past, I found that spiralizing was a way to have my cake and eat it, too—I could eat piping-hot bowls of noodles and still trim my waistline *and* get in the essential nutrients my body needed to thrive. I loved spiralizing for its health benefits, but also because of its versatility—a simple pasta dish could take on dozens of new flavors by simply swapping in a different spiralized vegetable. Talk about ditching the dinner rut!

After losing the weight, I went into maintenance mode and knew I needed to find more creative ways to cook vegetables to keep up the momentum and to adopt a lifelong healthy lifestyle, not just a diet.

I started experimenting, and so began the next phase of my healthy-eating journey. I looked at every vegetable in the grocery store as something that could be transformed into something else, or incorporated ingeniously into a meal. When I started posting my nonspiralized healthy creations on Instagram, instead of saying, "But this isn't spiralized!" my followers asked, "Where's the recipe?!"

Bursting at the seams, I could not be more excited (and ready!) to share those meals and recipes with you now. I've written this cookbook as a direct reflection of how I eat: healthfully and creatively, both spiralized and non-spiralized.

Say good-bye to your basic steamed veggies forever, and keep reading. We're about to go beyond Inspiralized—are you ready? I am.

HOW TO
GET INSPIRALIZED
& HOW TO
GO BEYOND

By now you know what Inspiralized is, but what does the "beyond" part mean? It means all the *other* creative techniques you can use to transform vegetables into deliciously healthy meals. I'll tell you all about them. In *Inspiralized & Beyond*, we're not just making vegetables taste good, we're turning them into meals that will inspire you and surprise both your mind and your taste buds. While most of the recipes feature fruits or vegetables used as substitutes for meats or processed foods (like bread), there are also some recipes that are just creative ways to prepare and cook vegetables. Produce is meant to be filling *and* fulfilling.

Let's go over some of the techniques we'll use throughout this book so you can get cooking!

SPIRALIZING

To spiralize, you use a gadget called a spiralizer to turn vegetables and fruits into noodles. Spiralizers started gaining popularity around 2013 and are now sold at almost all kitchenware stores and online. There are two main types of spiralizers: handheld and countertop. Handheld spiralizers allow you to spiralize only small, thin vegetables like zucchini, cucumbers, and carrots. Countertop spiralizers are more substantial and allow you to get to work on any vegetable that can be spiralized. There are many brands out there, but the one I use and recommend is the one I created: the Inspiralizer.

Spiralizing encourages you to eat seasonally, strolling farmer's markets and produce aisles for "spiralizable" vegetables (there's a full list of these on page 282). Spiralizing is easy and quick—with just three steps, you can create colorful noodles in seconds!

1   **PREPARE YOUR PRODUCE** / The only requirements are that the fruit or veggie has to be at least 1½ inches in diameter and at least 2 inches long, have a firm flesh (no squishy tomatoes!), and not have a hard core (like an avocado pit). If your fruit or vegetable has inedible skin, peel it. If the skin is edible, just scrub it well and leave it on—the skin usually contains many nutrients. Then, slice the ends off to create flat and even surfaces so the vegetable can be secured onto the spiralizer.

2   **SELECT YOUR NOODLE SHAPE** / While all spiralizers are different, most come with one to four blades, which yield different noodle shapes (see Box, opposite, for descriptions). Select a blade based on the dish you're making. In this cookbook, I'll tell you which blade to use in the ingredients list.

3   **LOAD YOUR PRODUCE AND SPIRALIZE** / Secure the vegetable onto the spiralizer and twist the vegetable (handheld) or spin the handle (countertop). The vegetable will transform into noodles instantly!

It really is as straightforward as 1–2–3, and the more you spiralize, the more comfortable you'll feel with different types of produce. I recommend starting with zucchini because it's easy to work with and can be used in pretty much any style and type of dish, from a casserole to a curry.

As spiralizing continues to grow in popularity, brands have popped up that sell packaged, prespiralized vegetables for those who may not have a spiralizer at home or are truly in a pinch and want to save a couple extra minutes. Some grocery chains such as Whole Foods and Trader Joe's offer these vegetable noodles at their salad bars and prepackaged as well.

SPIRALIZER BLADES

All spiralizers have different blade systems, so it's best to consult your product's manual. Here are general guidelines for most four-blade countertop spiralizers. If you're using the Inspiralizer, these letters will correspond to those on the tool. If not, follow the manufacturer's instructions, using these descriptions as a guide.

- **Blade A:** Yields thin, ribbonlike noodles similar to pappardelle.
- **Blade B:** Yields thicker noodles similar to bucatini or fettuccine.
- **Blade C:** Yields flatter, linguine-shaped noodles.
- **Blade D:** Yields classic spaghetti-shaped noodles.

BEYOND

Now let's go over some of the other main techniques used throughout this book.

Noodles

While spiralizing will always be my preferred way to mimic noodles, you can use many other creative techniques to always keep your taste buds guessing.

SPAGHETTI SQUASH

When cooked, the flesh of spaghetti squash can be scraped out with a fork or tongs into noodlelike strands. We use this technique for Spaghetti Squash Fideos with Shrimp and Chorizo (page 161), but it also makes a great substitute for a potato in dishes like the Cheesy Squashbrown Skillet with Bacon & Eggs on page 59.

To make spaghetti squash noodles, preheat the oven to 400 degrees. Halve the squash lengthwise. Scoop out and discard the seeds. Place the squash on a baking sheet, cut-side down. Bake for 35 to 45 minutes, or until fork-tender. Flip the squash over, flesh-side up, and let cool. When it's just cool enough to handle, use a fork or tongs to scrape the flesh out of the shell in strands.

BRUSSELS SPROUTS

It may sound like a bit of a stretch, but when Brussels sprouts are shaved, they become short crunchy tendrils that can be quickly sautéed and plated as pasta with your desired sauce and fixings.

To make Brussels sprout noodles, slice off the roots and pick off any outer browned leaves. Using a mandoline, carefully hold the sprout by the top and run it over the blade of the mandoline. Or prop the sprout up on its side and, using a very sharp chef's knife, slice it lengthwise as thin as possible.

ASPARAGUS

Asparagus spears can be shaved into noodles. They taste a bit earthy when raw, so they pair well with a dressing or sauce with a bolder flavor, such as a creamy pesto. The noodles can also be lightly sautéed with garlic and olive oil to cut some of the earthy flavor.

To make asparagus noodles, snap the woody bottoms off the spears. Lay an asparagus spear flat on the cutting board and, holding a vegetable peeler right below the tip, use medium pressure to peel toward the base. Repeat, turning the spear, until you've shaved off as much of the asparagus as possible, then repeat with the remaining spears. I like to chop off the tips afterward and toss them into the pasta.

FENNEL

Fennel has a strong flavor, so it's best to pair this noodle alternative with a bold sauce, such as the fra diavolo on page 154.

To make fennel noodles, halve the fennel bulb and use a mandoline or sharp knife to slice it into thin strips. When you add them to a hot pan, they'll wilt to an al dente texture.

LONG BEANS

Long beans are, well, *long* enough to mimic a noodle and can be sautéed with a sauce to create a healthy pasta or noodle dish. No extra prep needed!

Rice

Using various techniques, vegetables can also be broken down into rice-like bits and used to re-create your favorite rice dishes.

SPIRALIZED VEGETABLE RICE

I find spiralized rice to be the most rice-like alternative to true rice. Its consistency is firmer and more solid than a fluffy cauliflower rice, and because you can spiralize twenty-five to thirty different vegetables, you can make that many spiralized rice varieties! Select your spiralized vegetable based on what kind of dish and flavor you're going for.

Spiralize your vegetable of choice, then pack the noodles into a food processor and pulse until broken down into rice-like bits.

I recommend sautéing spiralized vegetable rice in a skillet a healthy oil, but it can also be simmered in soups like Tuscan White Bean and Chard Soup with Celeriac Rice (page 102) or baked into casseroles. Treat cooked spiralized rice just like you would regular rice.

CAULIFLOWER RICE

After spiralized vegetable rice, cauliflower rice is your next best bet for achieving a realistic consistency. While not as solid or chewy as regular rice, cauliflower rice is easily made in larger quantities (one large head of cauliflower can yield up to 4 cups rice!), and thanks to its muted taste, it goes with every different type of flavor, from Indian curries to Spanish paellas.

To make cauliflower rice, slice off and discard the stem of the cauliflower and separate the head into florets. Put the florets in a food processor and pulse until broken down into ricelike bits. Be careful not to overpulse and turn the cauliflower into mush. It tastes best when cooked—at the very least, toss it with olive oil and garlic and season with salt and pepper.

Cauliflower rice is now also sold at most grocery stores and produced by major brands, such as Green Giant Riced Cauliflower.

OTHER VEGGIE RICE

If you don't have a spiralizer but you want to make vegetable rice other than cauliflower, you can follow the same technique as with cauliflower rice; simply chop your chosen vegetable into ½-inch cubes first.

THE BEST VEGETABLES FOR SPIRALIZED RICE

Beet	Kohlrabi
Butternut Squash	Parsnips
Carrot	Rutabaga
Celeriac	Sweet Potato
Daikon Radish	Turnip
Jicama	

Bread, Toast, Crusts, Wraps & More

When trying to eat a less-processed, wholesome, clean diet, bread products may be your first hurdle. Breads, burger buns, tortillas, and pizza crusts are typically made with added sugars, dairy, preservatives, and, of course, processed wheat. With an open mind and some inventive use and manipulation of vegetables, you'll find yourself forgetting all about that crispy toast and spend more time enjoying what's on it or between it.

SPIRALIZED BUNS

Spiralized buns are best used as the base of open-faced sandwiches or, my personal favorite, as pizzas. To make a spiralized bun, first select your vegetable to spiralize. Sweet potatoes, white potatoes, parsnips, and rutabaga make the best noodle buns. Top these buns with burger patties, mashed avocado, cheese, or even bacon and a fried egg.

Spiralize the vegetable, sauté the noodles until wilted and al dente, and then toss the cooked noodles in a bowl with a large egg to coat. Pack the noodles into a ramekin or similar vessel. If you have time, let the ramekins sit in the refrigerator for 10 minutes to chill and set. Heat a large skillet over medium-high heat, flip the ramekin over, and tap the packed noodle bun out of the ramekin and into the skillet. (You can also just drop ⅓ cup of the noodle mixture into a pan and form it into a bun with a spatula. It won't be as pretty, but it will get the job done.) Cook for 3 to 4 minutes, until set on the bottom, then flip and cook for 3 minutes more, or until cooked through, browned, and firm.

VEGETABLE SLABS

Another healthy alternative for replacing toast or a bun is a vegetable slab, a ¼- to ½-inch-thick slice from a round vegetable, from zucchini to rutabaga. These can be used for sliders, mini pizzas, or even breakfast toast. While round cuts of vegetables do tend to work best, if you have another shaped vegetable, you can still make it work, as long as the vegetable is sturdy enough and the surface area can accommodate your desired toppings. These are thinner than spiralized buns, so they're better for closed sandwiches.

TORTILLAS AND TACOS

You can create healthier tortilla options by boiling certain starchy vegetables, mashing them, forming the mash into tortilla-size pieces, and baking. Try this with yucca (see the Yucca Tostadas with Veggies on page 223), plantains (Vegetarian Breakfast Quesadilla with plantain tortillas on page 58), and cauliflower.

Thin slices of jicama (⅛ to ¼ inch thick) can be gently folded and used as taco shells, as well as certain types of lettuces (see below).

LETTUCE AND COLLARD GREENS

Certain types of lettuces and greens can be used as alternatives for taco shells and sandwich wraps.

For use as a lettuce cup or tortilla for a taco, I recommend Boston or Bibb lettuce. The whole leaves are large and cup shaped, perfect for stuffing with something tasty, like Mushroom-Walnut Larb (page 146). You can also use romaine hearts—the extra-large leaves can be stuffed or used to wrap up cold cuts as well.

For a wrap, try collard greens or large cabbage leaves. Fill a large pot halfway with water, bring to a boil, and blanch the cabbage or collard leaves for a minute or two (for collard greens, trim the tough stem off the bottom first). This makes them easier to wrap and less crunchy.

CAULIFLOWER CRUST

Cauliflower is the most popular replacement for pizza crust. It can be a little floppy, so if your first try doesn't turn out great, adjust and give it another try. Cauliflower crust is made of cauliflower rice, egg, cheese, and herbs (see the recipe following). The crust is mixed together to form a dough, molded into a crust, and baked in the oven until firm.

CAULIFLOWER CRUST

SERVES 4

1 medium head cauliflower, cut into florets,
riced, and drained

1 teaspoon dried oregano

½ teaspoon dried basil

½ teaspoon garlic powder

2 large eggs, beaten

2 tablespoons grated Parmesan cheese

¼ cup almond flour

Salt and pepper

Preheat the oven to 425 degrees. Line a rimmed baking sheet or a
10-inch pizza pan with parchment paper.

In a large bowl, combine the cauliflower rice, oregano, basil, garlic
powder, eggs, Parmesan, and almond flour. Season with salt and pepper and
mix thoroughly until doughlike. Spread the dough over the prepared pan,
packing it in until it's about ½ inch thick all around.

Bake for 10 to 15 minutes, or until the crust is firm and lightly golden
brown on the edges. Remove from the oven and transfer the crust, on the
parchment paper, to a wire rack. Top with your desired toppings.

RIBBONED VEGETABLES

If you love spring or summer rolls, you're in luck; you can still enjoy those
favorite flavors, but in a more nourishing way, with veggie ribbons.

To make a cucumber or zucchini ribbon, use a mandoline to slice the
vegetable lengthwise into ⅛-inch-thick strips. Lay out the slices, top with
your desired fillings, and roll up. If you need some inspiration, start with the
Cucumber Summer Rolls with Avocado Mash on page 85.

Other vegetables can also be used to wrap up ingredients and make cooked
bite-size roll-ups, such as the slices of eggplant in Eggplant Rolls with Chicken
Schawarma & Tahini Drizzle (page 174).

BELL PEPPER CUPS

Bell pepper cups are another great vehicle for an open-faced sandwich. Slice the pepper in half lengthwise and remove the stem and seeds. Enjoy it crisp and raw, stuffed with whatever filling you'd like. For a more tender result, preheat the oven to 325 degrees and bake the pepper for 15 to 20 minutes, or until somewhat tender but still firm, before adding your topping or stuffing.

You can also simply slice the tops off bell peppers, remove any seeds, and stuff them whole. While not necessarily a direct sandwich replacement, it's still a healthy, veggie-forward way to make a meal.

PORTOBELLO MUSHROOM CAPS

These large, versatile mushroom caps can be transformed into the base for many meals and pizzas. Preheat the oven to 400 degrees. Scrape out the gills of the cap and stuff or top it as desired. Bake for 15 minutes or until tender, and use as a burger bun, mini pizza crust, or base for an open-faced sandwich.

BREADING & BREAD CRUMBS

Bread and flour aren't just used for sandwiches and pizzas; they're also found in most crunchy coatings. Try using toasted quinoa or a less-processed flour such as almond flour to encrust or bread meats.

Bread crumbs are also used to bind meat, as in meatballs. Try almond flour, pulsed broccoli florets, or even chia seeds as a healthier binder.

Meats

With the right seasonings and marinades, a vegetable can be substituted for an animal protein.

MUSHROOMS

Highly absorbent and easily softened, mushrooms of all kinds can be used in place of meat. Marinate portobello caps and use them like burger patties. Transform oyster and shiitake mushrooms into bacon by marinating them with soy sauce, liquid smoke, or maple syrup, and baking them at 350 degrees for 20 minutes, flipping halfway through.

LENTILS & QUINOA

Cooked with other vegetables, oats, and nuts, these grains make a good vegetarian stand-in for meatballs or Lentil Meat Loaf (page 186). Mixed with dried herbs and tomatoes, lentils and quinoa turn into vegetarian versions of meat ragus, like bolognese sauce.

CHICKPEAS

Another versatile all-star ingredient, chickpeas are a hearty source of dietary fiber and vegan protein. They absorb flavor well and can be seasoned to mimic the flavor of meat, and roasted until crispy as a vegetarian alternative. For instance, by mashing them with avocado and seasoning with Dijon mustard, salt, pepper, and some lemon juice, you can make a vegetarian version of classic tuna salad (see page 126).

The *liquid* from a can of chickpeas (called aquafaba) is even transformative! By taking aquafaba and whipping it at medium-high speed, you can create a cream with medium-stiff peaks that can be used in desserts and savory foods as an egg replacement or dairy-free version of cream.

WALNUTS

Pulsed until chunky-ground, sautéed with veggies, and seasoned appropriately, walnuts transform into a meat crumble—just try my jicama tacos (see page 206)!

JACKFRUIT & HEARTS OF PALM

Jackfruit and hearts of palm can be cooked until they're "shreddable" and thus turned into "pulled meat" with adequate glugs of barbecue sauce and liquid smoke.

HEARTY VEGETABLES

Thanks to their dense and firm texture, these vegetables are perfect for substituting meat. Try using cauliflower as a steak (see page 205), cooking broccoli Margherita-style (see page 70), serving cabbage as a main course (see page 84), and roasting marinated sunchokes like meat (see page 202).

Dairy

Creamy sauces are typically made with butter, cream, and other processed dairy-based ingredients. By soaking cashews and puréeing them with nutritional yeast, broth, and some spices, you can create the same consistency and even flavor. Coconut milk works similarly.

Many creamy soups are made using a roux (a mixture of white flour and fat, usually butter). To avoid these ingredients, you can steam vegetables like potatoes, cauliflower, and celeriac, then purée them to achieve the same thick consistency. Also, arrowroot starch or powder can be used as a healthy thickener. The general rule is to substitute about 2 teaspoons arrowroot powder for 1 tablespoon cornstarch, and 1 tablespoon arrowroot powder for every 1 tablespoon all-purpose flour.

For dressings and sandwich spreads made with mayonnaise, try puréeing an avocado with some Greek yogurt or oil until you reach the desired consistency.

As for cheese alternatives, nuts can be transformed into spreadable, tasty options. Almonds, macadamia, and cashews are the best nuts for this. To make a cheese out of nuts, soak 2 cups raw nuts in water to cover overnight or for at least 6 hours. Drain the nuts and put them in a food processor with nutritional yeast and whatever herbs you'd like to season the cheese with (for instance, for an Italian herbed cheese, use dried basil and oregano). Pulse until the nuts have broken down to a spreadable texture, using vegetable broth as needed to thin until the consistency is cheeselike.

STOCK UP & SET UP

By packing your fridge and pantry properly, you'll never be left with a "there's nothing to eat!" moment. Here are the essentials I always have on hand, including the accompanying cookware that gets the job done.

PANTRY

While my cooking and recipes focus largely on using fresh produce, having a well-stocked pantry is the backbone that pulls it all together. My pantry is never without the following items—and I do an inventory check every two or three weeks for any necessary restocking:

GARLIC / Necessary to start off most meals right; always keep at least one head of garlic in your kitchen.

RED & WHITE ONIONS / Onions are the base of so many meals. They're also great in stir-fries and salads, caramelized on burgers, and layered into sandwiches.

EXTRA-VIRGIN OLIVE OIL / My heart-healthy oil of choice, it is best for roasting, sautéing, and using in dressings.

EXTRA-VIRGIN COCONUT OIL / A great option for high-heat cooking and flavorful baking. Be sure to pick an unrefined coconut oil.

COOKING SPRAY / When greasing pans, ditch the standard vegetable oil spray and squeeze in more heart-healthy fats with an olive oil, avocado oil, or coconut oil spray.

SESAME OIL / Essential for Asian stir-fries. You can use toasted or not, depending on the intensity of flavor desired (toasted is bolder).

ASSORTED CANNED BEANS (NO SALT ADDED) / Black, kidney, and cannellini beans and chickpeas can be used in various types of cuisines and are a quick protein option when you forget to defrost that chicken breast.

LOW-SODIUM CHICKEN & VEGETABLE BROTH / Necessary for making soups and stews, braising, and puréeing; be sure to always opt for low-sodium.

LOW-SODIUM SOY SAUCE / Not only for Asian-inspired cooking, soy sauce can be used to add umami flavor to roasted vegetables and meats. If you're gluten-free, use coconut aminos or gluten-free tamari instead.

FLOURS / Tapioca starch, almond flour, coconut flour, and arrowroot powder are the flours I always have stocked for thickening sauces, lightly breading meats, and more nutritious baking.

VINEGARS / Keep red wine, rice, balsamic, and apple cider vinegars on hand for making marinades and dressings, and even roasting vegetables.

DRIED HERBS & SPICES / You can flavor foods without adding unnecessary processed ingredients, fats, sugars, and high amounts of sodium by using a simple mixture of on-hand spices. Chili powder, parsley, rosemary, thyme, basil, curry powder, coriander, oregano, paprika, cumin, garlic powder, red pepper flakes, bay leaves, onion powder, turmeric, and cinnamon are the bare necessities.

SEA SALT & PEPPERCORNS / Salt and pepper that have been preground can often come pre-processed. Using freshly ground salt and peppercorns not only adds richer flavor but is also healthier.

JARRED PASTA SAUCE / There are so many great brands of jarred pasta sauces out there now that unless you have the time, there's no need to make your own homemade sauce anymore. I like simmering jarred sauce over medium heat for 5 to 10 minutes to thicken and bring out the flavors before incorporating it into my dish. My favorite flavor is tomato-basil and I love Rao's or Victoria Fine Foods because their ingredients are wholesome.

CANNED COCONUT MILK / For curries, marinades, and baking, coconut milk is good to have on hand, especially when cooking Thai cuisine. There are two types: full-fat and "lite." The lite version has less fat and is not as creamy, so if you're trying to keep fat and calories down, choose that one. Full-fat is creamier and has more rich flavor, and it yields thick coconut cream solids when refrigerated overnight, which is useful in baking.

TAHINI / Made from ground sesame seeds and popular in Mediterranean and Middle Eastern cooking, it can be simply whisked together with some lemon juice, water, and garlic and used as a tasty sauce to drizzle on meats and vegetables.

NUT BUTTERS / I'm a nut butter lover and keep way too many varieties in my pantry, but almond or peanut is really all you need. Nut butters are great at breakfast and for snacking, and can be used in dressings and sauces. If you're allergic to nuts but want the same nut-buttery consistency, try sunflower butter, made from ground sunflower seeds.

NUTRITIONAL YEAST FLAKES / These magical flakes make anything taste cheesy. They're the vegan's secret ingredient for making dairy-free versions of classically cheesy, creamy sauces and dips.

HEALTHY GRAINS (BROWN RICE, QUINOA) / Two grains I always have in my pantry are brown rice and quinoa. Brown rice is an excellent source of fiber, helps lower cholesterol, and is a healthy way to add bulk to a vegetarian meal. Quinoa is a complete protein and my all-time favorite grain to mix into everything for an instant protein and nutrient boost—salads, soups, casseroles, even pasta sauces.

LENTILS / A hearty source of vegan protein, lentils are a must for creating filling meals. Lentils can be transformed in soups, lasagnas, salads, ragus, and much more.

MAPLE SYRUP & HONEY / These two are the only sweeteners I have in my home (unless I'm baking something special, in which case I will spring for some coconut sugar). Once you ditch standard sugar, you'll notice how sweet things start to taste, like honey.

DIJON MUSTARD / Essential for making salad dressing, but also convenient for spreading over seafood and using in sandwiches, Dijon mustard is less sour than yellow mustard and thus better for cooking. I typically keep country Dijon and regular Dijon on hand.

CANNED TOMATOES / Especially during the winter, when tomatoes are out of season, canned tomatoes (whole peeled, diced, crushed, or paste) are a hero pantry item. They show up everywhere—sauces, stews, rice dishes, chilies, and curries.

NUTS / Almonds, walnuts, pecans, and cashews can be used simply as a crunchy topping or in trail mix, but their versatility goes way beyond that. Cashews can be soaked and puréed as a substitute for cream and walnuts can be ground as a meat alternative. Nuts are full of proteins, antioxidants, and good fats.

CHIA SEEDS / This superfood isn't only for smoothies and chia puddings! Thanks to its high fiber content, this magical seed can absorb ten to twelve times its weight in water, making it a healthy binding agent for use in foods like meatballs and savory cakes.

COOKWARE

Aside from your basic necessities (skillets, saucepans, baking sheets, baking dishes, mixing bowls, oven mitts, a spatula, a slotted spoon, a quality knife set, a wooden spoon, a vegetable peeler, and a blender), here are some must-haves:

SPIRALIZER / The healthy cook's most essential kitchen tool! Whether handheld or countertop, don't leave your kitchen without one.

MINI FOOD PROCESSOR / If you're primarily cooking for one or two, a mini-chop is great to have on hand. You can make homemade marinades, pestos, dressings, purées, meatball mixes, homemade nut butters, hummus, and more. You can also make small batches of spiralized rice and cauliflower rice (see page 18 for more information). If you're serving more than two or three people, opt for a larger food processor.

WOK / If you love stir-fries or you cook for more than two, a wok is easiest to cook in when making spiralized meals.

SLOW COOKER / Of course, you can survive without a slow cooker, but life is easier with one. Slow cookers are made for busy people or people who don't love to cook but want to make healthier meals to last throughout the week or feed their family.

JULIENNE PEELER / If you don't want to purchase a spiralizer right away, julienne peelers are a good workaround—they're small handheld peelers (the size of a standard vegetable peeler) that turn your vegetable into matchstick-like strips. These small slices can be used as noodles, as crunchy toppings in sandwiches or salads, in slaws, and more.

MANDOLINE / For uniformly slicing vegetables into strips or rounds; ideal for creating gratins, lasagnas, chips, and more.

HOW TO USE
THIS BOOK

You just cook from it, right? Yes, of course! This book is meant to be broken in: stained with drips of olive oil and smudges of avocado, enthusiastically dog-eared and shared with loved ones. My dream is for you to find at least one recipe from this cookbook that you make almost every week, and many more to load up your "go-to" arsenal.

I've built in some extra special features to help you better navigate and decide what you want to make first. Because we all have such different diet preferences, culinary skill levels, time restraints, produce access, and health goals, I've used easy indicators to guide you through each recipe, which are also catalogued in Appendix A (page 276) for quick and easy reference.

Whether you're meal planning for the week ahead or guests are coming over in 20 minutes, you'll know exactly where to look!

DIET AND FEATURE CLASSIFICATION

The following indicators will classify the recipes by diet:

- **Vegan**
- **Vegetarian**
- **Gluten-Free**
- **Paleo**
- **Dairy-Free:** This recipe contains no dairy ingredients.
- **Dairy-Free (opt.):** The dairy in this recipe is not integral to the dish and can be omitted.

The following indicators will give you a bit more background information on each dish:

- **Spiralized:** You'll need a spiralizer to make this recipe.
- **Not Spiralized:** This recipe doesn't use spiralized veggies.
- **Low-Cal:** Under 300 calories per serving.
- **No-Cook:** Doesn't require any heated cooking, so it is mostly assembly-based.
- **Saves Well:** Works well as leftovers (great for meal planning and prepping!).
- **One-Pot:** Cooked in one pan or pot for easy cleanup: my favorite feature!

In addition, all recipes include the following nutritional information: calories, carbohydrates, protein, fat, saturated fat, fiber, and sugar. This information was calculated primarily using data from the USDA National Nutrient Database for Standard Reference.

DIFFICULTY LEVEL

The number of spirals signifies how difficult the recipe is to make even if the recipe is not spiralized.

- ⊚ **One spiral /** Very easy, no or not much cooking required, and if it's spiralized, it's basic spiralizing.

- ⊚⊚ **Two spirals /** Medium difficulty, more preparation and/or cooking required.

- ⊚⊚⊚ **Three spirals /** Most difficult, many steps required, and if it's spiralized, there's more handling of the spiralized vegetables.

Please don't let a three-spiral recipe discourage you from trying it! I'm a self-taught cook myself (thanks to my mother, grandparents, and good ol' Google), and I take pride in writing recipes that are easy and approachable. If I can do it, you can, too!

READING A SPIRALIZED RECIPE

You'll notice that the spiralized recipes have an additional section labeled "Also works well with." Here you'll find a list of a few vegetables that can be spiralized in place of the one in the main ingredient list. If you just really dislike sweet potatoes or can't find turnips at the farmer's market, you'll have other options to spiralize so you can still make the recipe.

In the recipes with spiralized ingredients, those ingredients will be written in this format: *1 medium zucchini, spiralized with Blade D, noodles trimmed*

This tells you which blade to use, and "noodles trimmed" means that the noodles should be cut into 7- to 8-inch pieces with a pair of clean kitchen shears (or a knife) so they're easier to eat. I've seen videos of people jump-roping their 5-foot-long zucchini noodles!

If a recipe includes spiralized rice or a certain type of noodle shape (such as a macaroni-shaped noodle), the indication will be included in the actual recipe directions itself, not the ingredient list.

Furthermore, if there's an instance where a non-spiralized recipe can easily be turned into a spiralized one, I will explain how in the Tip section.

LET'S COOK!

Now that you know what this book is all about and are ready to begin cooking more creatively with vegetables, it's time to start! You're equipped with everything you need to know to turn vegetables into hearty, nourishing, delicious meals.

The point of this cookbook is to get you more excited about eating vegetables. While the Lentil Meat Loaf with BBQ Sauce & Cauliflower Mash (page 186) may not taste just like your grandmother's meat loaf and mashed potatoes, it's not meant to. These lighter, heart-healthier options are meant to act as *alternatives* to your favorites, not replacements. By substituting one of these healthy dishes, you're still doing your taste buds good and doing your body even better. When you do eat more plants, you'll notice your taste buds change and you'll crave fried foods and sweets less often. You may even find yourself craving the plant-based option over the original. At least I do!

While this cookbook is omnivorous, just as I am, the main goal is this: the more veggies, the better! With the help of the recipes in this book, it's an attainable goal. Now, let's get Inspiralized—and beyond!

BREAKFAST

Spiralized / Vegetarian
Gluten-Free

NUTRITIONAL INFORMATION *Per serving*
Calories **346** / Fat **7g** / Sat Fat **2g** / Sodium **78mg**
Carbs **49g** / Fiber **7g** / Sugar **24g** / Protein **24g**

SPIRALIZED

CANTALOUPE & BLACKBERRY GREEK YOGURT BOWL

/ *with* / GOJI BERRY GRANOLA

TIME TO PREPARE
10 minutes

TIME TO COOK
20 minutes

SERVES 8

If prepping cantaloupe this way doesn't make you fall in love with spiralizing, I don't know what will. This fruit is often regarded as filler, but seeing it in this shape and texture truly exemplifies the magic of spiralizing. Not only is noodled cantaloupe easier to eat than large chunks or balls of it, but here, each melon strip also becomes coated in yogurt and granola, making every bite a perfect one. The blackberries complement the tartness of the Greek yogurt, balancing the sweetness in the granola for a well-harmonized bowl of flavors.

For the granola

Coconut oil, for greasing

2 cups gluten-free old-fashioned oats

⅓ cup slivered almonds

⅓ cup pepitas

½ teaspoon ground cinnamon

Pinch of salt

⅓ cup pure maple syrup or honey

1 teaspoon vanilla extract

⅓ cup goji berries

⅓ cup unsweetened coconut flakes

1 medium cantaloupe or honeydew melon (about 3½ pounds), peeled

8 cups nonfat plain Greek yogurt

2 cups blackberries or berry of your choice

Make the granola. Preheat the oven to 325 degrees. Lightly grease a baking sheet with coconut oil.

In a medium bowl, combine the oats, almonds, pepitas, cinnamon, and salt. Add the maple syrup and vanilla and mix well to coat the oats.

Spread out the granola on the prepared baking sheet and bake until golden brown, about 20 minutes, stirring once halfway through to ensure even cooking. Let cool, then transfer the granola to an airtight container along with the goji berries and coconut flakes. Toss well.

While the granola cooks, spiralize the peeled cantaloupe with Blade C. When you hit the seedy center, pull the cantaloupe off the spiralizer and scoop out the seeds with a spoon. Recenter the cantaloupe on the spiralizer and continue spiralizing with Blade C.

When the granola is finished, assemble the bowls. Place 1 cup of the Greek yogurt in each bowl and top each with ¼ cup granola, ¼ cup blackberries, and about 1 cup spiralized cantaloupe. Serve.

TIP / *When purchasing cantaloupe for spiralizing, grasp firmly around the melon. If your hands or fingertips make any imprints, it's overripe and will be too mushy to spiralize. If the cantaloupe is firm but gives just slightly, it's prime for spiralizing!*

Not Spiralized / No-Cook
Saves Well / Vegetarian
Gluten-Free

NUTRITIONAL INFORMATION *Per serving*
Calories **419** / Fat **23g** / Sat Fat **2g** / Sodium **23mg**
Carbs **48g** / Fiber **7g** / Sugar **38g** / Protein **13g**

NO-BAKE GREEK YOGURT TART
/ with / DATE-PECAN CRUST

TIME TO PREPARE
30 minutes

SERVES 6
◎ ◎ ◎

This tart is like a yogurt bowl that's been transformed into something much, much fancier, making it perfect to serve to guests. If you're planning a brunch and want something to make ahead, it also holds up well at room temperature and displays beautifully, especially if you take a little extra time with topping with the berries! You certainly won't miss a classic dough crust with this sweet and grainy date-pecan version—and with no cooking required, could it get any better?

For the crust

2 cups raw pecans

10 Medjool dates, pitted, chopped, soaked in warm water for 10 minutes, and drained

For the filling

1½ cups nonfat plain Greek yogurt

½ cup blueberries

4 strawberries, sliced

2 tablespoons honey

Make the crust. In a food processor, pulse the pecans until ground into a semi-fine meal. Add the dates and pulse until the mixture holds together when pinched and starts to look like dough.

Press the dough into the bottom of a 9½-inch tart pan with a removable bottom to form a flat, even crust. Chill in the freezer for 10 minutes.

Make the filling. Remove the crust from the freezer and carefully slide it onto a round serving platter. Spread the yogurt over the crust. Top the yogurt with the blueberries and strawberries, then drizzle with honey and serve.

TIP / *Make individual tarts by using six ramekins lined with parchment paper and dividing the ingredients accordingly.*

Not Spiralized / No-Cook
Vegetarian / Dairy-Free
Gluten-Free / Paleo

NUTRITIONAL INFORMATION *Per serving*
Calories **492** / Fat **20g** / Sat Fat **6g** / Sodium **174mg**
Carbs **74g** / Fiber **11g** / Sugar **43g** / Protein **14g**

APPLE PIE SMOOTHIE BOWL

TIME TO PREPARE
10 minutes

SERVES 1

Depending on the day, my body craves something either sweet or something savory in the morning—I switch back and forth. Since I'm not always going to grab a doughnut or a chocolate croissant to satisfy a morning sweet tooth, a dessert in a smoothie bowl makes a worthy and satisfying fix. Particularly in the fall when every store you walk into smells like spiced apple lattes and has cider for sale, apple pie is on the mind. This smoothie bowl uses all of the spices and ingredients for a pie, but leaves out the crust, sugar, and butter. Don't let morning sugar cravings ruin your day—make this smoothie instead!

1 large banana, peeled and frozen

½ cup coconut yogurt

1 cup frozen apples (I like Gala)

1 teaspoon ground cinnamon

⅛ teaspoon ground nutmeg

1 date, pitted

½ teaspoon vanilla extract

½ cup unsweetened almond milk

2 tablespoons maple-flavored gluten-free granola

1 tablespoon honey-flavored nut or seed butter

¼ teaspoon apple pie spice or additional cinnamon

In a high-speed blender, combine the banana, yogurt, apples, cinnamon, nutmeg, date, vanilla, and almond milk and purée until smooth. Pour into a medium bowl.

Top the smoothie with granola, nut butter, and apple pie spice. Serve.

TIP / *If you want to use your spiralizer here, spiralize an extra apple and use it as a topping for added crunch and apple flavor.*

Not Spiralized / Saves Well
Vegetarian / Gluten-Free
Paleo / Dairy-Free

NUTRITIONAL INFORMATION *Per cookie*
Calories **287** / Fat **20g** / Sat Fat **5g** / Sodium **73mg**
Carbs **23g** / Fiber **4g** / Sugar **7g** / Protein **5g**

CARROT CAKE BREAKFAST COOKIES

TIME TO PREPARE
15 minutes

TIME TO COOK
20 minutes

**MAKES ABOUT
10 COOKIES**

If you're the dessert-for-breakfast type, these cookies are packed with all the same flavors and ingredients of a classic carrot cake, without the flour or sugary cream cheese frosting. Portable and shareable, these cookies can be made in advance on a meal-prep day and enjoyed all week long. The oats and egg offer protein and fiber that's necessary to keep you fueled for whatever comes your way each day. The oats give these cookies an extra-chewy taste, making them even more cake-like. Who says you can't have dessert for breakfast?

2 cups pecans

2 cups gluten-free old-fashioned oats

1 cup grated carrots

1 teaspoon baking powder

½ teaspoon kosher salt

1 teaspoon ground cinnamon

½ teaspoon ground ginger

1 large egg

¼ cup pure maple syrup

3 tablespoons coconut oil, melted

1 teaspoon vanilla extract

Preheat the oven to 350 degrees. Line two baking sheets with parchment paper.

In a food processor, pulse 1¾ cups of the pecans until they resemble a coarse flour and are starting to stick together. Transfer to a large bowl. Pulse the remaining ¼ cup pecans until finely chopped, about 10 pulses. Add to the same bowl. Add the oats, carrots, baking powder, salt, cinnamon, and ginger and stir well to combine.

In a small bowl, lightly beat the egg, maple syrup, melted coconut oil, and vanilla until combined and pour over the dry ingredients. Stir until the dough is evenly combined.

For each cookie, pack the dough into a ¼-cup measure and turn it out onto the prepared baking sheets. With moistened hands, lightly press the rounds to about ½ inch thick.

Bake the cookies for 20 to 25 minutes, until golden and dry to touch. Let cool completely on the baking sheet before serving. The cookies can be refrigerated for up to 5 days or tightly wrapped and frozen for up to 1 month.

Not Spiralized / Saves Well
Vegan / Gluten-Free
Paleo / Dairy-Free

NUTRITIONAL INFORMATION *For each of 8 servings*
Calories **343** / Fat **17g** / Sat Fat **4g** / Sodium **276mg**
Carbs **37g** / Fiber **9g** / Sugar **12g** / Protein **10g**

BAKED PB&J OATMEAL

/ *with* / CHIA RASPBERRY JAM

TIME TO PREPARE
2 hours

TIME TO COOK
40 minutes

SERVES 6 TO 8

I don't know if my parents made me peanut butter and jelly sandwiches 24/7 while I was growing up or what, but a day never goes by that I don't yearn for one. I'm always craving this classic combination, so in an effort to avoid processed carbohydrates, I've become resourceful. This baked oatmeal has all the same flavors of a PB&J, but without the traditional sandwich bread. Each bite is a mini PB&J in itself with a more exciting texture and, of course, all the nutritional benefits of its clean ingredient list.

1 tablespoon coconut oil, melted and cooled room temperature, plus more for greasing

2 cups gluten-free old-fashioned oats

⅔ cup coarsely chopped walnuts

2 teaspoons ground cinnamon

1 teaspoon baking powder

¾ teaspoon fine sea salt

¼ teaspoon ground nutmeg

1¾ cups unsweetened almond milk, plus more for serving

⅓ cup pure maple syrup

2 large eggs

¼ cup creamy peanut butter or almond butter, plus more for serving

2 teaspoons vanilla extract

Chia Jam (recipe follows), for serving

Preheat the oven to 375 degrees. Grease a 10-inch ovenproof skillet or 9-inch square baking dish with coconut oil.

In a medium bowl, toss the oats, walnuts, cinnamon, baking powder, salt, and nutmeg to combine. In a small bowl, whisk together the almond milk, maple syrup, eggs, melted coconut oil, peanut butter, and vanilla.

Spread the dry oat mixture on the bottom of the prepared skillet, then pour the wet ingredients over the oats. Tip the baking dish back and forth to make sure the almond milk moves down through the oats. Bake for 35 to 40 minutes, until the top is golden.

For each serving spoon about ⅔ cup of the baked oatmeal into a bowl and top with ⅓ cup chia jam and some peanut butter. Serve hot, with a little more almond milk.

TIP / *You can make the chia raspberry jam the night before, or if you don't have time, sub in your favorite jelly or jam—just be careful of added sugars in the ingredient list.*

CHIA JAM

MAKES ABOUT 2 CUPS

10 ounces frozen raspberries

¼ cup chia seeds

1 tablespoon pure maple syrup

In a medium bowl, combine the raspberries, chia seeds, maple syrup, and 1 tablespoon water. Cover and let the mixture defrost for 2 hours at room temperature. Once the berries are defrosted, use the back of a fork to mash up the mixture until jamlike. Store in an airtight container in the refrigerator for up to 1 week.

TIP / *It's important that the apples are ¼-inch-thick slices—if they're thinner, they won't get tender and will just burn.*

Not Spiralized / Vegan
Gluten-Free / Paleo
Dairy-Free

NUTRITIONAL INFORMATION *Per serving*
Calories **374** / Fat **23g** / Sat Fat **18g** / Sodium **1mg**
Carbs **44g** / Fiber **11g** / Sugar **30g** / Protein **2g**

APPLE FRENCH TOAST
/ *with* / CINNAMON STREUSEL

TIME TO PREPARE
10 minutes

TIME TO COOK
10 minutes

SERVES 2

French toast connoisseurs beware, this is not meant to replace traditional French toast. It's merely an all-apple spin on it, using the same flavors. These apple pieces are cooked similarly with cinnamon, vanilla extract, and a sweet cooking fat (here, coconut oil instead of eggs and dairy). With every bite, you'll be amazed by how flavorful an apple can become. For a more complete breakfast, serve these with a side of scrambled eggs for a protein boost.

For the French toast

3 tablespoons coconut oil, melted, plus more for greasing

1 teaspoon ground cinnamon

½ teaspoon vanilla extract

¼ teaspoon ground nutmeg

2 medium to large apples (I like Gala), cored and sliced into ¼-inch-thick rounds

For the streusel

2 tablespoons almond flour

2 tablespoons coconut sugar

1 tablespoon coconut oil, melted and cooled to room temperature

½ teaspoon ground cinnamon

Pinch of salt

Pure maple syrup, for serving

Make the French toast. In a small baking dish, stir together 2 tablespoons of the melted coconut oil, the cinnamon, vanilla, and nutmeg. Add the apple rounds to the baking dish and turn to coat with the oil mixture.

Melt the remaining 1 tablespoon coconut oil in a large skillet over medium-high heat. When the oil is shimmering, add half the apple rounds and cook until browned on the bottom, 3 to 4 minutes. (Reduce the heat to medium as needed to prevent burning.) Flip and cook for 3 minutes more, until the apples are fork-tender. Transfer to a plate. Cook the remaining apples, using more coconut oil if needed to grease the pan.

Make the streusel. In a small bowl, stir together the almond flour, coconut sugar, coconut oil, cinnamon, and salt.

Divide the apple French toast between two plates, sprinkle with the streusel, and drizzle with maple syrup. Serve warm.

Not Spiralized / Saves Well
Vegetarian / Gluten-Free
Dairy-Free (opt.) / Low-Cal

NUTRITIONAL INFORMATION *Per serving*
Calories **174** / Fat **11g** / Sat Fat **4g** / Sodium **177mg**
Carbs **9g** / Fiber **2g** / Sugar **2g** / Protein **11g**

AUTUMN BRUSSELS SPROUT QUICHE

/ *with* / SWEET POTATO CRUST

TIME TO PREPARE
20 minutes

TIME TO COOK
45 minutes

SERVES 6

ⓘ ⓘ ⓘ

A formidable breakfast, lunch, *or* dinner, the quiche is a savory, pastry-crust dish that originated in France but has been adapted by many other cuisines. When I don't know what to serve for guests, I always default to a fluffy quiche with a big green salad on the side. My quiches are totally pastry-less; I use thinly sliced sweet potatoes that bake until tender but crispy, adding a slightly sweet flavor, striking orange color, and whole host of nutrients.

Cooking spray

1 large sweet potato, very thinly sliced, preferably with a mandoline

Fine sea salt and pepper

6 large eggs

⅓ cup unsweetened almond milk

½ cup shredded Gruyère cheese (optional)

1 tablespoon extra-virgin olive oil

½ cup diced white onion

2 garlic cloves, minced

1 cup Brussels sprouts, trimmed and sliced thinly

1 teaspoon fresh rosemary

Preheat the oven to 350 degrees. Grease a 9-inch pie plate with cooking spray.

Arrange the sweet potato slices in an overlapping pattern so they cover the bottom and sides of the prepared pie plate; slice the potatoes in half as needed. (The pieces will shrink as they bake so the slices can extend above the side of the pan.) Spray the sweet potatoes with more cooking spray and season lightly with salt and pepper.

Bake the sweet potato crust for 20 minutes, until tender. Let cool for 5 minutes. Keep the oven on.

Meanwhile, in a medium bowl, whisk together the eggs, almond milk, cheese, a large pinch of salt, and a few grinds of pepper.

Heat the olive oil in a large skillet over medium-high heat. When the oil is shimmering, add the onion, season with salt and pepper, and cook, stirring, until translucent, about 4 minutes. Add the garlic and cook until fragrant, about 30 seconds. Add the Brussels sprouts and a pinch each of salt and pepper and cook until soft, about 4 minutes. Stir in the rosemary and season with more salt and pepper as needed.

Spread the Brussels sprouts mixture over the sweet potato crust, and then pour the egg mixture on top. Bake for 30 to 35 minutes, until the eggs puff up and are set in the center. Remove the quiche from the oven and let cool for 5 minutes before slicing. Serve hot.

TIP / *To make this dish spiralized, slice the sweet potato halfway through lengthwise, being careful not to pierce through the center. Spiralize the sweet potato using Blade A to yield chip-like slices.*

Not Spiralized / Vegetarian
Gluten-Free / Paleo
Dairy-Free / Low-Cal

NUTRITIONAL INFORMATION *Per serving*
Calories **281** / Fat **19g** / Sat Fat **3g** / Sodium **54mg**
Carbs **19g** / Fiber **5g** / Sugar **11g** / Protein **11g**

FLOURLESS BREAKFAST CREPES
/ with / PEACHES & SUNFLOWER BUTTER

TIME TO PREPARE
5 minutes

TIME TO COOK
15 minutes

SERVES 4

One of my most vivid memories from visiting Paris for the first time was ordering a crepe from a vendor on the Champs-Élysées. I wanted to request peanut butter instead of Nutella ("when in Rome" doesn't apply in Paris, right?). But with only an amateur grasp of the French language, I ended up with a Nutella crepe with bananas—and still licked my paper plate clean, by the way. This healthier crepe with sunflower butter and peaches is a reflection of a healthier Ali—and to me, this one even tastes better, despite not being eaten in Paris. *C'est la vie!*

1 large banana

3 large eggs

Coconut oil cooking spray

½ cup sunflower butter, plus more for serving

2 small peaches, pitted and sliced into ¼-inch wedges

In a high-speed blender, purée the banana and eggs until smooth.

Heat a large nonstick skillet over medium-high heat and spray with cooking spray. When water flicked onto the skillet sizzles, pour about ¼ cup of the batter into the pan. Gently swirl the skillet to coat the bottom and form a thin crepe. Cook for 2 to 3 minutes, until the edges are completely set and the crepe starts to look dry on top. Reduce the heat if the crepes start browning too quickly. Carefully flip and cook for 1 minute more, until lightly browned on the bottom. Transfer the crepe to a plate and repeat with the remaining batter.

Divide the crepes among plates and gently spread 2 tablespoons of the sunflower butter over each. Top with the peach slices and roll up like a burrito, taking care not to tear the crepe. Spread with extra sunflower butter, if desired. Serve.

TIP / *If peaches aren't in season, you can use apples or pears instead.*

Spiralized / Saves Well
Vegetarian / Gluten-Free
Paleo / Dairy-Free
Low-Cal

NUTRITIONAL INFORMATION *Per serving*
Calories **161** / Fat **8g** / Sat Fat **2g** / Sodium **55mg** /
Carbs **18g** / Fiber **2g** / Sugar **8g** / Protein **5g**

CINNAMON-RAISIN SWEET POTATO BAGELS

/ *with* / MAPLE CASHEW CREAM CHEESE

TIME TO PREPARE
15 minutes
plus 3 hours soaking

TIME TO COOK
30 minutes

SERVES 6

You'll never get a Jersey girl to give up her bagel, because if you didn't know, New Jersey produces the world's best bagels. It's a fact. While walking through a kitchenware store, I spotted a doughnut pan and thought, "If I stuff these with spiralized veggies, they'll come out looking like bagels!" Allow me to introduce you to the spiralized bagel. This cinnamon-raisin version is made with sweet potato noodles and smeared with a vegan cream cheese made from cashews and sweetened with maple syrup. However you top your bagels, you'll love having these in your clean-eating breakfast arsenal.

For the bagels

Neutral oil or cooking spray

1 tablespoon extra-virgin olive oil

2 sweet potatoes, peeled and spiralized with Blade D

2 large eggs, beaten

½ teaspoon ground cinnamon

¼ cup raisins

For the maple cashew cream cheese

½ cup raw cashews, soaked for at least 3 hours or preferably overnight

3 tablespoons unsweetened almond milk, plus more as needed

¼ teaspoon ground cinnamon

½ teaspoon pure vanilla extract

2 teaspoons pure maple syrup

Pinch of salt

Preheat the oven to 400 degrees. Grease a nonstick doughnut pan with neutral oil or cooking spray.

Make the bagels. Heat the olive oil in a large skillet over medium-high heat. When the oil is shimmering, add the sweet potato noodles. Cook the noodles, tossing occasionally, until wilted, about 10 minutes. Transfer the noodles to a large bowl and refrigerate until cool, about 5 minutes.

Add the eggs, cinnamon, and raisins to the cooled sweet potato noodles and toss well to coat. Pack the noodles into the doughnut pan. Bake until the bagels are firm and the tops are crisp, about 15 minutes.

While bagels cook, make the maple cashew cream cheese. In a food processor, process the cashews, almond milk, cinnamon, vanilla, maple syrup, and salt until smooth. If the mixture is too thick to blend, add another tablespoon of almond milk.

Carefully pop the bagels out of the pan and let cool for 5 minutes. Spread with the maple cashew cheese and serve.

TIP / *If you want to make these bagels in your favorite traditional bagel flavor, use russet potatoes, skip the raisins, and season appropriately.*

Not Spiralized / Vegetarian
Gluten-Free / Paleo
Dairy-Free (opt.)

NUTRITIONAL INFORMATION *Per serving with toppings*

Calories **353** / Fat **14** / Sat Fat **6g** / Sodium **486mg**
Carbs **39g** / Fiber **8** / Sugar **11g** / Protein **17g**

HUEVOS RANCHEROS
/ with / BLENDER PLANTAIN TORTILLAS

TIME TO PREPARE
15 minutes (plus 35 minutes
to make tortillas)

TIME TO COOK
25 minutes

SERVES 4

True to his Puerto Rican roots, Lu can't get enough of plantains—topped with powdered sugar for dessert, sliced into chips, or mashed into mofongo (a Puerto Rican dish of mashed fried plantains), he loves it all. His favorite go-to breakfast dish at restaurants is huevos rancheros, so when I replaced the tortillas with my plantain version, he was certainly happy. The slight sweetness makes these huevos rancheros extra flavorful and certainly Lu-approved.

1 tablespoon extra-virgin olive oil

½ medium white onion, diced

1 (14.5-ounce) can no-salt-added diced tomatoes, with their juices

½ (6-ounce) can diced green chiles, drained

1 teaspoon chili powder

Fine sea salt and pepper

1 (15-ounce) can black beans

Cooking spray

4 large eggs

4 small Breakfast Blender Plantain Tortillas (recipe follows)

4 tablespoons crumbled cotija or feta cheese, for garnish (optional)

4 tablespoons chopped fresh cilantro, for garnish

Heat the olive oil in a medium pot over medium-high heat. When the oil is shimmering, add the onion and cook, stirring, for about 5 minutes, until translucent. Add the tomatoes with their juices, green chiles, and chili powder and season with salt and pepper. Bring to a simmer, stirring, then reduce the heat to medium-low and cook, stirring occasionally, for about 10 minutes, until thickened. Taste and season with salt and pepper as needed. Stir in the black beans. Keep the sauce over low heat until ready to use.

Heat a large nonstick skillet over medium-high heat and spray with cooking spray. When water flicked onto the skillet sizzles, crack in the eggs, working in batches as needed. Fry until the egg whites are set but the yolks are still runny, 3 to 5 minutes.

Arrange 1 plantain tortilla on each of four plates. Top each with the sauce and a fried egg. Garnish each with about 1 tablespoon each of the cheese (if using) and cilantro, then serve.

BREAKFAST BLENDER PLANTAIN TORTILLAS

Not Spiralized
Vegetarian / Gluten-Free
Paleo / Dairy-Free
Low-Cal

NUTRITIONAL INFORMATION
Per serving
Per 1 tortilla
Calories **111** / Fat **4g**
Sat Fat **3g** / Sodium **159mg**
Carbs **17g** / Fiber **0g**
Sugar **8g** / Protein **2g**

TIME TO PREPARE
15 minutes

TIME TO COOK
20 minutes

MAKES 8 TORTILLAS

◎ ◎

3 small yellow plantains (about 1½ pounds total), peeled and chopped into 1-inch pieces

1 large egg

2 tablespoons coconut oil, melted and cooled to room temperature

½ teaspoon fine sea salt

Preheat the oven to 400 degrees. Line two baking sheets with parchment paper.

In a high-speed blender, combine the plantains, egg, coconut oil, salt, and ¼ cup water and purée until smooth.

Scoop about ¼ cup of the batter onto a prepared baking sheet and spread it out into a circle, about 4 inches in diameter for small, thick tortillas or 6 to 7 inches in diameter for big, thin tortillas. Repeat with the remaining batter, leaving about 1 inch between each tortilla. (You will have to work in batches if making bigger tortillas.)

Bake for 10 minutes, until the bottom is set, then flip the tortillas and bake for about 10 minutes more, until golden brown.

Serve immediately or store in an airtight container, separated by wax or parchment paper, in the refrigerator for up to 3 days.

NUTRITIONAL INFORMATION *Per serving*
Calories **230** / Fat **16g** / Sat Fat **6g** / Sodium **884mg**
Carbs **8g** / Fiber **3g** / Sugar **4g** / Protein **18g**

ZUCCHINI CRUST BREAKFAST PIZZA

/ *with* / ARUGULA & SWEET PEPPERS

TIME TO PREPARE
15 minutes

TIME TO COOK
20 minutes

SERVES 4

ⓖ ⓖ ⓖ

½ cup almond flour, plus more for dusting

2 medium zucchini

4 large eggs

½ teaspoon dried basil

½ teaspoon dried oregano

½ teaspoon garlic powder

Fine sea salt and pepper

Cooking spray

1 cup thinly sliced small bell peppers

1 teaspoon extra-virgin olive oil, plus more for drizzling

1 cup shredded mozzarella cheese (about 4 ounces)

2 cups baby arugula

Given that 99 percent of the time I spiralize my zucchini, I often feel odd preparing it any other way. However, a zucchini crust is too good to pass up, especially as used in this breakfast pizza. Unlike a cauliflower crust, zucchini crust is firmer and doesn't break up as easily, so you get a more dough-like consistency. This one is topped simply with melted mozzarella, sweet peppers, and arugula, so you really taste the Italian herb–seasoned crust.

Preheat the oven to 450 degrees with racks in the top and bottom positions. Line a baking sheet with parchment paper and dust it with almond flour.

Lay out a large piece of cheesecloth or a clean kitchen towel and, using a box grater, grate the zucchini onto the towel. Gather the sides of the cheesecloth or towel and squeeze out excess liquid over the sink. Put the zucchini in a large bowl.

Beat 2 of the eggs and add them to the bowl, along with the almond flour, basil, oregano, garlic powder, ½ teaspoon salt, and a few grinds of pepper. Mix well until it takes on a dough-like texture. If the mixture is too wet, add a tablespoon or two more almond flour.

Transfer the dough to the baking sheet and form it into a 10-inch round or two 5-inch rounds. Lightly spray the crust(s) with cooking spray and bake on the lower rack of the oven for about 15 minutes, until the edges are browned and the crust is firm.

In a small bowl, toss the peppers with the olive oil.

Remove the pizza from the oven and sprinkle with the mozzarella. Scatter evenly with the peppers and carefully crack the remaining 2 eggs on top, nestling them among the peppers. Bake the pizza on the top rack of the oven for about 7 minutes, until the cheese melts and the egg whites are just set but the yolks are still runny.

Garnish with the arugula and drizzle with olive oil. Season with a little more salt and pepper and serve hot.

Not Spiralized
Vegetarian / Gluten-Free
Dairy-Free (opt.)

NUTRITIONAL INFORMATION *Per serving*
Calories **472** / Fat **25g** / Sat Fat **7g** / Sodium **329mg**
Carbs **35g** / Fiber **16g** / Sugar **3g** / Protein **28g**

DELICATA SQUASH EGG CUP BAKE

/ *with* / LENTILS & FETA

TIME TO PREPARE
15 minutes

TIME TO COOK
45 minutes

SERVES 4

When delicata squash comes into season in the fall, I always love picking one up to display on my countertop. One of the reasons that fall is my favorite time of year is because of the stunning squashes that start popping up in grocery store displays and at farmer's markets. This elegant one deserves an equally elegant preparation and presentation, like in this egg bake with lentils and salty feta. This heart-healthy protein- and veggie-packed breakfast dish is gorgeously plentiful and may just be enough to make autumn your favorite time of year, too!

2 small delicata squash, each about 8 inches long, sliced crosswise into 2-inch-thick rounds and seeded

3 tablespoons extra-virgin olive oil

Fine sea salt and pepper

1 bay leaf

1 cup dry green lentils, rinsed

2 tablespoons fresh lemon juice

1½ teaspoons ground cumin

2 tablespoons chopped fresh parsley

⅓ cup crumbled feta cheese (optional)

8 large eggs

Preheat the oven to 425 degrees. Line two baking sheets with parchment paper.

Arrange the delicata squash on the prepared baking sheets, brush with 1 tablespoon of the olive oil, and season with salt and pepper. Bake until the squash is fork-tender, about 35 minutes.

Meanwhile, in a medium pot, combine 3 cups water, the bay leaf, lentils, and a large pinch of salt and bring to a boil over high heat. Reduce the heat to medium-low and simmer until the lentils are tender but not mushy, 15 to 20 minutes. Drain any excess water and discard the bay leaf.

In a medium bowl, whisk together the lemon juice, cumin, parsley, and remaining 2 tablespoons olive oil. Add the cooked lentils, then fold in the feta, if desired. Season with salt and pepper. Transfer to a platter.

When the squash is tender, crack an egg into each round. Return the squash to the oven and cook for 7 to 8 minutes for a runny yolk or 10 minutes to set completely.

Serve the squash over the lentils.

Not Spiralized / Vegetarian
Gluten-Free

NUTRITIONAL INFORMATION *Per quesadilla*
Calories **580** / Fat **35g** / Sat Fat **18g** / Sodium **1255mg**
Carbs **46g** / Fiber **5g** / Sugar **20g** / Protein **21g**

VEGETARIAN BREAKFAST QUESADILLA

TIME TO PREPARE
15 minutes (plus 35
minutes to make tortillas)

TIME TO COOK
15 minutes

MAKES 4 QUESADILLAS

Whether as breakfast for dinner or a festive weekend brunch, these breakfast quesadillas are not only chock-full of vegetables and real ingredients, but they're also more flavorful than your average quesadilla. The plantain tortillas have a slightly sweet flavor, complementing the gooey cheese and fluffy eggs. Served simply with avocados, these quesadillas demonstrate how with a little bit of prep, meals can be both delicious and good for you.

1 tablespoon extra-virgin olive oil

1 small white onion, diced

1 green bell pepper, diced

1 red bell pepper, diced

1 plum tomato, seeded and diced

½ jalapeño, seeded and diced

Fine sea salt and pepper

1 large garlic clove, minced

4 large eggs, beaten

8 large Breakfast Blender Plantain Tortillas (see page 53)

2 cups shredded Mexican cheese blend or cheddar cheese

1 large ripe avocado, pitted, peeled, and very thinly sliced

Heat the olive oil in a medium nonstick skillet over medium-high heat. When the oil is shimmering, add the onion, bell peppers, tomato, and jalapeño. Season with salt and black pepper and cook until the vegetables are softened, about 5 minutes. Add the garlic and cook until fragrant, about 30 seconds. Transfer to a medium bowl.

Add the eggs to the pan and cook, stirring them with a spatula to scramble, until set, about 5 minutes. Transfer to a plate.

Wipe the skillet clean and place it over medium-high heat. Add one of the plantain tortillas. When the bottom is heated, 30 seconds to 1 minute, flip the tortilla. Top with ¼ cup of the cheese and about ¼ cup of the vegetable mixture. Add ¼ cup of the scrambled eggs and another ¼ cup of the cheese. Top with another plantain tortilla. When the cheese on the bottom has melted, carefully flip the quesadilla over and flatten it with a spatula. Cook until all the cheese has melted, 3 to 5 minutes. Set aside and repeat with the remaining ingredients to make four quesadillas.

Slice each quesadilla in half or quarters, for easy eating. Top with avocado slices and serve.

TIP / *Instead of serving the avocado in slices, try mashing it in a medium bowl with some lime juice and serving it on top of the quesadilla.*

NUTRITIONAL INFORMATION *Per serving*
Calories **234** / Fat **14g** / Sat Fat **5g** / Sodium **354mg**
Carbs **15g** / Fiber **3g** / Sugar **6g** / Protein **14g**

CHEESY SQUASHBROWN SKILLET

/ *with* / **BACON & EGGS**

TIME TO PREPARE
10 minutes

TIME TO COOK
20 minutes

SERVES 4

While hash browns are made from potatoes and potatoes are indeed vegetables, they can often leave you feeling stuffed thanks to their starchiness and high carbohydrate content. By substituting spaghetti squash, you get "squashbrowns," a lighter take on the beloved breakfast side. The squash combines with the cheese for a savory, salty, gooey bite to complement the crunchy bacon and fluffy eggs. This is a complete breakfast, so you won't miss the potatoes—and may end up preferring this spaghetti squash version because of how much lighter you feel afterward!

4 bacon slices

2 garlic cloves, minced

¼ cup chopped fresh chives

4 cups cooked spaghetti squash (see page 17), squeezed of excess moisture

Fine sea salt and pepper

½ cup shredded cheddar cheese

Cooking spray

4 large eggs

Cook the bacon in a large nonstick or cast-iron skillet over medium heat until crispy, flipping halfway through, about 7 minutes. Transfer the bacon to a paper towel–lined plate to drain.

Pour off all but 1 tablespoon of the bacon grease in the pan. Immediately add the garlic, chives, and spaghetti squash and season with salt and pepper. Cook until the squash starts to brown, about 10 minutes.

Sprinkle the squash with the cheese and let it melt, 3 to 5 minutes. Stir to combine the melty cheese with the squash. Transfer to a plate and cover to keep warm.

Wipe the skillet clean and set it over medium-high heat. Spray with cooking spray and crack in the eggs. Fry until the egg whites are set but the yolks are still runny, 3 to 5 minutes.

On each of four plates, serve ½ cup of the squash-browns with 1 piece of bacon and a fried egg.

TIP / *Plan ahead! Make spaghetti squash for dinner (try my Spaghetti Squash Fideos with Shrimp & Chorizo on page 161) and save any leftover unseasoned squash for this recipe the next morning. Just be sure to squeeze out any excess moisture from the squash before using.*

ALSO WORKS WELL WITH
Zucchini / Broccoli
White Potato

Spiralized / Gluten-Free
Paleo / Dairy-Free
Low-Cal

NUTRITIONAL INFORMATION *Per serving*
Calories **186** / Fat **12g** / Sat Fat **4g** / Sodium **239mg**
Carbs **3g** / Fiber **1g** / Sugar **1g** / Protein **15g**

SHEET PAN OMELET
/ *with* / SPIRALIZED BELL PEPPERS, ONIONS & HAM

TIME TO PREPARE
15 minutes

TIME TO COOK
35 minutes

SERVES 8

If you haven't tried cooking your eggs on a sheet pan, get ready. This is the best thing you can do when entertaining a group of people for breakfast or brunch. Just pop the sheet pan of eggs into the oven, forget about it (well, set a timer!), and then slice your perfectly cooked eggs into square portions to serve in bagels, over toast, or as omelets for your guests. It's a nifty presentation and doesn't require as much attention as pan-cooked eggs do, making your life easier—and your guests more impressed.

Olive oil, for greasing

18 large eggs

1 green bell pepper, spiralized with Blade A, noodles trimmed

1 red bell pepper, spiralized with Blade A, noodles trimmed

½ red onion, peeled, spiralized with Blade A, noodles trimmed

⅔ cup cubed ham

Salt and pepper

Hot sauce, for serving

Preheat the oven to 300 degrees. Grease a large rimmed baking sheet.

In a large bowl, beat together the eggs, then add the bell peppers, onion, and ham. Season with salt and black pepper. Pour the mixture into the prepared pan, making sure the vegetables and ham are distributed evenly.

Bake for about 35 minutes, until the eggs are just set. Remove from the oven and let rest for 5 minutes. Slice into 6 to 8 pieces and serve with hot sauce.

Spiralized / Vegetarian
Gluten-Free / Paleo
Dairy-Free

NUTRITIONAL INFORMATION *Per serving*
Calories **422** / Fat **21g** / Sat Fat **5g** / Sodium **435mg**
Carbs **47g** / Fiber **14g** / Sugar **12g** / Protein **15g**

EGGS BENEDICT

/ *with* / **AVOCADO HOLLANDAISE & PARSNIP CAKES**

TIME TO PREPARE
15 minutes

TIME TO COOK
25 minutes

SERVES 4

My mother and sister love poached eggs, so they both love eggs Benedict—but they don't love the buttery hollandaise sauce that leaves them feeling sluggish afterward. This version of the creamy sauce is made with avocado and lemon juice for a bright kick. It pairs well with the parsnip cakes I snuck into this dish to replace the usual toast. I can't wait for my mom and sister to try this dish—they had better make me a plate, too!

2 tablespoons extra-virgin olive oil

4 large parsnips, peeled, spiralized with Blade D, noodles trimmed

½ teaspoon salt, plus more as needed

½ teaspoon pepper, plus more as needed

7 large eggs

Dash of distilled white vinegar

1 avocado, pitted and peeled

¼ cup fresh lemon juice

1 cup hot water

Microgreens, for garnish (optional)

Heat 1 tablespoon of the olive oil in a large skillet over medium heat. When the oil is shimmering, add the parsnip noodles and season with salt and pepper. Cook, tossing, for about 7 minutes, until warmed through.

Transfer the noodles to a medium bowl. Beat 3 eggs in a small bowl and pour them over the noodles. Toss to combine. Fill four ramekins halfway with the noodles. Cover each with a piece of foil or wax paper, pressing it down firmly onto the noodles to compress them. If you have time, refrigerate for 10 minutes.

In the same skillet, heat the remaining 1 tablespoon olive oil over medium heat. When the oil is shimmering, add the parsnip cakes two at a time, flipping each out of its ramekin into the skillet and patting the bottom until the bun falls out. Cook for 3 minutes, until set, being sure to push in any stray noodles or snip them with kitchen shears. Carefully flip and cook, pressing down with the back of a spatula to compress the cakes, for 2 to 3 minutes more, until the cakes are completely set and browned on both sides. Repeat with the remaining cakes.

Meanwhile, fill a medium pot halfway with water and bring to a steady simmer over high heat. Add the vinegar.

In a food processor or high-speed blender, combine the avocado, lemon juice, hot water, salt, and pepper in a food processor or high-speed blender and purée until smooth.

Crack the remaining 4 eggs individually into ramekins or small cups. When the water is simmering, create a gentle whirlpool in the water and slowly tip in 1 of the eggs, white first. Cook for 3 minutes, until medium firm when poked at, then remove with a slotted spoon and place gently on a paper towel–lined plate to drain. Repeat with the remaining eggs.

Arrange 1 parsnip cake on each plate, top with a poached egg, and drizzle with the avocado hollandaise. Garnish with microgreens, if desired.

Not Spiralized / Vegetarian
Gluten-Free / Paleo
Dairy-Free

NUTRITIONAL INFORMATION *Per serving*
Calories **472** / Fat **29g** / Sat Fat **6g** / Sodium **322mg**
Carbs **26g** / Fiber **9g** / Sugar **1g** / Protein **14g**

SESAME BAGEL YUCCA

/ *with* / SCRAMBLED EGGS & GARLICKY CHARD

TIME TO PREPARE
15 minutes

TIME TO COOK
35 minutes

SERVES 4

When my husband and I first moved in together, he asked me to make one of the dishes his mother used to make for him—boiled yucca with eggs. Unfamiliar with yucca, I went to the grocery store with a Google image printed out, but left the store empty-handed because the veggie that looked most similar was labeled "cassava," not yucca. Don't make the same mistake I did: cassava *is* yucca. This root vegetable tastes like a potato, making it a great breakfast food. Thanks to its starchiness, yucca absorbs flavors well, so each yucca wedge in this dish tastes like a piece of a sesame bagel.

Fine sea salt

2 medium yucca, peeled and cut into fries about 3 inches long and ⅔ inch thick

¼ cup plus 1 tablespoon extra-virgin olive oil

2 teaspoons sesame seeds

1¼ teaspoons garlic powder

1 teaspoon onion powder

Pepper

1 large garlic clove, minced

8 cups chopped Swiss chard leaves (from about 2 small bunches)

8 large eggs, lightly beaten

Preheat the oven to 450 degrees. Line a baking sheet with parchment paper.

Fill a medium pot halfway with lightly salted water and bring to a boil over high heat. Add the yucca and cook until fork-tender, about 7 minutes.

Meanwhile, in a large bowl, whisk together 3 tablespoons of the olive oil, the sesame seeds, garlic powder, onion powder, ½ teaspoon salt, and ¼ teaspoon pepper.

When the yucca is tender, drain it and transfer to the bowl with the spice mix. Toss to coat.

Spread out the yucca on the prepared baking sheet and roast for about 10 minutes, until the bottoms are browned. Flip the fries and roast for about 10 minutes more, until browned all over and crisped on the edges.

Meanwhile, heat 1 tablespoon of the olive oil in a large nonstick skillet over medium-high heat. When the oil is shimmering, add the garlic and cook until fragrant, about 30 seconds. Add the chard and a tablespoon or two of water and cook until wilted and tender, 3 to 5 minutes. Season with salt and pepper. Divide the chard among four plates.

In the same skillet, heat the remaining 1 tablespoon olive oil over medium heat. Add the eggs and cook, stirring with a spatula to scramble, until just set, about 2 minutes. Season with salt and pepper and transfer to the plates with the chard.

Serve the eggs and greens with the yucca.

ALSO WORKS WELL WITH
Sweet Potato / Rutabaga
White Potato

Spiralized / Vegetarian
Gluten-Free / Paleo
Dairy-Free

NUTRITIONAL INFORMATION *Per serving*
Calories **351** / Fat **26g** / Sat Fat **5g** / Sodium **84mg**
Carbs **24g** / Fiber **7g** / Sugar **7g** / Protein **8g**

PARSNIP EGGS-IN-A-HOLE

TIME TO PREPARE
5 minutes

TIME TO COOK
15 minutes

SERVES 2

An egg-in-a-hole is an egg fried in a slice of bread with the center cut out. A clever and visually interesting way to prepare otherwise straightforward eggs and toast, egg-in-a-hole is a quick and easy yet fun breakfast dish. With this spiralized version, I've replaced the bread with parsnip noodles that are cooked around the egg, almost like a nest. The slightly nutty and sweet veggie infuses this breakfast with more flavor and nutrients. When the broken egg coats the noodles, it creates an almost pasta-like situation with the yolk as a sauce.

3 tablespoons extra-virgin olive oil

2 parsnips, peeled, spiralized with Blade D

Fine sea salt and pepper

2 large eggs

Chopped fresh chives, for garnish

Heat 1 tablespoon of the olive oil in a large skillet over medium-high heat. When the oil is shimmering, add the parsnip noodles and season with salt and pepper. Cook, tossing, until al dente, about 5 minutes. Transfer the noodles to a plate.

In the same skillet, heat the remaining 2 tablespoons olive oil over medium-high heat. Mold the parsnip noodles into two mounds and arrange them in the skillet. As the bottoms fry, carefully create an indent in the center of each mound.

When the parsnips are set on the bottom, crack 1 egg into the center of each, cover the pan with a lid, and cook until the egg whites set, about 5 minutes.

Transfer each parsnip nest to a plate and serve warm, garnished with chives.

Not Spiralized / Vegetarian
Gluten-Free / Paleo
Dairy-Free / Low-Cal

NUTRITIONAL INFORMATION *For each of 2 servings*
Calories **250** / Fat **16g** / Sat Fat **5g** / Sodium **112mg**
Carbs **18g** / Fiber **5g** / Sugar **9g** / Protein **11g**

THREE-INGREDIENT MATCHA PANCAKES
/ *with* / TOASTED COCONUT

TIME TO PREPARE
5 minutes

TIME TO COOK
10 minutes

SERVES 1 OR 2

Welcome to my 2016 discovery and forever obsession: the two-ingredient pancake. If you haven't tried making these yet, definitely don't turn the page. The first time I made these pancakes, I reacted similarly to the way I did when I first discovered spiralizing, shouting in between mouthfuls, "How did I not know about this?!" While they don't have quite the same fluff as classic pancakes, the flavor and general consistency are spot-on. This matcha version kicks it up a notch, adding metabolism-boosting and detoxifying benefits, high antioxidant levels, and, of course, a pretty green color! Topped with toasted coconut and a drizzle of maple syrup, these pancakes will change the way you do breakfast.

1 large banana

3 large eggs

1 teaspoon matcha powder

Cooking spray

Pure maple syrup, for drizzling

2 tablespoons unsweetened coconut flakes, toasted, for serving

TIP / *If the earthy flavor of matcha doesn't bother you, increase the amount to 1 tablespoon for more nutritional benefits—and a greener pancake.*

In a high-speed blender, combine the banana, eggs, and matcha and purée until smooth.

Heat a large nonstick skillet over medium-high heat and spray with cooking spray. When water flicked onto the skillet sizzles, pour the batter into the pan to create 2- to 3-inch rounds. Cook until the batter sets on the bottom, 2 to 3 minutes. Carefully flip the pancakes and cook until the batter sets, 1 to 2 minutes more. Reduce the heat if the pancakes are browning too fast. Transfer to a plate and repeat with the remaining batter. (You will have 6 to 8 pancakes.)

Divide the pancakes among plates. Drizzle with maple syrup, top with toasted coconut, and serve immediately.

APPETIZERS & SIDES

Not Spiralized / Saves Well
One-Pot / Vegetarian
Gluten-Free / Low-Cal

NUTRITIONAL INFORMATION *Per serving*
Calories **260** / Fat **19g** / Sat Fat **5g** / Sodium **439mg**
Carbs **13g** / Fiber **5g** / Sugar **4g** / Protein **11g**

MARGHERITA-STYLE

CHARRED BROCCOLI SLABS

TIME TO PREPARE
10 minutes

TIME TO COOK
20 minutes

SERVES 4

If you've only ever eaten broccoli florets, neatly separated from their stem, prepare to be wowed. Treating the broccoli like a steak and slicing it to keep most of the stem intact makes it heartier and gives you more surface area on which to load seasonings and toppings, as here with marinara sauce, basil, and cheese. Kind of like a pizza and kind of like a vegetable Parmigiana, these broccoli slabs can star as the main course when served with a side of mashed cauliflower (see page 187) or as a side served alongside a protein like some roasted chicken or steak. Either way, you'll appreciate broccoli on a whole new level.

1 large head broccoli

3 tablespoons extra-virgin olive oil

Fine sea salt and pepper

2 garlic cloves, sliced

1 cup prepared tomato-basil sauce or marinara sauce

⅔ cup shredded mozzarella cheese

¼ cup grated Parmesan cheese

¼ cup shredded fresh basil leaves

Preheat the oven to 450 degrees.

Trim off and discard the dried, tough part of the broccoli stem (about ½ inch). Working from the stem end, slice the broccoli lengthwise into 4 slabs.

Arrange the broccoli slabs in a single layer in a 9 × 13-inch baking dish. Drizzle with the olive oil, turning to coat, and season lightly with salt and pepper. Nestle the garlic slices among and under the broccoli slabs. Roast for 10 minutes. Flip and roast for 10 minutes more, until tender and browned.

Top the broccoli with the tomato-basil sauce and the mozzarella. Bake until the cheese is melted and bubbling, 5 to 8 minutes more.

Immediately garnish with the Parmesan and basil. Serve warm.

Spiralized / Saves Well
Vegan / Gluten-Free
Paleo / Dairy-Free
Low-Cal

NUTRITIONAL INFORMATION *Per serving*
Calories **298** / Fat **14g** / Sat Fat **2g** / Sodium **590mg**
Carbs **43g** / Fiber **1g** / Sugar **11g** / Protein **2g**

SALT & VINEGAR SPIRALIZED POTATOES

TIME TO PREPARE
15 minutes

TIME TO COOK
15 to 30 minutes

SERVES 4

Nothing screams "summer" like a lobster roll and a bag of Cape Cod Sea Salt & Vinegar potato chips. Those addictingly salty and tangy chips are irresistible, but unfortunately, not the best for a healthy you. Before the vinegar is added to the chips, it's processed into a dry, powdery substance that sticks to the chip. Ick! This spiralized version skips all that, leaving your fingertips oil-free. Serve these at your next summer party alongside lobster and your guests will be amazed!

2 russet potatoes, peeled, spiralized with Blade C, noodles trimmed

1½ cups distilled white vinegar

1½ cups cold water

¼ cup extra-virgin olive oil

Fine sea salt and pepper

Place the potato noodles in a large bowl with the vinegar and cold water. Cover and refrigerate for 30 minutes, stir, then refrigerate for 30 minutes more.

Heat the olive oil in a large skillet over medium-high heat. When the oil is shimmering, use tongs to remove the potato noodles from the bowl, pat dry, and add to the pan. Season with salt and pepper. Cook, tossing, until cooked through and browned, 10 to 15 minutes. Serve warm.

TIP / *To use even less oil, cook the noodles in the oven instead of frying them. Preheat the oven to 425 degrees. After the noodles chill in the vinegar, lay them out on a parchment paper–lined baking sheet and pat them dry. Season with salt and pepper and toss with 2 tablespoons olive oil. Roast for 25 to 30 minutes, until crispy, shaking the pan halfway through. Let cool for 5 to 10 minutes to crisp up, then serve warm.*

Not Spiralized / Vegetarian
Gluten-Free / Dairy-Free
Low-Cal

NUTRITIONAL INFORMATION *Per sausage with 2 tablespoons hummus*
Calories **204** / Fat **16g** / Sat Fat **2g** / Sodium **506mg**
Carbs **10g** / Fiber **4g** / Sugar **2g** / Protein **6g**

ARTICHOKE & OLIVE SAUSAGES
/ *with* / HUMMUS

TIME TO PREPARE
15 minutes

TIME TO COOK
30 minutes

MAKES 6 SAUSAGES

Hours before I'm having friends or family over for drinks, I'm always Googling "appetizer ideas." You'd think I'd have a well-developed list of go-to appetizers to serve when guests come over, but surprisingly, I don't, and I always end up defaulting to the same meat, cheese, crudité, and cracker display. Since marinated artichokes and olives are a must on such a platter, I figured why not combine the two and make finger foods out of them?

Cooking spray

1½ cups pitted green olives

8 jarred marinated artichoke quarters (or 2 whole jarred marinated artichokes)

3 tablespoons fresh parsley

Pepper

1 large egg, beaten

½ cup almond flour, plus more as needed

¾ cup hummus, store-bought or homemade (recipe follows)

Preheat the oven to 375 degrees. Line a baking sheet with parchment paper and spray with cooking spray.

In a food processor, combine the olives, artichokes, parsley, and pepper and pulse until finely chopped. Add the egg and almond flour and pulse until the mixture holds together when packed. Add more almond flour if needed for binding.

Using your hands, form the mixture into 6 sausage-like shapes and place them on the prepared baking sheet. Spray the sausages with cooking spray and bake for about 30 minutes, until firm and golden brown. Let cool for 5 minutes.

Serve the sausages with about 2 tablespoons hummus per serving.

/ recipe continues

EXTRA-SMOOTH HUMMUS

TIME TO PREPARE
25 MINUTES

MAKES
1½ TO 2 CUPS

1 (15-ounce) can chickpeas, drained and rinsed

½ cup tahini

Juice of 1 lemon (2 to 3 tablespoons)

2 small garlic cloves (or more, if you like garlicky hummus),
coarsely chopped

1 tablespoon extra-virgin olive oil

½ teaspoon salt, plus more as needed

Peel the chickpeas by taking each between your thumb and first two fingers and popping them out of their skins. Put the chickpeas in a food processor and process for 1 minute, until smooth, stopping to scrape down the sides as needed. Add the tahini, lemon juice, garlic, olive oil, and salt and process until puréed. Add water by the tablespoon until you achieve a smooth and creamy texture. Taste and adjust the flavors to your preference (more lemon, salt, etc.). Store in an airtight container in the refrigerator for 3 to 5 days.

Not Spiralized / Saves Well
Vegetarian / Gluten-Free
Low-Cal

NUTRITIONAL INFORMATION *Per veggie tot*
Calories **27** / Fat **2g** / Sat Fat **1g** / Sodium **59mg**
Carbs **1g** / Fiber **0g** / Sugar **0g** / Protein **2g**

ANY-VEGGIE TOTS

TIME TO PREPARE
15 minutes

TIME TO COOK
25 minutes

MAKES ABOUT 12 TOTS
ⓖ ⓖ ⓖ

You don't have to have a tot to make these veggie tots! But if you do, this is a much cleaner version of the tater classic that you can feel good about serving to your little ones—and yourself. The beauty of these is that they can be made with many different types of vegetables (or a combo) to yield golden brown oven-baked finger foods perfect for packing in lunches, baking into casseroles, enjoying as a midafternoon snack, dipping into ketchup, and so on. My personal favorite? A broccoli-cauliflower combo!

1 cup grated or shredded vegetable (broccoli, cauliflower, zucchini, and sweet potato are good choices)

¼ cup finely diced white onion

1 large garlic clove, minced, or ½ teaspoon garlic powder

⅓ cup almond flour

⅓ cup grated Parmesan cheese

3 tablespoons chopped fresh parsley

1 large egg, lightly beaten

Fine sea salt and pepper

Mustard, ketchup, and/or hummus (store-bought or homemade, opposite), for serving

Preheat the oven to 400 degrees. Line a baking sheet with parchment paper.

If you're using a watery vegetable, like zucchini, put it in cheesecloth or a clean kitchen towel, gather the sides of the cheesecloth or towel, and squeeze out excess liquid over the sink.

In a medium bowl, combine the grated vegetable, onion, garlic, almond flour, Parmesan, parsley, egg, ½ teaspoon salt, and a few grinds of pepper. Add a little more almond flour if the mixture seems too wet. Mix well. Form the mixture into tot shapes and place on the prepared baking sheet.

Bake the tots for 25 to 30 minutes, flipping halfway through, until golden brown and crisp around the edges. Let cool for 5 minutes before serving.

Serve with your favorite condiment for dipping.

Not Spiralized / Vegan
Dairy-Free / Low-Cal

NUTRITIONAL INFORMATION *Per slider*
Calories **28** / Fat **2g** / Sat Fat **0g** / Sodium **29mg**
Carbs **2g** / Fiber **1g** / Sugar **0g** / Protein **1g**

SMOKY, SAVORY

BRUSSELS SPROUT MINI SLIDERS

/ *with* / **TOFU**

TIME TO PREPARE
15 minutes

TIME TO COOK
20 minutes

MAKES 20 SLIDERS

Adorable, bite-size, and good for you, these little appetizers may take some care to assemble, but they're guaranteed to impress even the biggest tofu skeptics. Brussels sprouts are sliced in half to be used like a bun, sandwiching the marinated tofu. The combination of the soy sauce, liquid smoke, and garlic gives these a BBQ potato chip flavor without the potatoes, processed oils, or frying.

2 tablespoons extra-virgin olive oil

1 tablespoon low-sodium soy sauce (use coconut aminos or gluten-free tamari, if gluten-free)

2 garlic cloves, pressed

½ teaspoon ground cumin

¼ teaspoon cayenne pepper

¼ teaspoon liquid smoke or smoked paprika

20 large Brussels sprouts, ends trimmed and halved lengthwise

6 ounces tofu, drained (see Tip) and cut into ¼-inch-thick slices

Dijon mustard, for serving

Preheat the oven to 375 degrees. Line two baking sheets with parchment paper.

In a small bowl, combine the olive oil, soy sauce, garlic, cumin, cayenne, and liquid smoke. Brush the Brussels sprouts on both sides with about half the olive oil mixture and set them cut-sides down on one of the prepared baking sheets. Brush the tofu on both sides with the remaining olive oil mixture and arrange on the other prepared baking sheet.

Bake the tofu and Brussels sprouts for 10 minutes, then flip each piece and return to the oven, switching which baking sheet is on which rack. Bake until the tofu is well browned, 10 minutes more, and the Brussels sprouts are tender, 10 to 15 minutes more. Let cool slightly.

Smear the cut sides of the Brussels sprouts with mustard and sandwich a piece of tofu between 2 halves. Secure with a toothpick and serve.

TIP / *To drain tofu, lay it down on a clean kitchen towel or a double layer of paper towels. Top the tofu with another layer of towels. Using firm pressure, press down on the tofu to release excess moisture. You may need to repeat this two or three times until the tofu is drained. Alternatively, once you've added the second layer of towels, place a heavy object on top and let the tofu sit for about 15 minutes to drain.*

Not Spiralized / Vegetarian
Gluten-Free

NUTRITIONAL INFORMATION *Per ⅔ cup*
Calories **330** / Fat **16g** / Sat Fat **7g** / Sodium **524mg**
Carbs **36g** / Fiber **7g** / Sugar **5g** / Protein **13g**

SWEET POTATO SKIN NACHOS

TIME TO PREPARE
20 minutes

TIME TO COOK
1 hour

SERVES 4 TO 6
🍥 🍥

My father loves traditional nachos, but he has two daughters who don't really eat beef and a health-conscious wife, so he rarely gets to order them when we're out, unless my husband or brother-in-law is with us. I love nachos, too (who doesn't?), but what I don't like is that I can't read the ingredient list on the tortilla chips, and I'm very particular about my toppings. For these nachos, I crisp the skins of sweet potatoes in the oven and then top them with all the good stuff: cheese, jalapeños, beans, tomatoes, avocado, and plenty of cilantro. I could eat these nachos all day, every day—and my dad loves them!

4 medium sweet potatoes

2 tablespoons extra-virgin olive oil

Fine sea salt and pepper

1 (15-ounce) can pinto beans, drained and rinsed

½ cup no-salt-added canned corn kernels, drained and rinsed

2 cups shredded Mexican cheese blend, or more, as needed

1 large jalapeño, sliced into thin rounds

1 medium tomato, seeded and diced

1 to 2 avocados, pitted, peeled, and cubed

¼ cup chopped cilantro

¼ cup sliced scallions

¼ cup finely chopped white onion

1 lime, quartered, for serving

Preheat the oven to 400 degrees with a rack in the center position.

Pierce each potato 4 times with a fork. Place the potatoes directly on the oven rack and bake until the skins are crisp and the flesh is fork-tender, 45 to 55 minutes. Let cool for about 10 minutes, until cool enough to handle. Turn the broiler to high.

Halve each potato lengthwise, then cut each half in half crosswise. Using a spoon, scoop out the flesh, leaving about ¼ inch intact. Reserve the flesh for another use (or snack on it now).

Brush the skins on both sides with the olive oil and season with salt and pepper. Arrange them skin-side up on a baking sheet, spacing them apart, and broil until the skins start to crisp, 2 to 3 minutes, monitoring them closely so they don't burn. Flip the potato skins over and broil until the top edges just start to brown, 2 to 3 minutes more.

Reduce the oven temperature to 400 degrees. Push the skins together on the baking sheet so they are just touching. Top with the beans and corn. Sprinkle the cheese evenly over the top and bake until the cheese melts, about 5 minutes.

Immediately garnish with the jalapeño, tomato, avocado, cilantro, scallions, and white onion. Season with salt. Serve warm, with lime wedges.

TIP / *If you do want to use meat, add ⅓ cup of your cooked meat of choice (I'd suggest pulled chicken or ground beef) on top of the nachos before you add the cheese so the cheese melts onto it.*

Not Spiralized / No-Cook
Saves Well / Vegan
Gluten-Free / Paleo
Dairy-Free / Low-Cal

NUTRITIONAL INFORMATION *Per serving*
Calories **255** / Fat **13g** / Sat Fat **2g** / Sodium **392mg**
Carbs **27g** / Fiber **10g** / Sugar **6g** / Protein **9g**

LIME-JICAMA CHIPS
/ *with* / CASHEW DIP

TIME TO PREPARE
15 minutes
plus 3 hours soaking

TIME TO COOK
15 minutes

SERVES 4

Every football season, queso dips pop up. Partygoers crowd around bowls of the cheesy dip, usually accompanied by salty tortilla chips and sourdough pretzel bites. Between the processed ingredients in the chips and the dairy in the queso, guests are left in a cheesy carb coma long before halftime. With a little creative thinking and a clean ingredient list, I've given this favorite party staple a healthy revamp. By making the dip out of spiced puréed soaked cashews and using seasoned jicama slices as the vehicle for dunking, you've got yourself a touchdown on both flavor and health.

1 cup raw cashews, soaked for at least 3 hours, drained, and rinsed

3 tablespoons nutritional yeast

3 tablespoons tomato paste

2 tablespoons fresh lemon juice

½ teaspoon smoked paprika

¼ teaspoon onion powder

½ teaspoon fine sea salt, plus more as needed

½ cup vegetable broth or water

1½ teaspoons chili powder

1 medium jicama, peeled and sliced into chips

½ lime

In a food processor, combine the cashews, nutritional yeast, tomato paste, lemon juice, smoked paprika, onion powder, salt, broth, and 1 teaspoon of the chili powder and process until smooth. Taste and season with more salt, if needed. If desired, warm the queso in a small saucepan over medium heat until bubbling. Transfer to a small serving bowl.

Arrange the jicama chips in a serving bowl or on a serving plate. Squeeze the lime over the chips and dust them with the remaining ½ teaspoon chili powder. Serve the chips alongside the queso.

Not Spiralized / Vegetarian
Gluten-Free / Low-Cal
Dairy-Free (opt.)

NUTRITIONAL INFORMATION *Per 1 smashed kohlrabi*
Calories **179** / Fat **9g** / Sat Fat **2g** / Sodium **176mg**
Carbs **21g** / Fiber **12g** / Sugar **9g** / Protein **8g**

WHOLE ROASTED SMASHED KOHLRABI
/ *with* / THYME & GARLIC

TIME TO PREPARE
5 minutes

TIME TO COOK
70 minutes

SERVES 4

Kohlrabi is that alien-looking vegetable you find in your CSA box and have no idea what to do with. Most people peel, cube, and roast it or serve it julienned and raw in a slaw. Yawn! Here I treat them like potatoes—*smashed* potatoes, that is. I'm kind of famous (in my family . . .) for my smashed potatoes, which I parboil, mash, and roast until crispy and golden. I can't wait to test out my smashed kohlrabi at our next holiday get-together!

8 small kohlrabi

2 tablespoons extra-virgin olive oil, plus more for drizzling

1 teaspoon garlic powder

Fine sea salt and pepper

¼ cup grated Parmesan cheese (optional)

2 tablespoons fresh thyme leaves

Preheat the oven to 450 degrees.

Using scissors, snip off all the kohlrabi stems as close to the bulb as possible. Trim the tough bottom but try to leave the skin intact.

Place the kohlrabi on a baking sheet and toss with the olive oil. Season with the garlic powder and salt and pepper to taste. Roast for 60 to 75 minutes, flipping the kohlrabi halfway through, until well browned on the outside and fork-tender.

Remove the kohlrabi from the oven and turn the broiler to high. Smash the kohlrabi with a potato masher or heavy plate and sprinkle with the Parmesan, if desired. Return to the oven and broil for 3 to 4 minutes, until the edges crisp up.

Transfer the kohlrabi to a serving platter. Sprinkle with the thyme and serve warm, drizzled with more olive oil, if desired.

TIP / *Buy small kohlrabi to mimic the size of the Yukon Gold or red potatoes that are typically used for smashed potatoes. This recipe doesn't use the stems and leaves, but you can save them for another use, cooking them like spinach.*

*Not Spiralized / Vegan
Dairy-Free*

NUTRITIONAL INFORMATION *Per serving*
Calories **306** / Fat **18g** / Sat Fat **3g** / Sodium **735mg**
Carbs **23g** / Fiber **5g** / Sugar **9g** / Protein **14g**

SOY-GLAZED ROASTED CABBAGE STEAKS

/ *with* / **EDAMAME PURÉE**

TIME TO PREPARE
20 minutes

TIME TO COOK
30 minutes

SERVES 4

Not quite a steak but not quite a salad wedge, these roasted cabbage steaks will make you respect this leafy green on a whole new level. The cabbage is roasted with oil and soy sauce for an umami flavor that finally puts this veg in the limelight. Each bite has a subtly spicy kick from the wasabi in the velvety smooth edamame purée. If you're having a homemade sushi night or making Asian food for dinner, start off with these cabbage steaks, but don't be surprised if they steal the show.

For the cabbage

1 head green cabbage

¼ cup extra-virgin olive oil

3 tablespoons low-sodium soy sauce (use coconut aminos or gluten-free tamari, if gluten-free)

Pepper

For the purée

2½ cups frozen shelled edamame, cooked according to the package instructions

2 tablespoons fresh lime juice

1 tablespoon low-sodium soy sauce (use coconut aminos or gluten-free tamari, if gluten-free)

2 teaspoons wasabi paste

Fine sea salt and pepper

Make the cabbage. Preheat the oven to 400 degrees. Line a baking sheet with parchment paper.

Stand the cabbage up so that the root end is on a cutting board. Cut ½-inch-thick slices lengthwise, holding the leaves together as you slice. Arrange the cabbage steaks on the prepared baking sheet.

In a small bowl, whisk together the olive oil and soy sauce. Generously brush the tops of the cabbage steaks with half the soy sauce mixture and lightly season each with pepper. Roast for 15 minutes, turn over carefully, brush with the remaining soy sauce mixture, and roast for 15 to 20 more minutes, until soft.

Meanwhile, make the purée. In a food processor, combine the edamame, lime juice, soy sauce, wasabi paste, and ⅓ cup water and process until smooth. Taste and season with salt and pepper.

Divide the edamame purée among four plates. Top each with a cabbage steak and serve.

Not Spiralized / No-Cook
Vegan / Gluten-Free
Paleo / Dairy-Free
Low-Cal

NUTRITIONAL INFORMATION *Per roll*
Calories 46 / Fat 4g / Sat Fat 1g / Sodium 6mg
Carbs 4g / Fiber 2g / Sugar 1g / Protein 1g

CUCUMBER SUMMER ROLLS
/ *with* / AVOCADO MASH

TIME TO PREPARE
20 minutes

MAKES 12 ROLLS

If you ever find yourself craving something crunchy and refreshing on a hot day, make these veggie rolls. Instead of using rice paper, these are rolled in cucumber for even more vegetable love. Although a bit messier than a standard summer roll, you can pack more into each roll and they'll be more colorful on the serving plate. With a glass of rosé alongside, you can't ask for a better summer-afternoon snack.

2 avocados, pitted and peeled

Juice of 1 lime, plus more to taste

Fine sea salt and pepper

1 seedless cucumber, at least 13 inches long

¼ cup cilantro leaves

1 large carrot, cut into thin matchsticks (at least 1 cup)

1 yellow bell pepper, thinly sliced into small matchsticks (at least 1 cup)

Dijon mustard, for garnish

In a medium bowl, mash the avocado with the lime juice. Season with salt and pepper.

Trim the ends of the cucumber and halve it crosswise. Using a mandoline, thinly slice the cucumber halves lengthwise into at least 12 flat, bendable pieces.

Arrange the cucumber strips on a clean surface. Spread an even layer of the avocado mash on each strip, leaving about 1 inch on one of the ends. Sprinkle with some of the cilantro. Arrange the carrots, followed by the bell peppers, in an even layer on the cucumber strips and then top with more cilantro. Working from the end with the carrots, roll up the cucumber and pierce with a toothpick to hold the roll together.

Arrange the rolls on a platter. Garnish each roll with a dollop of Dijon mustard on top for extra kick. Serve.

Not Spiralized / Vegan
Gluten-Free / Paleo
Dairy-Free / Low-Cal

NUTRITIONAL INFORMATION *Per serving*
Calories 252 / Fat 19g / Sat Fat 2g / Sodium 453mg
Carbs 18g / Fiber 14g / Sugar 3g / Protein 9g

TOMATO TARTARE

/ *with* / GARLIC-ROSEMARY FLAXSEED CRACKERS

TIME TO PREPARE
40 minutes

TIME TO COOK
25 minutes

SERVES 4

When I was pregnant, I *really* missed sushi, and especially raw tuna. I order tuna tartare any time I see it on a restaurant menu. I love fresh, sushi-grade tuna—*and* the accompanying chips or crackers that come with it. Since I couldn't have it during my pregnancy, I had to become resourceful and thus, a tomato tartare was born! The tomato is finely chopped, chilled, and tossed with seasonings and ingredients to give it that tuna tartare taste. The salty flax crackers have a slight umami taste, bringing even more life to the tartare.

For the crackers

1½ cups ground flaxseeds

½ teaspoon fine sea salt

1 teaspoon crushed dried rosemary

½ teaspoon garlic powder

Flaky sea salt (optional)

Pumpkin seeds, for sprinkling (optional)

For the tartare

4 large tomatoes, peeled (see Tip)

1 small shallot, minced (about 1 tablespoon)

1 tablespoon capers, coarsely chopped

1 tablespoon finely chopped fresh parsley

1 tablespoon Dijon mustard, plus more to taste

3 dashes of Worcestershire sauce, plus more to taste

Pinch of salt

Pinch of pepper

Make the crackers. Preheat the oven to 350 degrees. Line a baking sheet with parchment paper.

In a large bowl, combine the ground flaxseeds, salt, rosemary, and garlic powder. Add ½ cup water and stir until a dough forms. Transfer the dough to a sheet of parchment paper and cover with another sheet of parchment paper. Gently roll the dough to about ¹⁄₁₆ inch thick. Trim the edges so they are even and cut the dough into rectangles.

Place the rectangles on the prepared baking sheet, leaving about ¼ inch between each. Re-roll and cut the scraps and add them to the baking sheet (use two baking sheets, if needed). Sprinkle the dough with flaky salt and press pumpkin seeds into the rectangles, if desired. Bake until the crackers are dry and hard to the touch, 25 to 35 minutes. Transfer to a rack and let cool completely.

Meanwhile, make the tomato tartare. Finely dice the peeled tomatoes, removing and discarding as many of the seeds as you can with your fingers. Transfer the tomatoes to a fine-mesh strainer set over a medium bowl and refrigerate until well chilled, at least 30 minutes.

Discard the liquid in the bowl, then rinse the bowl and dry well. Add the drained tomatoes to the bowl, then fold in the shallot, capers, parsley, mustard, Worcestershire, salt, and pepper.

Serve the tomato tartare with the crackers.

TIP / *If you don't have a tomato peeler, you can remove the skins this way: Bring a large pot of water to a boil. Score an X in the bottom of each tomato with a paring knife. Add the tomatoes to the boiling water and cook for about 20 seconds, until the skins start to peel back. Transfer to a colander and run under cold water. Peel off the skins.*

Not Spiralized / No-Cook
Saves Well / Vegan
Gluten-Free / Paleo
Dairy-Free / Low-Cal

NUTRITIONAL INFORMATION *Per serving of ¼ cup cheese plus 1 endive*
Calories **215** / Fat **14g** / Sat Fat **2g** / Sodium **139mg**
Carbs **18g** / Fiber **5g** / Sugar **6g** / Protein **7g**

PISTACHIO & CRANBERRY

VEGAN CHEESE BALL

/ *with* / ENDIVE CHIPS

TIME TO PREPARE
50 minutes plus 3 hours
soaking

SERVES 4 TO 6

Around the holidays, your standard meat-and-cheese display needs a little sprucing up, whether it's adding a few pomegranates next to the Brie or a silver-painted sprig of holly next to the prosciutto. But why not dress up the actual food? That's what I did with this cheese ball. There's no better time than the holidays to go big and this appetizer is guaranteed to be the center of attention, not just because it's elegantly garnished but because . . . it's vegan! Skeptics will double-dip this cashew-based cheese alternative and then rejoice when they learn it's healthy.

1½ cups raw cashews, soaked for at least 3 hours, drained, and rinsed

¼ teaspoon lemon zest

2 tablespoons fresh lemon juice

1 tablespoon nutritional yeast

1 garlic clove

¼ teaspoon onion powder

¼ teaspoon fine sea salt, plus more as needed

¼ teaspoon pepper

1½ teaspoons dried thyme

1½ teaspoons dried rosemary

¼ cup shelled roasted and salted pistachios, chopped

¼ cup dried cranberries

4 to 6 Belgian endives, ends trimmed and leaves separated

In a food processor, combine the cashews, lemon zest, lemon juice, nutritional yeast, garlic, onion powder, salt, and pepper and process until smooth, about 2 minutes, scraping down the sides with a spatula every so often. Add the thyme and rosemary and pulse until the herbs are well distributed. Taste and season with more salt as needed.

Line a small bowl with cheesecloth or plastic wrap and add the cheese. Using the cheesecloth or plastic, form the cheese into a ball. Refrigerate until firm, at least 30 minutes.

Spread the pistachios and cranberries over a shallow baking dish or large plate.

Remove the cloth or plastic from the cheese ball and gently roll the cheese over the pistachios and dried cranberries, pressing them in. Continue until the cheese ball is coated all the way around.

Transfer the finished cheese ball to a serving platter and serve with the endive leaves.

Not Spiralized / No-Cook
Gluten-Free / Low-Cal

NUTRITIONAL INFORMATION *Per crostini*
Calories **49** / Fat **1g** / Sat Fat **1g** / Sodium **23mg**
Carbs **9g** / Fiber **2g** / Sugar **7g** / Protein **1g**

RICOTTA & FIG GOLDEN BEET CROSTINI
/ *with* / HONEY

TIME TO PREPARE
20 minutes

**MAKES 8 TO
10 CROSTINI**

Golden beets have a naturally crisp, mild taste and are durable enough to use as a substitute for crostini for a lighter, veggie-forward version of this classic appetizer. The crunchiness of the raw golden beet with the creamy ricotta cheese and velvety fresh figs makes for an intriguing combination of textures. Even better— these no-cook appetizers will hold their form in the heat, so bring them to your next outdoor get-together!

**1 large golden beet
(about 6 ounces),
peeled and sliced into
⅛-inch-thick rounds**

¼ cup ricotta cheese

5 fresh figs, diced

Honey, for drizzling

Arrange the beet slices on a serving platter and spread about 1 teaspoon of the ricotta on each. Top evenly with the chopped figs and drizzle very lightly with honey. Serve.

TIP / *If you can't find fresh figs, use dried Turkish figs instead—they're a little tougher to dice, but they taste great and work just as well!*

Not Spiralized / Vegetarian
Gluten-Free / Paleo
Dairy-Free / Low-Cal

NUTRITIONAL INFORMATION *Per pretzel ring*
Calories **65** / Fat **3g** / Sat Fat **1g** / Sodium **243mg**
Carbs **4g** / Fiber **1g** / Sugar **2g** / Protein **5g**

CAULIFLOWER PRETZEL RINGS
/ *with* / **MUSTARD**

TIME TO PREPARE
15 minutes

TIME TO COOK
25 minutes

MAKES 6 PRETZELS

Cauliflower is an all-star vegetable that can be used to make just about anything. So why not pretzels? Pretzels are typically made with yeast, flour, and sugar, while this cleaner version is made with real ingredients, like cauliflower, eggs, and almond flour. Chia seeds help the dough form and have the added bonus of superfood benefits, like fiber and essential omega-3 fatty acids. The pretzels are finished off with whole pink Himalayan salt for added minerals and that classic salty taste.

Cooking spray

3 to 4 cups cauliflower florets (from 1 medium head)

¼ cup almond flour

2 large eggs, lightly beaten

½ teaspoon onion powder

½ teaspoon garlic powder

1 tablespoon chia seeds

Fine sea salt and pepper

½ teaspoon whole pink Himalayan salt

Dijon mustard, for serving

Preheat the oven to 400 degrees. Line a baking sheet with parchment paper and spray with cooking spray.

In a food processor, pulse the cauliflower florets until rice-like, working in batches as needed. Transfer the cauliflower to a clean kitchen towel. Gather the sides of the towel and squeeze out excess liquid over the sink. Place the cauliflower rice in the large bowl and add the almond flour, eggs, onion powder, garlic powder, chia seeds, ½ teaspoon sea salt, and a few grinds of pepper. Mix well.

Form the dough into 6 balls and arrange them on the prepared baking sheet. Using your hands, flatten and shape each round so it's ½ inch thick. Using your finger, poke a hole in the middle of each. Form each round so the hole in each is about 1½ inches wide. Carefully sprinkle the tops of the rings with the Himalayan salt and press the salt into the dough.

Spray the tops of the rounds with cooking spray and bake for 10 to 15 minutes, until golden brown on the bottom. Carefully flip the rounds, spray again with cooking spray, and bake for about 10 minutes, until browned on the bottom. Let cool for 5 to 10 minutes, until the rounds are somewhat firm.

Serve the cauliflower pretzel rings with mustard.

Not Spiralized / Saves Well
Vegetarian / Gluten-Free
Low-Cal

NUTRITIONAL INFORMATION *Per biscuit*
Calories **196** / Fat **11g** / Sat Fat **5g** / Sodium **412mg**
Carbs **10g** / Fiber **6g** / Sugar **5g** / Protein **13g**

CHEESY CAULIFLOWER BISCUITS

TIME TO PREPARE
15 minutes

TIME TO COOK
35 minutes

MAKES 6 BISCUITS
ⓖ ⓖ ⓖ

These cheesy cauliflower biscuits are your healthy answer to Southern comfort food. Having gone to college in North Carolina, I ate my fair share of biscuits—buttermilk biscuits, chive biscuits, and, of course, cheesy biscuits. Biscuits were in the dining halls and filled the bread basket at many restaurants. I'd never had a biscuit until I got to college, and once I discovered them, well, let's just say they were a contributing factor to my "freshman 15." This wholesome cauliflower version is not quite as fluffy as the original, but it's just as flavorful. Serve these at breakfast or with dinner for a bit of nutritious Southern comfort.

8 cups cauliflower florets (from 1 medium head)

2 large eggs

¼ cup almond flour, plus more as needed

¼ cup minced fresh chives

½ teaspoon garlic powder

¼ teaspoon onion powder

½ teaspoon fine sea salt

1 cup plus 2 tablespoons shredded cheddar cheese

1 tablespoon extra-virgin olive oil

Preheat the oven to 400 degrees. Line a baking sheet with parchment paper.

In a food processor, pulse the cauliflower until it reaches a rice-like consistency, working in batches as needed. Transfer the rice to a clean kitchen towel. Gather the sides and squeeze out excess liquid over the sink. Transfer the cauliflower to a large bowl and add the eggs, almond flour, chives, garlic powder, onion powder, and salt. Using a spatula, stir to combine. Add a little more almond flour if the mixture seems too wet.

Scoop 6 large mounds of the cauliflower mixture, about ⅓ cup each, onto the prepared baking sheet. Place 2 tablespoons of the cheddar cheese in the center of each mound. Fold the cauliflower mixture to enclose the cheese and form it into a biscuit shape. Space the biscuits apart evenly on the baking sheet and brush the tops with the olive oil.

Bake the biscuits for about 30 minutes, until golden brown. Remove the pan from the oven. Turn the broiler to high. Sprinkle another tablespoon of cheese over each biscuit. Return to the oven and broil for 1 to 2 minutes, until the cheese melts. Remove the biscuits from the oven, transfer to a rack, and let cool slightly. Serve warm.

TIP / *For meat lovers out there, add a heaping ⅓ cup bacon bits to the batter for extra salty, savory flavor.*

Not Spiralized / Vegan
Dairy-Free / Low-Cal

NUTRITIONAL INFORMATION *Per 1 mini salad*
Calories **87** / Fat **5g** / Sat Fat **1g** / Sodium **332mg**
Carbs **8g** / Fiber **2g** / Sugar **5g** / Protein **4g**

MINI WEDGE SALADS

/ *with* / TOFU BACON BITS & HEARTS OF PALM DRESSING

TIME TO PREPARE
15 minutes

TIME TO COOK
25 minutes

**MAKES 8 MINI OR
4 FULL-SIZE SALADS**

I've tried all types of bacon alternatives—eggplant bacon, coconut bacon, even bacon using three different types of mushrooms. For bacon bits, however, the key is crumbled tofu. It crisps up in the oven to achieve the perfect bacon-bit texture and flavor—your brain will second-guess your taste buds. The bacon is the perfect finish to this party-friendly mini version of the classic wedge salad. The biggest surprise? The creamy dairy-free dressing, made with a secret ingredient: hearts of palm!

For the tofu bacon bits

2 tablespoons low-sodium soy sauce (use gluten-free tamari or coconut aminos, if gluten-free)

2 tablespoons liquid smoke

2 tablespoons pure maple syrup

¼ teaspoon smoked paprika

6 ounces extra-firm tofu, drained (see Tip, page 76)

For the dressing

1 (14-ounce) can hearts of palm, drained

Zest and juice of 1 lemon

2 tablespoons extra-virgin olive oil

¼ teaspoon salt

Pepper

1 head iceberg lettuce

12 cherry tomatoes, halved

Fine sea salt and pepper

Make the tofu bacon bits. Preheat the oven to 425 degrees. Line a baking sheet with parchment paper.

In a medium bowl, whisk together ¼ cup water, the soy sauce, liquid smoke, maple syrup, and smoked paprika. Roughly crumble the tofu into bits into the bowl, being sure not to make any pieces too tiny. Stir to coat. Spread the tofu in an even layer on the prepared baking sheet. Bake until browned and crispy, flipping the tofu halfway through, about 20 minutes. Be sure to watch the tofu and remove any pieces that are burning.

Meanwhile, make the dressing. In a food processor, combine the hearts of palm, lemon zest, lemon juice, olive oil, salt, and pepper to taste and pulse until creamy, adding water, 1 tablespoon at a time, as needed to loosen the dressing. Taste and adjust the seasoning if needed.

Prepare the salad wedges. Halve the head of lettuce through its core. Cut each half into 2 wedges. To make a mini salad wedge, cut each wedge in half again.

Spear 3 tomato halves onto each of 8 toothpicks and secure each into a lettuce wedge. Drizzle with dressing, top with tofu bacon bits, and season with salt and pepper.

TIP / *These wedges don't have to be mini. Serve this as a main salad by slicing the lettuce into quarters and topping with the tomatoes, dressing, and tofu bacon.*

Not Spiralized / Saves Well
Low-Cal

NUTRITIONAL INFORMATION *Per dumpling*
Calories **60** / Fat **3g** / Sat Fat **1g** / Sodium **233mg**
Carbs **4g** / Fiber **1g** / Sugar **3g** / Protein **4g**

ZUCCHINI PORK DUMPLINGS

TIME TO PREPARE
30 minutes

TIME TO COOK
15 minutes

MAKES
18 TO 20 DUMPLINGS

"Should we get the dumplings?" If you've ever found yourself asking that of your takeout partner-in-crime, you're not alone. Although delicious, this classic Chinese staple isn't the best choice health-wise, on account of its starchy dough wrapping that's fried in oil. By replacing the wrapper with zucchini strips and oven-baking, you have a healthy alternative to satisfy your takeout cravings. Seasoned pork and veggies are wrapped in zucchini strips to create beautiful dumpling pouches with a pillowy consistency and more dietary fiber in every spoonful. A sprinkling of scallions, spicy red pepper flakes, and soy sauce for dipping finish off this takeout makeover.

12 ounces napa cabbage leaves, roughly chopped

1 teaspoon salt

2/3 pound lean ground pork

1 tablespoon grated fresh ginger (using a zester)

1/4 cup minced green onions (white and green parts), plus 1/4 cup finely minced, green parts only, for serving

1/2 teaspoon ground white pepper

1 1/2 tablespoons soy sauce, plus more for serving

1 tablespoon rice wine

2 teaspoons sesame oil

5 to 6 medium zucchini (about 1 1/2 inches in diameter)

Crushed red pepper flakes, for serving

Preheat the oven to 400 degrees.

In a food processor, add the cabbage and pulse until finely minced. Set aside on a large, thin kitchen towel in the sink. Sprinkle with salt and let stand for 10 to 15 minutes. Wrap the cabbage up in the towel and wring out excess moisture over the sink (should eliminate about 1/3 cup of moisture). Set the cabbage aside.

Meanwhile, wipe out the food processor and add in the pork, ginger, green onions, pepper, soy sauce, rice wine, and sesame oil and pulse to mix the ingredients well, being careful not to overpulse. (You don't want the mixture to become paste-like.) Transfer to a large bowl and add the cabbage. Mix together with your hands to combine thoroughly. Set aside.

Using a mandoline or vegetable peeler, peel the zucchini into 1/8-inch-thick strips. Set 1 strip down and then set another one down on top of it to create a cross shape. Repeat with 2 more zucchini strips on an angle to create an 8-cornered star shape.

/ recipe continues

Use zucchini that are 1½ inches in diameter so that the zucchini strips are large enough for wrapping the pork filling but small enough to remain dumpling-sized. Each zucchini should yield enough noodles to make 4 dumplings.

Spoon about 2 tablespoons of filling onto the center of the zucchini star. Bring the ends of the zucchini together, laying them over the filling. Flip the dumpling over so the seam side is down. Arrange on a baking sheet and repeat with remaining zucchini strips and dumpling filling, lining them up on the baking sheets as you go. You should create 18 to 20 total dumplings.

Bake for 15 minutes, or until dumplings are firm and edges start to brown and crisp up.

Transfer the zucchini dumplings to serving platters, and sprinkle with green onions and red pepper flakes. Serve with soy sauce.

SOUPS & SALADS

ALSO WORKS WELL WITH
Turnip / Rutabaga

Spiralized / Saves Well
Vegetarian / Gluten-Free
Dairy-Free (opt.) / Low-Cal

NUTRITIONAL INFORMATION *Per each of 6 servings*
Calories **220** / Fat **5g** / Sat Fat **1g** / Sodium **847mg**
Carbs **37g** / Fiber **11g** / Sugar **8g** / Protein **11g**

TUSCAN WHITE BEAN & CHARD SOUP

/ *with* / CELERIAC RICE

TIME TO PREPARE
20 minutes

TIME TO COOK
15 minutes

SERVES 4 TO 6

Whenever my husband's sick with the "man flu," he orders vegetable and orzo soup from our local diner. He says it's a cure-all. Orzo is a small rice-shaped pasta made from processed flour, so while it may taste soothing, you're filling your body with some not-so-curing ingredients. For an equally comforting but more nutrition-forward meal, this white bean and chard soup has fiber and protein in the beans and all the benefits from leafy greens in the chard. The celeriac rice fulfills that textural need for rice that many of us desire in these types of soups. The few tablespoons of Parmesan cheese added at the end give the soup the perfect salty and savory finish. Man flu cured!

1 small celeriac, peeled, spiralized with Blade D

1 tablespoon extra-virgin olive oil

¾ cup diced white onion

2 carrots, diced

2 large garlic cloves, minced

¼ teaspoon red pepper flakes, or more to taste

Fine sea salt and pepper

6 cups low-sodium vegetable broth (or chicken broth, if not vegetarian)

Leaves from 4 sprigs thyme

1 (15-ounce) can white beans, drained and rinsed

6 cups chopped Swiss chard leaves

4 to 6 tablespoons grated Parmesan cheese, for garnish (optional)

Place the celeriac noodles in a food processor and pulse until rice-like.

Heat the olive oil in a large pot over medium-high heat. When the oil is shimmering, add the onion and carrots and cook until softened, about 5 minutes. Add the garlic and cook until fragrant, about 30 seconds. Season with the red pepper flakes and salt and black pepper to taste. Stir in the broth.

Add the thyme, bring to a boil, then reduce the heat to medium-low. Add the celeriac rice, beans, and chard. Simmer for 5 to 7 minutes, until the celeriac rice is no longer crunchy.

Ladle the soup into bowls and top each with 1 tablespoon of the Parmesan, if desired.

ALSO WORKS WELL WITH
Jicama

Spiralized / Saves Well
Gluten-Free / Dairy-Free
Low-Cal

NUTRITIONAL INFORMATION *Per serving*
Calories **277** / Fat **11g** / Sat Fat **1g** / Sodium **1326mg**
Carbs **36g** / Fiber **11g** / Sugar **5g** / Protein **17g**

CHORIZO & CHICKPEA STEW

/ *with* / KOHLRABI

TIME TO PREPARE
10 minutes

TIME TO COOK
20 minutes

SERVES 4

Since I eat a primarily plant-based diet, when I do eat meat, it's as an addition to a vegetarian dish, not the star. This way, I get to enjoy the robustness of a meat like chorizo while still eating plenty of vegetables. By adding an extra bit of smoked paprika to this stew, the chorizo's flavors are highlighted even more, making the dish that much more full-bodied. Paired with mild kohlrabi and soft chickpeas to soak up the broth, this dish is my kind of balance.

1 tablespoon extra-virgin olive oil

4 ounces fresh (Mexican) chorizo, casing removed

1 small yellow onion, diced

3 garlic cloves, minced

1 (14.5-ounce) can crushed tomatoes

½ teaspoon ground cumin

4 cups low-sodium chicken broth or vegetable broth

1 (15-ounce) can chickpeas, drained and rinsed

½ teaspoon paprika

½ teaspoon smoked paprika

1 medium kohlrabi, peeled, spiralized with Blade C, noodles trimmed

Fine sea salt and pepper

Chopped fresh parsley, for garnish

Heat the olive oil in a large pot over medium-high heat. When the oil is shimmering, add the chorizo and cook, stirring and breaking up with a wooden spoon as it cooks, until browned, about 7 minutes. Using a slotted spoon, transfer the chorizo to a plate.

Add the onion and garlic to the pot and cook until the onion is softened, 3 to 5 minutes. Add the tomatoes and cumin and cook, stirring, for 2 minutes, until the tomatoes soften. Add the broth, chickpeas, paprika, and smoked paprika. Increase the heat to high and bring to a boil, then reduce the heat to medium-low and simmer the soup, partially covered, for 10 minutes. Uncover and stir in the kohlrabi and chorizo and cook until the kohlrabi is tender, about 10 minutes more. Season with salt and pepper.

Divide the soup among four bowls, garnish with parsley, and serve.

ALSO WORKS WELL WITH
Zucchini

Spiralized / Vegetarian
Gluten-Free / Low-Cal
One-Pot

NUTRITIONAL INFORMATION *Per serving*
Calories **136** / Fat **8g** / Sat Fat **3g** / Sodium **729mg**
Carbs **3g** / Fiber **1g** / Sugar **1g** / Protein **13g**

STRACCIATELLA SOUP

/ *with* / **BROCCOLI NOODLES**

TIME TO PREPARE
5 minutes

TIME TO COOK
15 minutes

SERVES 4

Stracciatella is an Italian word that can be used for three entirely different types of food (soup, ice cream, and cheese). Here we have the soup, which typically includes a meat broth and wisps of egg. I like to think of it as the Italian version of Chinese egg drop soup, and I love eating it on chilly days. It's comforting, salty, savory, and filling. My version also includes spiralized broccoli for added crunch and a boost of calcium.

4 cups low-sodium vegetable broth

1 garlic clove

2 large broccoli stems, spiralized with Blade D, noodles trimmed

4 large eggs

⅓ cup grated Parmesan cheese

1 tablespoon chopped fresh parsley

½ teaspoon fine sea salt

Pepper

2 cups baby spinach

Pinch of red pepper flakes, for garnish

In a medium pot, bring the broth to a boil with the garlic over high heat. Add the broccoli noodles, reduce the heat to medium, and cook for 5 minutes, until al dente.

Meanwhile, in a medium bowl, whisk together the eggs, Parmesan, parsley, salt, and a few grinds of black pepper.

While stirring the broth, slowly pour in the egg mixture. Continue to stir until the eggs are set, about 1 minute—the eggs will become wispy. Stir in the spinach and let wilt, about 1 minute more.

Serve immediately with red pepper flakes.

ALSO WORKS WELL WITH
Kohlrabi

Spiralized / Saves Well
Gluten-Free / Dairy-Free
One-Pot

NUTRITIONAL INFORMATION *Per each of 6 servings*
Calories **329** / Fat **6g** / Sat Fat **0g** / Sodium **549mg**
Carbs **34g** / Fiber **12g** / Sugar **4g** / Protein **26g**

CHICKEN CHILI STEW

/ *with* / **JICAMA NOODLES**

TIME TO PREPARE
15 minutes

TIME TO COOK
30 minutes

SERVES 4 TO 6

If you love tortilla soup, you'll love this chicken stew. This dish has it all—just enough tang, plenty of spice, and tons of protein from the chicken and beans. The jicama noodles give it a satisfying crunch while adding more veggies and lots of dietary fiber. It saves well, so you may want to double up on the ingredients to ensure you have some leftovers!

2 (14-ounce) cans great northern beans, drained and rinsed

1 tablespoon extra-virgin olive oil

1 large white onion, chopped

1 medium jalapeño, minced

2 medium poblano peppers, seeded and diced

3 garlic cloves, minced

1 tablespoon ground cumin

1 teaspoon ground coriander

½ teaspoon chili powder

Fine sea salt and pepper

8 cups low-sodium chicken broth

Juice of 2 limes

1 medium jicama, peeled, spiralized with Blade D, noodles trimmed

4 cups shredded rotisserie or other cooked chicken

¼ cup chopped fresh cilantro

Place half the beans in a medium bowl. Using the back of a fork or a potato masher, mash until a chunky-smooth consistency is reached. Add the remaining beans and stir together.

Heat the olive oil in a large pot over medium-high heat. When the oil is shimmering, add the onion, jalapeño, poblano, and garlic and cook until softened, about 5 minutes. Add the cumin, coriander, and chili powder and season with salt and pepper. Cook, stirring, until fragrant, about 1 minute. Add the broth and lime juice, increase the heat to high, and bring to a strong simmer. Reduce the heat to medium, add the beans, and simmer for 20 minutes.

Taste the soup and add more salt if needed. Stir in the jicama and chicken and simmer until the jicama softens slightly, about 5 minutes. Stir in the cilantro.

Divide the stew among four to six bowls and serve.

Not Spiralized / No-Cook
Saves Well / One-Pot
Vegan / Gluten-Free
Paleo / Dairy-Free
Low-Cal

NUTRITIONAL INFORMATION *Per ⅔ cup*
Calories **108** / Fat **6g** / Sat Fat **1g** / Sodium **396mg**
Carbs **13g** / Fiber **6g** / Sugar **3g** / Protein **4g**

HEARTS OF PALM CEVICHE

TIME TO PREPARE
30 minutes plus
30 minutes to chill

SERVES 2 TO 4

When Lu and I went on our honeymoon in Mexico, we ate ceviche every single day. Like clockwork, around three in the afternoon, we'd order another round of margaritas and the "ceviche of the day," beachside. As absolutely sensational as the seafood in the ceviche was, I found myself looking forward to the chopped veggies that always ended up in the bottom of the bowl, soaked in the leftover juices. With this seafood-free version, you'll get that same refreshingly tangy taste. Unfortunately, Mexico's beaches are not included.

1 (20-ounce) jar hearts of palm, drained and chopped into chunks

1 medium tomato, diced

¼ red onion, diced

2 jalapeños, seeded and minced

½ orange bell pepper, diced

½ yellow bell pepper, diced

½ seedless cucumber, diced

1½ tablespoons fresh lime juice, plus more as needed

1½ tablespoons fresh orange juice (from about 1 orange)

Fine sea salt and pepper

1 ripe avocado, pitted, peeled, and diced

¼ cup chopped fresh cilantro

Lettuce cups or tortilla chips, for serving

In a large bowl, toss together the hearts of palm, tomato, onion, jalapeños, bell peppers, and cucumber. Add the lime juice and orange juice and toss well. Taste and adjust with more lime juice, if needed, and season with salt and pepper. Refrigerate for at least 30 minutes or up to 4 hours.

Fold in the avocado and cilantro just before serving. Serve in lettuce cups or with tortilla chips alongside.

Spiralized / Gluten-Free
Paleo / Dairy-Free
Low-Cal

NUTRITIONAL INFORMATION *Per serving*
Calories **289** / Fat **12g** / Sat Fat **4g** / Sodium **1162mg**
Carbs **12g** / Fiber **4g** / Sugar **7g** / Protein **32g**

BEEF PHO

/ *with* / ZUCCHINI NOODLES

TIME TO PREPARE
15 minutes

TIME TO COOK
30 minutes

SERVES 4

Beef noodle soup, aka pho (pronounce *fuh*), is one of the most globally recognized noodle dishes from Vietnam—and for good reason. It's easy to fall in love with. With fresh zucchini noodles in place of the rice noodles and tender slices of beef, this pho not only has a richly flavored broth, but great texture as well. Whether you're curling up with a bowl after a hard day at work or warming up with it on a weekend afternoon, pho never disappoints.

12 ounces lean beef sirloin, fat trimmed

Fine sea salt and pepper

1 tablespoon extra-virgin olive oil

1 large onion, halved

1 (4-inch) piece fresh ginger, halved

3 cups low-sodium beef broth

2 star anise pods

1 cinnamon stick

2 tablespoons fish sauce

2 medium zucchini, spiralized with Blade D, noodles trimmed

1 red jalapeño or other mild chile, thinly sliced

1 green jalapeño, thinly sliced

3 scallions, thinly sliced

½ cup fresh cilantro

1 cup fresh bean sprouts

1 lime, quartered

Poke the meat all over with a fork to tenderize it. Season generously with salt and pepper. Heat the olive oil in a large pot over high heat. When the oil is shimmering, add the meat and sear until charred on the outside but still rare within, 2 to 3 minutes per side. Transfer to a plate.

Add the onion and ginger to the pot and cook for 3 to 5 minutes, until the onion begins to soften. Add the broth, star anise, cinnamon stick, and 1 cup water and bring to a simmer. Reduce the heat to medium-low and cook for 15 to 20 minutes to let the flavors develop.

Meanwhile, thinly slice the meat against the grain.

Add the fish sauce to the broth, increase the heat to high, and bring to a boil. Boil for 5 minutes. Using a slotted spoon, remove and discard the star anise, ginger, and cinnamon stick. Transfer the onion to a cutting board. Add the zucchini noodles to the pot and cook until al dente, 3 to 5 minutes.

While zucchini noodles cook, thinly slice the onion.

Divide the soup and noodles among four bowls. Top each with beef, onion, jalapeño, scallions, cilantro, and bean sprouts. Serve with lime wedges for squeezing.

TIP / *Can't find star anise? It's okay to skip it, though I highly recommend using it if you can get it.*

Not Spiralized / Vegan
Gluten-Free / Paleo
Dairy-Free

NUTRITIONAL INFORMATION *Per serving*
Calories **373** / Fat **22g** / Sat Fat **5g** / Sodium **452mg**
Carbs **30g** / Fiber **13g** / Sugar **10g** / Protein **15g**

BUFFALO CAULIFLOWER SALAD

/ *with* / **AVOCADO & VEGAN RANCH**

TIME TO PREPARE
30 minutes
plus 3 hours soaking

TIME TO COOK
40 minutes

SERVES 6

When I worked my corporate job right after college, I always looked forward to lunchtime so I could take my contractually promised hour-long break. Most days, I would drive to a popular local deli where I'd stand in line, listening to everyone's orders before mine, and eavesdrop on the corporate lunch chatter. One day, I specifically remember a man ordering a "Buffalo chicken salad" because his wife had put him on a diet. He ordered the salad with extra croutons, extra ranch, and "yes, I'll have a slice of bread with that." In that moment, months before quitting to pursue Inspiralized, I remember thinking, *This is why I need to start Inspiralized—I need to show people how you can still have these same flavors while sticking to a healthy diet.* I wish I could share this *actually* healthy buffalo cauliflower salad with that man I stood behind in line years ago—I bet he'd be impressed!

For the cauliflower

½ cup unsweetened almond milk

¾ cup almond flour

2 teaspoons garlic powder

2 teaspoons onion powder

1 teaspoon ground cumin

1 teaspoon paprika

¼ teaspoon fine sea salt

¼ teaspoon pepper

8 cups cauliflower florets (from 2 medium heads)

1 tablespoon coconut oil, melted

½ cup hot sauce (I like Frank's RedHot)

Make the cauliflower. Preheat the oven to 450 degrees. Line a baking sheet with parchment paper.

In a large bowl, whisk together the almond milk, almond flour, garlic powder, onion powder, cumin, paprika, salt, pepper, and ½ cup water. Add the cauliflower and toss to coat, making sure to get the batter into all the crevices. Place the cauliflower florets on the prepared baking sheet and roast until browned in spots, about 20 minutes. Remove from the oven, but keep the oven on.

In a separate large bowl, whisk the coconut oil with the hot sauce. Add the hot cauliflower and toss to coat. Replace the parchment paper with a clean sheet. Return the cauliflower to the baking sheet and roast for about 20 minutes, until the sauce is browned.

/ ingredients & recipe continue

TIP / *If you're not
strictly dairy-free, add
crumbled blue cheese to
this salad for a more
authentic Buffalo chicken
experience.*

For the ranch dressing

1 cup raw cashews, soaked for at least 3 hours, drained, and rinsed

¾ cup unsweetened almond milk

2 large garlic cloves

2 tablespoons fresh lemon juice, plus more to taste

2 tablespoons white wine vinegar

1 teaspoon Dijon mustard

Fine sea salt and pepper

For the salad

12 cups spinach, coarsely chopped

2 carrots, shaved into strips with a vegetable peeler

2 celery stalks, chopped

2 ripe avocados, pitted, peeled, and cubed

¼ cup roasted salted pepitas (pumpkin seeds)

Meanwhile, make the ranch dressing. In a high-speed blender, combine the cashews, almond milk, garlic, lemon juice, vinegar, and mustard and blend until creamy. Season with salt and pepper.

Make the salad. Pour ½ cup of the dressing into a clean large bowl. Add the spinach, carrots, celery, and avocado and toss well. Divide the salad among four plates and top with the Buffalo cauliflower and the pepitas. Drizzle with more of the dressing and serve, passing any remaining dressing at the table.

Not Spiralized /
Gluten-Free

NUTRITIONAL INFORMATION *For each of 6 servings*
Calories **357** / Fat **23g** / Sat Fat **7g** / Sodium **1509mg**
Carbs **35g** / Fiber **6g** / Sugar **15g** / Protein **13g**

FRENCH ONION SOUP

/ *with* / RUTABAGA TOAST

TIME TO PREPARE
15 minutes

TIME TO COOK
40 minutes

SERVES 4 TO 6

ᓂ ᓂ ᓂ

I love what's underneath the cheesy toast in French onion soup—beautifully caramelized onions cooked in beef broth with thyme and red wine. By substituting a slab of rutabaga for the bread, you still get to enjoy that classic flavor and texture with a little more health.

3 tablespoons extra-virgin olive oil

4 yellow onions, thinly sliced (see Tip)

Fine sea salt

1 small rutabaga, peeled and sliced into ¼-inch-thick rounds

Cooking spray

½ cup dry red wine

6 cups low-sodium beef broth

2 bay leaves

1 teaspoon dried thyme

Pepper

1 cup grated Gruyère cheese

2 tablespoons chopped fresh parsley

TIP / *You can use Blade A to spiralize the onions instead of slicing them.*

Preheat the oven to 425 degrees. Line a baking sheet with parchment paper.

Heat the olive oil in a large pot over medium heat. When the oil is shimmering, add the onions and ¼ teaspoon salt. Cook, stirring, until the onions are translucent, about 5 minutes. Reduce the heat to medium-low and cook, stirring, until the onions have reduced by half and are browned and softened, 20 to 30 minutes more.

Meanwhile, arrange the rutabaga slabs on the prepared baking sheet. Spray with cooking spray and roast until fork-tender, 25 to 30 minutes. Remove the pan from the oven and turn the oven to broil.

When the onions are cooked, add the wine and scrape up any browned bits from the bottom of the pot with a wooden spoon. Add the broth, bay leaves, and thyme and season with salt and pepper. Stir once, then simmer, partially covered, for 15 minutes to let the flavors develop. Taste and add more salt as needed.

When the soup is almost done, sprinkle the cooked rutabaga evenly with the Gruyère. Broil until the cheese is bubbling and golden brown, 3 to 5 minutes.

Remove the bay leaves and divide the soup among four to six bowls. Top each bowl with a cheesy rutabaga slab, cheese-side up. Garnish with the parsley and serve.

Spiralized / No-Cook
Saves Well / One-Pot
Vegetarian / Gluten-Free
Dairy-Free (opt.)

NUTRITIONAL INFORMATION *Per serving*
Calories **238** / Fat **13g** / Sat Fat **2g** / Sodium **736mg**
Carbs **22g** / Fiber **8g** / Sugar **5g** / Protein **13g**

MEDITERRANEAN
ZUCCHINI PASTA SALAD

TIME TO PREPARE
20 minutes

TIME TO COOK
5 minutes

SERVES 6
◉ ◉

In my first cookbook, I shared a recipe for Italian Zucchini Pasta Salad that might be the most popular of all my cookbook and blog recipes—ever! It's always being made in the summertime and brought to potluck dinners and BBQ parties. After making it dozens of times, I knew I had to come up with something just as easy and shareable, but with different flavors. So this vegetarian version was born, made with a Mediterranean flair instead of Italian. Chock-full of salty flavor from olives and chickpeas and filled with plenty of vegetables, this zucchini pasta salad is going to give the Italian version a run for its money!

For the dressing

¼ cup extra-virgin olive oil

2 tablespoons red wine vinegar

1 tablespoon fresh lemon juice

1 teaspoon dried oregano

½ teaspoon dried parsley

½ teaspoon garlic powder

1 teaspoon Dijon mustard

Fine sea salt and pepper

For the salad

2 medium zucchini

1 small red onion

1 (14-ounce) can quartered artichoke hearts, drained

½ cup halved pitted kalamata olives

1 (15-ounce) can chickpeas, drained and rinsed

½ cup crumbled feta cheese (optional)

2 cups baby spinach

1 cup cherry tomatoes, halved

Make the dressing. In a medium bowl, whisk together the olive oil, vinegar, lemon juice, oregano, parsley, garlic powder, and mustard. Taste and season with salt and pepper.

Make the salad. Slice the zucchini halfway through lengthwise, being careful not to pierce through the center. Spiralize the zucchini with Blade C and put them in a large bowl. Slice the onion halfway through lengthwise, being careful not to pierce through the center. Spiralize the onion with Blade A and add half the onion noodles to the bowl with the zucchini noodles. (Save the rest for another use.) Add the artichokes, olives, chickpeas, feta (if using), spinach, and tomatoes to the bowl.

Pour the dressing over the salad and toss well to combine. Serve immediately or refrigerate until ready to serve.

TIP / *This salad is best the next day, when the zucchini has softened and absorbed all the flavors of the dressing.*

Not Spiralized / Vegetarian
Gluten-Free

NUTRITIONAL INFORMATION *Per serving*
Calories **436** / Fat **42g** / Sat Fat **7g** / Sodium **332mg**
Carbs **7g** / Fiber **2g** / Sugar **2g** / Protein **13g**

CACIO E PEPE KALE

/ *with* / FRIED EGG

TIME TO PREPARE
20 minutes

TIME TO COOK
10 minutes

SERVES 4

Cacio e pepe means "cheese and pepper" in Italian and is the name of a classic pasta dish usually made with spaghetti or bucatini. The hot pasta noodles are tossed with olive oil, cheese, and lots of freshly cracked black pepper to create a simple but memorable meal. With this dish, I've turned a beloved pasta into a salad, using the same ingredients in the classic dish but tossing it with chopped kale instead of noodles. The fried egg's yolk runs into the kale and cheese, creating a carbonara-like sauce that will transport you right to Italy.

For the dressing

1 large egg yolk

3 tablespoons unsweetened almond milk

1 teaspoon apple cider vinegar

1 small garlic clove, minced

½ cup extra-virgin olive oil

2 tablespoons grated Parmesan cheese, plus more for dusting

3 tablespoons grated Pecorino Romano cheese, plus more for dusting

¾ teaspoon coarsely cracked black peppercorns, plus more for garnish

¼ teaspoon fine sea salt, plus more to taste

¼ cup raw pine nuts

Cooking spray

4 large eggs

8 cups shredded curly kale leaves (about 8 ounces)

Make the dressing. In a food processor, combine the egg yolk, almond milk, vinegar, and garlic and process until combined. With the motor running, drizzle in the olive oil until incorporated. Add the cheeses and peppercorns and process until smooth. Season with the salt. Taste and adjust the seasoning as needed.

Toast the pine nuts in a large nonstick skillet over medium-high heat until golden brown and fragrant, about 3 minutes. Transfer the nuts to a small bowl.

Return the skillet to the heat and spray with cooking spray. Working in batches as needed, crack in the eggs. Cover and cook until the egg whites set, about 3 minutes.

Pour the dressing into a large bowl and add the kale. Toss well to combine. Divide the kale among four plates. Top each salad with an egg. Garnish each with an extra teaspoon of cheese, some freshly cracked pepper, and the pine nuts.

Spiralized / Saves Well
Gluten-Free / Dairy-Free
Low-Cal

NUTRITIONAL INFORMATION *For each of 8 servings*
Calories **196** / Fat **4g** / Sat Fat **1g** / Sodium **100mg**
Carbs **40g** / Fiber **3g** / Sugar **7g** / Protein **7g**

CORN CHOWDER SALAD

/ *with* / BACON & POTATOES

TIME TO PREPARE
20 minutes

TIME TO COOK
20 minutes

SERVES 8 TO 10 AS A SIDE SALAD

With my creative thinking cap on, I have reimagined this classic New England soup into a salad, eliminating the need for the butter, cream, milk, and flour that typically make this chowder decadent. By turning this dish into a salad, it becomes shareable at a BBQ or a summer dinner. The potato noodles soak up the salty bacon flavors and give this salad a hearty, savory taste. Unlike a proper corn chowder, this salad can be prepped ahead of time, making it even better for those warm summer nights.

4 thick-cut bacon slices, cut into ½-inch pieces

1 pound Yukon Gold potatoes, spiralized with Blade D, noodles trimmed

1 medium red onion, peeled, spiralized with Blade A, noodles trimmed

2 red bell peppers, spiralized with Blade A, noodles trimmed

¼ teaspoon red pepper flakes

1 teaspoon garlic powder

¼ teaspoon paprika

Fine sea salt and pepper

Kernels from 6 ears corn

¼ cup apple cider vinegar

2 tablespoons finely chopped fresh parsley

Cook the bacon in a large skillet over medium-low heat until crisp, 5 to 7 minutes, flipping halfway through. Transfer to a paper towel–lined plate to drain.

Pour off all but 2 tablespoons of the bacon fat from the skillet. Set the skillet over medium-high heat and add the potatoes, onion, bell peppers, and red pepper flakes. Add the garlic powder and paprika and season with salt and black pepper. Cook until the potatoes are browned and cooked through, about 10 minutes. Add the corn and cook until warmed through, about 3 minutes.

Transfer the mixture to a large serving bowl and add the vinegar and bacon. Season with salt and black pepper. Toss well to combine, garnish with the parsley, and serve.

NUTRITIONAL INFORMATION *Per serving*
Calories **561** / Fat **42g** / Sat Fat **24g** / Sodium **837mg**
Carbs **12g** / Fiber **1g** / Sugar **5g** / Protein **29g**

SPICY PORK COCONUT CURRY SOUP

/ *with* / **DAIKON NOODLES**

TIME TO PREPARE
10 minutes

TIME TO COOK
30 minutes

SERVES 4

I love spicy food. In fact, I love the kind of spicy food that clears your sinuses, especially spicy soups with lots of toppings that offset the spice, like an Asian curry soup with noodles. This dish has plenty of fixings to absorb the spiciness from the red curry paste and hot ground pork. The coconut broth balances the spicy pork and the crunchy daikon noodles absorb all the curry's flavors and soften just enough to mimic a true curry noodle bowl.

For the curry

1 tablespoon coconut oil

2 tablespoons red curry paste

1 shallot, minced

3 garlic cloves, minced

2 (14-ounce) cans lite coconut milk

2 cups low-sodium chicken broth or vegetable broth

Fine sea salt

1 tablespoon fish sauce

2 to 3 daikon radishes, peeled, spiralized with Blade D, noodles trimmed

For the pork

1 tablespoon coconut oil

1 pound lean ground pork

Fine sea salt

1 (1-inch) piece fresh ginger, peeled and minced

1 garlic clove, minced

2 to 3 teaspoons sambal oelek or Sriracha

4 scallions, chopped

4 hard-boiled eggs, halved

Fresh cilantro, for garnish

1 lime, quartered

Make the curry. Melt the coconut oil in a large pot over medium heat. When the oil is shimmering, add the curry paste, shallot, and garlic and cook, stirring continuously, for 4 to 5 minutes, until the vegetables soften. Add the coconut milk and broth and season generously with salt. Bring the mixture to a boil, then reduce the heat to medium-low and simmer for 20 minutes. Add the fish sauce and daikon noodles and cook until the daikon softens, about 5 minutes.

Meanwhile, make the pork. Melt the coconut oil in a large skillet over medium-high heat. When the oil is shimmering, add the pork and season with salt. Cook, breaking up the meat with a wooden spoon as it cooks, until browned, about 7 minutes. Add the ginger and garlic and cook until fragrant, 1 to 2 minutes. Stir in the sambal oelek and cook for 1 minute more. Remove the skillet from the heat.

Divide the curry evenly among four bowls. Top evenly with the pork, scallions, and eggs and garnish with cilantro. Serve immediately with lime wedges for squeezing.

TIP / *Sambal oelek is a spicy chile-vinegar paste common in Southeast Asian cuisine. If you can't find it, Sriracha will do just fine.*

Not Spiralized / Vegan
Dairy-Free / Low-Cal

NUTRITIONAL INFORMATION *Per serving*
Calories **273** / Fat **10g** / Sat Fat **1g** / Sodium **716mg**
Carbs **43g** / Fiber **11g** / Sugar **10g** / Protein **10g**

BEET POKĒ BOWL
/ *with* / SEAWEED

TIME TO PREPARE
40 minutes

TIME TO COOK
45 minutes

SERVES 4

◉ ◉ ◉

When planning a vacation to Hawaii for our babymoon, I couldn't help but be disappointed by one thing: I would be going to the motherland of pokē, a delicious raw fish salad, and wouldn't be able to have any. After a few weeks of early-onset FOMO, I decided to take matters into my own hands. One day, while at a Whole Foods salad bar, I saw "sesame marinated beets with seaweed" and thought, *That looks like pokē!*, inspiring the creation of this vegetarian (and pregnancy-friendly) pokē bowl.

3 medium Chiogga or golden beets

2 tablespoons dried hijiki seaweed

¼ cup mirin

For the beet marinade

2 tablespoons low-sodium soy sauce

1 teaspoon toasted sesame oil

1 tablespoon rice vinegar

1 teaspoon finely grated fresh ginger

1 teaspoon white sesame seeds

¼ cup chopped scallions

⅛ teaspoon fine sea salt, plus more to taste

For the radishes

3 tablespoons rice vinegar

½ teaspoon salt

½ teaspoon honey

4 small Cherry Belle radishes, thinly sliced

To assemble

1⅓ cups cooked brown rice or spiralized zucchini rice (see page 18)

1 cup steamed shelled edamame

1 large carrot, shaved into thin strips with a vegetable peeler

1 large ripe avocado, pitted, peeled, and thinly sliced

TIP / *If you can't find hijiki seaweed, you can use a premade seaweed salad instead.*

Preheat the oven to 400 degrees.

Wrap the beets in aluminum foil and place on a baking sheet. Roast until fork-tender, about 45 minutes. Remove the foil and let cool. When cool enough to handle, peel the beets and cut them into cubes.

While the beets are roasting, in a small bowl, soak the hijiki in ½ cup cold water until rehydrated and softened, about 30 minutes. Drain, add the mirin, and soak for 5 minutes more. Drain again.

Marinate the beets. In a medium bowl, whisk together the soy sauce, sesame oil, vinegar, ginger, sesame seeds, scallions, and salt. Add the beets, toss, and set aside to marinate for at least 20 minutes and up to 1 hour.

Marinate the radishes. In a separate medium bowl, whisk together the vinegar, salt, and honey. Add the radishes and toss to coat. Let marinate alongside the beets.

Assemble the bowls. Divide the rice among four bowls. Working in a circle, arrange the edamame, seaweed, carrots, radishes, and avocado on top of the rice. Using a slotted spoon, add the beets to the center of each bowl, dividing them evenly. Drizzle each bowl with marinade remaining in the bowl and serve.

Spiralized / Saves Well
Vegetarian / Dairy-Free

NUTRITIONAL INFORMATION *Per serving*
Calories **420** / Fat **26g** / Sat Fat **3g** / Sodium **595mg**
Carbs **43g** / Fiber **5g** / Sugar **15g** / Protein **13g**

THAI CASHEW CHOPPED SALAD
/ *with* / SESAME-GARLIC DRESSING

TIME TO PREPARE
30 minutes

TIME TO COOK
15 minutes

SERVES 4

Lu and I went to Thailand for our first wedding anniversary. We wanted to go somewhere neither of us had been that was exotic with beautiful beaches. While the stunning mountainous islands in the middle of the ocean and emerald green water were certainly unforgettable, the food made the longest-lasting impression. With fresh fish, colorful vegetables, and fragrant ginger and fish sauce, almost every meal left us talking for hours afterward about it. What I noticed the most was how crisp and refreshing Thai chopped salads were. After returning home, I found myself craving them. This salad is my best attempt at re-creating one of those spectacular dishes.

For the dressing

2 tablespoons avocado oil or extra-virgin olive oil

3 tablespoons sesame oil

3 tablespoons low-sodium soy sauce (use coconut aminos or gluten-free tamari, if gluten-free)

2 tablespoons rice vinegar

1 teaspoon fresh lime juice

2 tablespoons honey

1 tablespoon grated fresh ginger

3 garlic cloves, chopped

For the salad

⅓ cup roasted cashews

12 ounces shelled edamame, steamed

4 cups shredded rainbow chard leaves

1 large carrot, spiralized with Blade D, noodles coarsely chopped

2 scallions, chopped

1 red bell pepper, spiralized with Blade A, noodles chopped into 2-inch pieces

1 yellow bell pepper, spiralized with Blade A, noodles chopped into 2-inch pieces

2 cups spiralized red cabbage (use Blade A; about ½ small cabbage)

½ cup fresh cilantro, coarsely chopped

½ cup cooked red quinoa, preferably chilled

1 tablespoon white sesame seeds, for garnish

Make the dressing. In a food processor, combine the avocado oil, sesame oil, soy sauce, vinegar, lime juice, honey, ginger, and garlic and process until smooth. Transfer to a small bowl. Clean out the food processor bowl and blade.

Make the salad. In the clean food processor, combine the cashews and edamame and pulse until minced. Transfer to a large bowl. Add the chard, carrot, scallions, bell peppers, cabbage, cilantro, and quinoa.

Drizzle the dressing around the rim of the bowl, toss the salad well to coat, garnish with the sesame seeds, and serve.

Not Spiralized / No-Cook
Vegan / Gluten-Free
Dairy-Free / Low-Cal

NUTRITIONAL INFORMATION *Per serving*
Calories **282** / Fat **11g** / Sat Fat **1g** / Sodium **803mg**
Carbs **42g** / Fiber **15g** / Sugar **1g** / Protein **13g**

CHICKPEA "TUNA" SALAD
/ with / AVOCADO & SUNFLOWER SEEDS

TIME TO PREPARE
15 minutes

SERVES 2

When I have to travel somewhere for work, I love bringing my mother along. We don't have much one-on-one time, so when there's an excuse to be together for a few days, we make the most of it. One such trip took us to St. Petersburg, Florida, where I filmed a live segment on HSN for my Inspiralizer. On a lunch break, after scrolling through Yelp for a few minutes, I found a vegan café named Love Food Central in a nearby hip neighborhood. My mother and I both ordered the same thing: the garbanzo mash. The menu description explained that it was a "vegan tuna salad on toast." Curious, we dug in—and were pleasantly surprised at how much it tasted like tuna salad. Made with mashed chickpeas and sunflower seeds for a salty kick, it had excellent flavor and a similar consistency to real tuna salad. Although the café's version was made with a vegan mayonnaise, I wanted to create a less processed version, using avocado as the creamy element.

1 (15-ounce) can chickpeas, drained and rinsed

½ ripe avocado, pitted, peeled, and mashed (about ¼ heaping cup)

1 tablespoon whole-grain mustard

1 tablespoon fresh lemon juice

¼ cup diced celery

¼ cup diced red onion

½ teaspoon Old Bay seasoning

1 tablespoon sunflower seeds

Fine sea salt and pepper

Bibb lettuce cups or chopped greens, for serving

In a medium bowl, mash the chickpeas with a fork until chunky-smooth. Add the avocado, mustard, lemon juice, celery, onion, Old Bay seasoning, and sunflower seeds. Season with salt and pepper, and stir well to combine.

Serve in lettuce cups or over chopped greens.

TIP / *Spread this over a roasted rutabaga slab (see page 139) for a sandwich.*

SANDWICHES

Not Spiralized
Gluten-Free / Paleo
Dairy-Free / Low-Cal

NUTRITIONAL INFORMATION *Per sandwich*
Calories **76** / Fat **4g** / Sat Fat **3g** / Sodium **398mg**
Carbs **6g** / Fiber **1g** / Sugar **0g** / Protein **6g**

KIELBASA & SAUERKRAUT SANDWICHES

/ *on* / POTATO "BUNS"

TIME TO PREPARE
20 minutes

TIME TO COOK
35 minutes

SERVES 12
as an appetizer or 4 as a
main course

This potato bun was inspired by mafrum, a Libyan dish popular in Jewish cooking. Typically, this stuffed potato dish consists of a mixture of ground beef and spices sandwiched inside a potato and cooked in a tomato sauce. When I first saw mafrum, I thought the potato part would work perfectly as a hamburger or hot dog bun alternative. Instead of ground beef, I stuff these potatoes with kielbasa sausage and top them with sauerkraut and mustard for a totally healthy spin on mafrum. Incorporating sauerkraut into your diet helps aid in digestion, as it contains microorganisms that feed the good bacteria in your gut.

Cooking spray

2 large russet potatoes, peeled

1½ tablespoons extra-virgin olive oil

½ teaspoon garlic powder

Fine sea salt and pepper

2 kielbasa sausages

1½ cups prepared sauerkraut

Dijon mustard, for serving

Preheat the oven to 425 degrees. Spray a large nonstick baking sheet with cooking spray.

Slice ½ inch off the sides of the potatoes and discard. Cut the potatoes crosswise into ½-inch-thick slices—each potato, depending on its size, should yield about 6 slices. Cut each round crosswise down the middle, being careful not to pierce through the slice entirely, just enough to create the center of the "bun" where you'll stuff the sausage and filling. Brush the potatoes with the olive oil and season both sides with the garlic powder and salt and pepper to taste. Arrange the potatoes on one side of the prepared baking sheet and the sausages on the other.

Roast together until the sausages are cooked through, 20 to 25 minutes. Remove the sausages and return the baking sheet to the oven. Roast the potatoes for 5 to 10 minutes more, until browning and cooked through. Meanwhile, halve the sausages lengthwise and then crosswise into thirds to create 12 pieces.

Let the potatoes cool for 5 minutes, until cool enough to handle. Spoon about 2 tablespoons of the sauerkraut onto each potato round and top each with a sausage piece.

Serve with mustard on the side.

Not Spiralized / Vegetarian
Gluten-Free / Low-Cal

NUTRITIONAL INFORMATION *Per sandwich*
Calories **263** / Fat **16g** / Sat Fat **6g** / Sodium **238mg**
Carbs **27g** / Fiber **7g** / Sugar **10g** / Protein **6g**

OPEN-FACED

ROASTED VEGGIE & HAVARTI RUTABAGA MELTS

TIME TO PREPARE
20 minutes

TIME TO COOK
30 minutes

MAKES 4 SANDWICHES

Comfort food at its finest, these roasted veggie melts are all about the gooey cheese! Havarti, a semisoft Danish cow's-milk cheese, has a distinctively rich, buttery taste and melts beautifully on top of these savory roasted vegetables. By using slabs of rutabaga as the base for this open-faced melt, you get an extra kick of veggies. The Dijon mustard is the proverbial cherry on top for a quick hit of spice at the end. You may want to halve these and serve them as appetizers to share.

1 small rutabaga, sliced into four ½-inch-thick slabs (see Tip)

2 tablespoons extra-virgin olive oil

Fine sea salt and pepper

1 red onion, sliced into rings

2 large carrots, sliced into ¼-inch-thick rounds

2 large parsnips, peeled and sliced into ¼-inch-thick rounds

1 tablespoon fresh thyme

1 tablespoon Dijon mustard

4 slices Havarti cheese

TIP / *Slice the rutabaga lengthwise if you'd like longer sandwiches (like a baguette) or crosswise if you prefer rounder sandwiches (like a ciabatta).*

Preheat the oven to 425 degrees. Line two baking sheets with parchment paper.

Arrange the rutabaga slabs on one of the baking sheets, brush with one-third of the olive oil, and season lightly with salt and pepper. On the other baking sheet, spread out the onion, carrots, and parsnips. Drizzle with the remaining oil, season with the thyme and salt and pepper to taste, and toss well to coat. Roast together for 25 to 30 minutes, until the rutabaga is fork-tender and the veggies are fork-tender and browned. Remove from the oven, but keep the oven on.

On each rutabaga slab, spread a thin layer of the mustard. Pile roasted veggies on top, dividing them evenly, then top each with a slice of cheese. Return to the oven and roast for 5 to 7 minutes, until the cheese melts. Serve hot.

Not Spiralized / Vegetarian
Gluten-Free / Low-Cal

NUTRITIONAL INFORMATION *Per serving*
Calories **192** / Fat **12g** / Sat Fat **4g** / Sodium **258mg**
Carbs **12g** / Fiber **4g** / Sugar **8g** / Protein **10g**

VEGETARIAN MEATBALL SUB
/ *in* / ZUCCHINI

TIME TO PREPARE
20 minutes

TIME TO COOK
30 minutes

SERVES 4

◎ ◎ ◎

When thinking imaginatively about eating veggies and fruits, it's easy to go for shock value and come up with the craziest things you can do with them. Maybe you've seen avocados used as burger buns—not exactly practical, but certainly creative. While the thought of stuffing zucchini with meatballs may seem over the top, it's not only a delicious way to eat zucchini but also a great way to reduce food waste and thus, *very* practical.

4 medium zucchini

1 tablespoon extra-virgin olive oil

1 garlic clove, minced

½ cup almond flour

1 small egg, beaten

2 tablespoons grated Parmesan cheese

½ teaspoon dried oregano

¼ teaspoon dried basil

Fine sea salt and pepper

Cooking spray

½ cup prepared marinara sauce (I like Victoria Fine Foods)

½ cup shredded mozzarella cheese

¼ cup chopped fresh basil

Preheat the oven to 375 degrees. Line two baking sheets with parchment paper.

Line a medium bowl with cheesecloth or a kitchen towel. Slice the zucchini in half lengthwise. Using a spoon or melon baller, scoop out the flesh, leaving enough skin to keep the zucchini intact, about ⅛ inch, and transfer the flesh to the lined bowl. Twist the cloth over the sink to squeeze out as much of the liquid from the flesh as possible.

Transfer the zucchini shells to one of the prepared baking sheets and arrange them cut-side up.

Heat the olive oil in a large skillet over medium-high heat. When the oil is shimmering, add the garlic and cook until fragrant, about 30 seconds. Add the drained zucchini and cook, stirring occasionally and mashing the flesh with a wooden spoon as it cooks, until all the liquid has evaporated, about 5 minutes.

/ recipe continues

TIP / *Try these "zucchini boats" another (not vegetarian) way: lay a sausage link in a hollowed-out zucchini half instead of meatballs, top with cheese and sauce, and you have a whole new meal!*

Transfer the zucchini mixture to a large bowl and let cool slightly. Use a fork to mash any remaining large chunks. Add the almond flour, egg, cheese, oregano, basil, ¼ teaspoon salt, and a few grinds of pepper. Mix well and, using your hands, form the mixture into 12 balls, rolling them tightly. Transfer to the other prepared baking sheet.

Spray the tops of the meatballs with cooking spray and bake until firm and browned, about 20 minutes. Transfer the zucchini shells to the oven at the same time and bake until mostly softened but still firm, about 20 minutes.

Stuff 3 meatballs each into 4 of the zucchini shells. Top with marinara sauce and sprinkle with the mozzarella. Return to the oven and bake until the cheese melts, about 5 minutes.

Garnish the stuffed zucchini halves with the fresh basil. Transfer to plates and top with the unstuffed zucchini halves to finish your meatball subs. Serve hot.

ALSO WORKS WELL WITH
Parsnip / White Potato

Spiralized / Vegetarian
Gluten-Free / Low-Cal

NUTRITIONAL INFORMATION *Per one half*
Calories **143** / Fat **6g** / Sat Fat **3g** / Sodium **262mg**
Carbs **16g** / Fiber **2g** / Sugar **3g** / Protein **7g**

SWEET POTATO WAFFLE GRILLED CHEESE

TIME TO PREPARE
10 minutes

TIME TO COOK
20 minutes

SERVES 2
◉ ◉ ◉

The "will it waffle?" trend definitely had some merit—one of my favorites was the grilled cheese. Trust me: A waffled grilled cheese truly is a fun spin on the original! Of course, with just cheese and bread, there's not much nutritional value, so I set out to make a healthier spiralized version—using my spiralized sweet potato waffles! Sweet potatoes add a sweet flavor to complement the savory cheese and bring added nutritional benefits, such as vitamins A and C and potassium. See— even grilled cheese can become a healthy treat!

1 tablespoon extra-virgin olive oil

1 large sweet potato, peeled, spiralized with Blade D, noodles trimmed

Fine sea salt and pepper

1 large egg, beaten

Cooking spray

1 or 2 slices white cheddar cheese

Preheat a waffle iron according to the manufacturer's instructions.

Heat the olive oil in a large skillet over medium heat. When the oil is shimmering, add the sweet potatoes and season with salt and pepper. Cook, tossing, for about 10 minutes, until the noodles are warmed through. Transfer the noodles to a large bowl and add the egg. Toss to coat.

Spray the preheated waffle iron with cooking spray and carefully pack in the noodles. Cook the waffle according to the manufacturer's instructions. Carefully remove the waffle and transfer to a plate. Repeat with the remaining noodles to make a second waffle.

Spray the waffle iron with cooking spray again and return one waffle to the iron, fitting it into the grooves. Top with the cheese and place the other waffle on top. Close the waffle iron (it's okay if it doesn't close completely) and cook until the cheese melts and oozes from the sides, about 5 minutes.

Carefully remove the waffle grilled cheese and cut it in half with a sharp knife before serving.

Spiralized / Vegetarian
Gluten-Free / Low-Cal

NUTRITIONAL INFORMATION *Per reuben*

Calories **247** / Fat **15g** / Sat Fat **6g** / Sodium **633mg**
Carbs **18g** / Fiber **4g** / Sugar **10g** / Protein **9g**

OPEN-FACED
RED CABBAGE REUBEN

TIME TO PREPARE
15 minutes

TIME TO COOK
40 minutes

SERVES 4 TO 6

This hot sandwich typically contains corned beef, sauerkraut, Russian dressing, and Swiss cheese. It usually comes stacked high on rye bread with globs of dressing dripping down the sides. While this kind of sandwich has its time and place, sometimes it's better to find your own healthy, creative alternative that you can enjoy all the time—and then when you *do* splurge on the real deal, you appreciate it that much more. This vegetarian Reuben uses red cabbage seasoned with horseradish and balsamic vinegar to mimic the sauerkraut–corned beef combo and doesn't skimp on the Swiss cheese, because #balance.

1 small rutabaga, peeled and cut into ⅛-inch-thick slices

2 tablespoons extra-virgin olive oil

2 cups spiralized purple cabbage (use Blade A; about ½ small cabbage)

3 cups baby spinach

¼ cup prepared horseradish

¼ cup balsamic vinegar

Fine sea salt and pepper

4 to 6 tablespoons whole-grain mustard

4 to 6 slices Swiss cheese

Preheat the oven to 425 degrees. Line a baking sheet with parchment paper.

Arrange the rutabaga slabs on the prepared baking sheet. Brush with 1 tablespoon of the olive oil and roast until fork-tender, about 25 minutes. Remove the rutabaga slabs from the oven and set aside, but keep the oven on.

Meanwhile, heat the remaining 1 tablespoon olive oil in a large skillet over medium-high heat. When the oil is shimmering, add the cabbage and cook for 5 minutes, until wilted. Add the spinach, horseradish, vinegar, and salt and pepper to taste and cook for about 3 minutes, until the liquid has reduced. Remove the pan from the heat and set aside.

Spread 1 tablespoon of the mustard over each rutabaga slab. Top with the cabbage and then a slice of cheese. Return to the oven and bake for 5 to 7 minutes more, until the cheese melts. Remove from the oven and serve.

Not Spiralized
Gluten-Free / Paleo
Dairy-Free / Low-Cal

NUTRITIONAL INFORMATION *Per slider*
Calories **201** / Fat **12g** / Sat Fat **3g** / Sodium **209mg**
Carbs **20g** / Fiber **5g** / Sugar **5g** / Protein **5g**

BLT SWEET POTATO SLIDERS

/ *with* / CILANTRO LIME AVOCADO MAYO

TIME TO PREPARE
15 minutes

TIME TO COOK
20 minutes

MAKES 4 SLIDERS

Every time Lu and I go out for our favorite BLT sandwich down the street in our neighborhood, we face the inevitable question, "Would you like fries or salad with that?" To take some temptation off the table (literally), Lu will order sweet potato fries and I'll order a side salad and we'll split both. Here there's no compromise, and every bite is full of nourishing real foods. We love this meal especially because of the addicting salty-and-sweet combo from the sweet potatoes and bacon. And no sharing needed, because these sliders are made from all good-for-you ingredients, like this avocado "mayo."

2 large sweet potatoes, each sliced into eight ½-inch-thick rounds

1 tablespoon extra-virgin olive oil

4 bacon slices, cut into thirds

1 small ripe avocado, pitted and peeled

Juice of ½ lime

2 tablespoons chopped fresh cilantro

Fine sea salt and pepper

2 romaine lettuce leaves, chopped into 2-inch pieces

2 small beefsteak tomatoes, each sliced into 4 rounds

Preheat the oven to 425 degrees. Line a baking sheet with parchment paper.

Arrange the sweet potato rounds on the prepared baking sheet. Brush with the olive oil and roast until fork-tender, 20 to 25 minutes. Let cool for about 5 minutes.

Meanwhile, cook the bacon in a large skillet over medium heat until crispy, about 10 minutes, flipping halfway through. Transfer to a paper towel–lined plate to drain.

While the bacon cooks, in a mini food processor, combine the avocado, lime juice, and cilantro and pulse until creamy; add water as needed, 1 tablespoon at a time, to thin the mixture. Taste and season with salt and pepper as needed.

Smear 1 side of each sweet potato with the avocado mayo and top with some lettuce, followed by a slice of tomato. Top with a slice of bacon and then another sweet potato round. Pierce with a toothpick to secure. Repeat to make 4 sliders. Serve.

Spiralized / Saves Well
Gluten-Free

NUTRITIONAL INFORMATION *1 full bell pepper cup sandwich*
Calories **489** / Fat **31g** / Sat Fat **16g** / Sodium **546mg**
Carbs **10g** / Fiber **5g** / Sugar **2g** / Protein **41g**

PHILLY CHEESESTEAKS

/ *in* / BELL PEPPER CUPS

TIME TO PREPARE
10 minutes

TIME TO COOK
35 minutes

SERVES 4 TO 8

When I was in high school, I went on a date and had my first Philly cheesesteak. This was before my healthy enlightenment, when I ate anything I wanted. It was a classic case of "ignorance is bliss." We went to Geno's—I'll say *one of* the spots where they serve the best cheesesteaks to avoid taking sides in that classic Philly debate! It was absolutely delicious, but I distinctly remember thinking there was too much bread. See, I've always been a filling kinda gal—I like my sandwiches packed so full that I can barely fit my mouth around them. This bell pepper cup version completely eliminates that issue and lets you focus on the steak, onions, and provolone cheese that make this Philadelphia-born sandwich one of a kind.

Cooking spray

4 green bell peppers, halved

1 tablespoon extra-virgin olive oil

1 pound sirloin steak, thinly sliced

2 garlic cloves, minced

1 large white onion, peeled, spiralized with Blade A, noodles trimmed

1 pound cremini mushrooms, sliced

Fine sea salt and pepper

8 slices provolone cheese

Preheat the oven to 325 degrees. Coat a large baking dish with cooking spray.

Place the bell peppers in the prepared baking dish and bake until tender, 15 to 20 minutes. Remove from the oven, set aside, and turn the broiler to high.

While peppers roast, heat the olive oil in a large skillet over medium-high heat. When the oil is shimmering, add the steak and cook until browned on both sides, 6 to 7 minutes. Using tongs, transfer to a plate. Immediately add the garlic, onion, and mushrooms to the skillet and season with salt and black pepper. Cook for 5 to 7 minutes, until the onions are tender. Return the beef to the skillet. Stir to combine.

Stuff the beef-and-onion mixture carefully into each bell pepper half. Top each with a slice of provolone. Return to the oven and broil for 3 minutes, until the cheese is melted and bubbling. Serve immediately.

Not Spiralized / Vegetarian
Dairy-Free / Low-Cal

NUTRITIONAL INFORMATION *Per roll*
Calories **218** / Fat **10g** / Sat Fat **1g** / Sodium **851mg**
Carbs **34g** / Fiber **7g** / Sugar **13g** / Protein **6g**

TERIYAKI

EGGPLANT NORI BURRITO ROLL

TIME TO PREPARE
20 minutes

TIME TO COOK
10 minutes

SERVES 4

Eggplant is a versatile ingredient, especially as a meat replacement. It absorbs flavor well, softens well, and can take on the personality of certain meats with the right marinades and seasonings. After transforming eggplant into teriyaki meat, I stuffed it into a nori roll and came up with this trendy sushirito (sushi burrito).

For the eggplant

¼ cup low-sodium soy sauce (use coconut aminos or gluten-free tamari, if gluten-free)

¼ cup fresh orange juice

1 tablespoon rice vinegar

1 tablespoon sesame oil

1 tablespoon honey

1 teaspoon hot sauce, or pinch of red pepper flakes

1½ teaspoons grated fresh ginger

1 garlic clove, pressed or minced

4 mini eggplants (about 5 inches long) or Japanese eggplants, stemmed and sliced lengthwise into ½-inch-thick strips

1 tablespoon white sesame seeds

For the avocado cream

1 ripe avocado, pitted and peeled

2 teaspoons fresh lime juice

1½ teaspoons wasabi powder

Salt

For the burritos

4 nori sheets

½ cup julienned cucumbers

½ cup julienned carrots

Make the eggplant. In a small bowl, whisk together the soy sauce, orange juice, vinegar, sesame oil, honey, hot sauce, ginger, and garlic. Pour half the mixture into a 10-inch skillet and bring to a simmer over medium heat. Add the eggplant, cover, and cook until golden brown on the bottom, about 5 minutes. Flip, add the rest of the sauce, cover, and cook for 5 to 7 minutes more, until caramelized. Stir in the sesame seeds, and remove the skillet from the heat.

Meanwhile, make the avocado cream. In a mini food processor, combine the avocado, lime juice, and wasabi powder and process until smooth. Taste and adjust the seasoning with more wasabi powder, if desired, and salt.

Assemble the burritos. Set a nori sheet on a clean surface, with one short side facing you. Working on the part closest to you, spread one-quarter of the avocado cream over one-third of the nori, leaving 1 inch on the bottom of the piece. Top with one-quarter of the cucumbers and carrots. Using tongs, arrange one-quarter of the teriyaki eggplant on top.

Roll up the nori to enclose the filling, applying pressure and tucking as you roll. Slice the roll in half and, if desired, slice off the ends to make it look neater. Repeat with the remaining ingredients.

Pour any teriyaki sauce from the skillet into a dipping bowl and serve it alongside the burritos.

Spiralized / Vegan
Gluten-Free / Dairy-Free
Low-Cal

NUTRITIONAL INFORMATION *Per wrap*
Calories **225** / Fat **12g** / Sat Fat **2g** / Sodium **885mg**
Carbs **25g** / Fiber **10g** / Sugar **6g** / Protein **6g**

COLLARD GREEN FAJITA WRAPS

/ *with* / BLACK BEAN-AVO MASH

TIME TO PREPARE
15 minutes

TIME TO COOK
15 minutes

MAKES 4 WRAPS

I work very hard and I love what I do, but I've learned to practice self-care and take time off throughout the day—for both mental sanity and work quality. Each day I have a proper lunch away from my computer. For one month, I made something different for lunch every day. My favorite? This fajita wrap. It has all the great flavors of fajitas with a healthy lightness thanks to the collard greens and the fiber and nutritious fats from the veggies and avocado.

For the fajita seasoning

¼ teaspoon cayenne pepper

1 teaspoon chili powder

¼ teaspoon paprika

½ teaspoon smoked paprika

½ teaspoon onion powder

¼ teaspoon ground cumin

½ teaspoon salt

¼ teaspoon dried oregano

For the fajitas

4 collard greens, stems trimmed

1 tablespoon extra-virgin olive oil

2 red bell peppers, spiralized with Blade A, noodles trimmed

2 green bell peppers, spiralized with Blade A, noodles trimmed

1 large white onion, peeled, spiralized with Blade A, noodles trimmed

1 (15-ounce) can refried black beans

1 ripe avocado, pitted and peeled

Juice of 1 lime

Fine sea salt and pepper

Make the fajita seasoning. In a small bowl, mix together the cayenne, chili powder, paprika, smoked paprika, onion powder, cumin, salt, and oregano.

Make the fajitas. Fill a large pot one-third of the way with water and bring to a boil over high heat. Once boiling, add the collard green leaves and blanch to soften the cores, about 2 minutes. Remove and drain in a colander.

Heat the olive oil in a large skillet over medium-high heat. When the oil is shimmering, add the bell peppers, onion, and fajita seasoning; toss to coat. Cook until the vegetables are tender, 5 to 7 minutes.

Meanwhile, place the black beans and avocado in a medium bowl. Mash together with a fork until chunky-smooth. Add the lime juice and season with salt and black pepper. Stir to combine.

Pat the collard leaves dry and spread them out on a clean surface. Divide the black bean mixture evenly among the collard leaves and spread it over each leaf in an even layer, leaving a 1-inch border. Top with the bell pepper mixture. Fold the bottom and top edges of each leaf in and then roll like a burrito, tucking as you go. Slice the rolls in half and pierce each side with a toothpick to hold the roll together. Serve.

Not Spiralized / Gluten-Free
Saves Well / Vegan
Dairy-Free / Low-Cal

NUTRITIONAL INFORMATION ⅔ cup larb + 2 or 3 lettuce cups
Calories **189** / Fat **10g** / Sat Fat **4g** / Sodium **812mg**
Carbs **19g** / Fiber **7g** / Sugar **10g** / Protein **9g**

MUSHROOM-WALNUT LARB
/ in / LETTUCE CUPS

TIME TO PREPARE
20 minutes

TIME TO COOK
20 minutes

SERVES 4

One of Lu's closest friends is Marc Forgione, a successful chef in New York City. Marc helped his former sous-chef Soulayphet Schwader open his own dream restaurant, Khe-Yo, to honor his Laotian background. Dining at Khe-Yo for the first time, I couldn't believe how unique everything tasted—the sauces, the spices, and the freshness of the ingredients. Inspired, I started researching Southeast Asian food and discovered larb, a ground meat dish flavored with fish sauce, lime, and fresh herbs. It's often served over lettuce, as it is here, but I've put a spin on the traditional filling, using a mushroom-walnut mixture to mimic the texture of ground meat. With tangy lime juice and salty fish sauce, these vegetarian larb lettuce cups will definitely get you interested in Laotian food!

8 ounces button mushrooms, sliced

4 cups chopped cauliflower florets (from ½ medium head)

⅔ cup chopped raw walnuts

⅓ cup fresh lime juice (from about 3 limes)

2 tablespoons fish sauce (or less, if you don't like the taste)

1 teaspoon honey

2 to 3 teaspoons Thai chile paste or Sriracha, depending on how much spice you like

1 tablespoon coconut oil

1 garlic clove, sliced

3 scallions, thinly sliced, white and green parts kept separate

½ cup chopped fresh cilantro

⅓ cup chopped fresh mint

2 small heads Boston lettuce, leaves separated

½ small red onion, halved and thinly sliced

2 Thai chiles, very thinly sliced (optional)

In a food processor, pulse the mushrooms until finely chopped. Set aside in a medium bowl. Put the cauliflower in the food processor and pulse until finely chopped, being careful not to overpulse into mush. Transfer to the bowl with the mushrooms. Repeat with the walnuts and add them to the bowl.

In a small bowl, stir together the lime juice, fish sauce, honey, and chile paste.

Melt the coconut oil in a large skillet over medium-high heat. When the oil is shimmering, add the garlic and the white parts of the scallions and cook until softened, about 2 minutes. Add the vegetable-walnut mixture and stir well to combine. Add the sauce and cook, stirring occasionally, until the liquid has been absorbed and the vegetables start to brown, about 15 minutes.

Remove the skillet from the heat and let cool for about 10 minutes. Stir in the green parts of the scallions, the cilantro, and the mint.

Transfer the mixture to a serving bowl and serve with the lettuce leaves, red onion, and Thai chiles, if desired, for assembly at the table.

TIP / *Feel free to substitute ground chicken, pork, or beef for the mushroom-walnut mixture if you'd like to try a more authentic version.*

Not Spiralized / Vegetarian
Gluten-Free / Dairy-Free
Low-Cal

NUTRITIONAL INFORMATION *Per toast*
Calories **198** / Fat **13g** / Sat Fat **2g** / Sodium **113mg**
Carbs **16g** / Fiber **5g** / Sugar **2g** / Protein **7g**

POTATO TOAST

/ *with* / GREEN PEA–AVOCADO MASH,
SHAVED EGG & RADISHES

TIME TO PREPARE
20 minutes

TIME TO COOK
25 minutes

SERVES 6

During the summertime, Lu and I love walking over to one of our favorite Jersey City cafés, Short Grain, grabbing a table outside, and ordering iced coffees and avocado toasts. The avocado toast comes with radishes, a fried egg, and feta on top. After about a dozen trips for this same dish, I started making it at home, with some tweaks, such as omitting the feta and using a hard-boiled egg instead, which breaks apart nicely when mashed with a fork. I then discovered that you can easily shred egg with a grater, which really mimics that quintessential crumbly cheese texture. The buttery warm potato slab replaces the toast, resulting in a totally new, healthier breakfast dish!

2 medium russet potatoes, sliced lengthwise into six ½-inch-thick slabs

1 tablespoon extra-virgin olive oil

Fine sea salt and pepper

4 large hard-boiled eggs, peeled

¼ cup frozen sweet peas, cooked and cooled to room temperature

2 ripe avocados, pitted, peeled, and cubed

1 large jalapeño, minced

1 large garlic clove, minced

Juice of 1 lime, plus more as needed

3 tablespoons chopped fresh cilantro

2 Cherry Belle radishes, thinly sliced

Preheat the oven to 425 degrees. Line a baking sheet with parchment paper.

Arrange the potato slabs on the prepared baking sheet. Brush with one-third of the olive oil and season with salt and pepper. Roast until fork-tender, 25 to 30 minutes. Let cool for 5 minutes.

While the potatoes roast, grate the eggs on the large holes of a box grater into a medium bowl.

In a separate medium bowl, mash the peas with a fork or potato masher until chunky. Add the avocado and lightly mash, leaving a little bit of texture. Gently fold in the jalapeño, garlic, lime juice, and cilantro. Season with salt.

Top the potato slabs with the avocado mash. Sprinkle with the grated egg. Finish with the radish slices and serve.

PASTA & NOODLES

ALSO WORKS WELL WITH
Broccoli / Turnip
Zucchini / Kholrabi
Parsnip

Spiralized /
Gluten-Free / Paleo
Dairy-Free

NUTRITIONAL INFORMATION *Per serving*
Calories **390** / Fat **24g** / Sat Fat **3g** / Sodium **669mg**
Carbs **23g** / Fiber **5g** / Sugar **8g** / Protein **25g**

SPAGHETTI AL TONNO

/ *with* / CELERIAC NOODLES

TIME TO PREPARE
15 minutes

TIME TO COOK
20 minutes

SERVES 2

When I first launched Inspiralized, for a while I tried to have "theme days" on the blog—for example, "Skinny Sundays" or "Farmer's Market Thursdays." One of my favorite premises was "5-Minute Pasta," where I'd time myself and attempt to make a spiralized pasta in five minutes or less. This particular challenge led to my first version of spaghetti al tonno, an Italian pasta dish that features canned tuna cooked into tomatoes. The original dish was literally jarred marinara sauce, canned tuna, and zucchini noodles tossed together in a pan for five minutes. While tasty, it didn't exactly take you to Italy, so I've re-created it in a slightly more sophisticated, much tastier way. I promise, this version is well worth the extra few minutes.

2 tablespoons extra-virgin olive oil

1 medium celeriac, peeled, spiralized with Blade D, noodles trimmed

Fine sea salt and pepper

1 tablespoon capers

1 large garlic clove, minced

1 (14.5-ounce) can crushed tomatoes

¼ teaspoon red pepper flakes

1 (6-ounce) can Italian tuna in oil, drained

3 tablespoons chopped fresh parsley

Heat 1 tablespoon of the olive oil in a large skillet over medium-high heat. When the oil is shimmering, add the celeriac noodles and season with salt and black pepper. Cook, tossing frequently, until cooked through and softened, about 10 minutes. Set aside.

Meanwhile, heat the remaining 1 tablespoon olive oil in a large pot over medium-high heat. When the oil is shimmering, add the capers and garlic and cook, stirring, until the garlic is golden, about 1 minute. Add the tomatoes and red pepper flakes, and season with salt and black pepper. Bring the mixture to a simmer, then reduce the heat to medium-low and cook until reduced by half, about 5 minutes. Add the tuna and cook for 5 minutes more, until the tuna is heated through. Stir in the parsley.

Divide the celeriac noodles among two plates. Top with the tuna sauce and serve.

NUTRITIONAL INFORMATION *Per serving*

Calories **406** / Fat **25g** / Sat Fat **4g** / Sodium **1161mg**
Carbs **18g** / Fiber **2g** / Sugar **12g** / Protein **41g**

SPICY SHRIMP
CABBAGE PAD THAI

TIME TO PREPARE
15 minutes

TIME TO COOK
15 minutes

SERVES 2

The moment we landed in Chiang Mai, Thailand, for the first leg of our one-year anniversary trip, I dragged poor jet-lagged Lu to a street fair to get some pad thai. As a lifelong lover of this noodle dish, I couldn't bear to go even one day in Thailand without trying some. That night, I tasted real pad thai—the fish sauce just seemed fresher and sharper, but perhaps it was because I was enchanted by the fact that I was having a truly authentic experience. At all our other meals, we ordered a side order of pad thai because we wanted to taste as many varieties as possible. Hands down, my favorite was a spicy cabbage version with shrimp that I had in southern Thailand—I was pleased to see a "noodle alternative" on the menu and relished the one low-carb meal I ate on that trip. Just like I didn't, you won't miss the noodles in this dish.

1 tablespoon plus
2 teaspoons sesame oil

2 garlic cloves, minced

2 teaspoons minced
fresh ginger

4 cups spiralized green
cabbage (use Blade A;
about ½ cabbage)

2 tablespoons fresh
lime juice

1½ tablespoons low-
sodium soy sauce (use
coconut aminos or
gluten-free tamari, if
gluten-free)

1 tablespoon honey

1 teaspoon fish sauce,
plus more to taste

Pinch of red pepper
flakes

2 large eggs, beaten

1 teaspoon Sriracha or
Thai chile sauce, plus
more for serving

½ pound medium raw
shrimp, shelled and
deveined

Fine sea salt and
pepper

¼ cup chopped raw
peanuts

Heat 1 tablespoon of the sesame oil in a large skillet over medium-high heat. When the oil is shimmering, add the ginger and garlic and cook until fragrant, about 1 minute. Add the cabbage and cook, stirring frequently, until crisp-tender, about 7 minutes.

Meanwhile, in a small bowl, whisk together the lime juice, soy sauce, honey, fish sauce, and red pepper flakes.

When the cabbage is crisp-tender, push it to the sides of the skillet to make a well in the center. Add the eggs and cook, stirring with a spatula to scramble them, until set, about 3 minutes. Stir the eggs into the cabbage, combining all the ingredients in the skillet. Add the soy sauce mixture and cook, tossing to coat. Taste and season with more fish sauce as needed. Stir in the cilantro and divide the cabbage between two plates. Wipe the skillet clean.

In a medium bowl, whisk together the Sriracha and remaining 2 teaspoons sesame oil. Add the shrimp and toss to coat. Season lightly with salt and pepper. Set the skillet over medium-high heat. When it's hot, add the shrimp in a single layer and cook, turning once, until opaque, 1 to 2 minutes per side.

Top each plate with the shrimp and peanuts and serve.

Not Spiralized /
Gluten-Free / Paleo
Dairy-Free / Low-Cal

NUTRITIONAL INFORMATION *Per serving*
Calories **237** / Fat **8g** / Sat Fat **1g** / Sodium **103mg**
Carbs **25g** / Fiber **9g** / Sugar **14g** / Protein **21g**

CRAB FRA DIAVOLO

/ *with* / **FENNEL NOODLES**

TIME TO PREPARE
10 minutes

TIME TO COOK
25 minutes

SERVES 4

After a few victorious but mostly failed attempts at spiralizing fennel, I started slicing fennel lengthwise into thin strips and cooking it like noodles that way. The fennel softens, and its licorice flavor becomes milder. The more it heats, the more it absorbs the flavors of this fra diavolo, a spicy tomato sauce. The fennel noodles become the perfect vehicle for the sauce, absorbing its flavors and complementing its spiciness. The crab is pillowy and blends smoothly in this pasta, giving us yet another way to enjoy pasta—without the pasta.

3 large fennel bulbs

2 tablespoons extra-virgin olive oil

Salt and black pepper

1 medium yellow onion, diced

2 large garlic cloves, minced

½ teaspoon red pepper flakes, plus more to taste

1 (28-ounce) can no-salt-added crushed tomatoes

¾ pound jumbo lump crabmeat

¼ cup chopped fresh curly parsley

Trim and discard the tough bottom from the fennel. Remove the stalks and fronds and discard or save for another use. Quarter the fennel bulb and carefully slice out the core. Slice the fennel lengthwise into ¼- to ½-inch-thick pieces.

Heat 1 tablespoon of the olive oil in a large skillet over medium-high heat. When the oil is shimmering, add the fennel and season with salt and pepper. Cover and cook until the fennel softens to al dente, about 7 minutes. Remove the fennel from the skillet.

Add the remaining 1 tablespoon olive oil and the onion to the pan and cook until softened, 3 to 4 minutes. Add the garlic and red pepper flakes and cook until fragrant, about 30 seconds. Add the tomatoes and bring to a boil, then reduce the heat to medium-low and simmer until thickened, 10 to 15 minutes. Stir in the crab and fennel and cook until just heated through, about 2 minutes. Season with salt and more red pepper flakes to taste.

Divide the fra diavolo among four plates, garnish with the parsley, and serve.

TIP / *Be sure to slice your fennel into thin pieces per the recipe (¼ to ½ inch); otherwise, you'll have tougher noodles.*

RUTABAGA NOODLE VEGETABLE STIR-FRY

TIME TO PREPARE
10 minutes

TIME TO COOK
25 minutes

SERVES 4

Everyone needs a go-to stir-fry. The perfect, satisfying meal for busy weeknights, stir-fries are quick and easy, and that's exactly what this rutabaga version aims to be. Don't be fooled by the rutabaga noodle; it's very adaptable, and although it seems like a root vegetable that would be better suited for heartier dishes, it's quite versatile, especially in stir-fries. When cooked, rutabaga becomes soft like an udon or rice noodle and absorbs the sauce, making every bite flavorful.

2 medium rutabaga, peeled, spiralized with Blade C, noodles trimmed

Cooking spray

Salt and pepper

2 garlic cloves, minced

1 (1-inch) piece fresh ginger, peeled and minced

2 tablespoons rice vinegar

⅓ cup low-sodium soy sauce (use coconut aminos or gluten-free tamari, if gluten-free)

1 tablespoon arrowroot powder

1 tablespoon toasted sesame oil

3 scallions, chopped

1 red bell pepper, spiralized with Blade D, noodles trimmed

1 large carrot, peeled, spiralized with Blade D, noodles trimmed

4 ounces shiitake mushrooms, stems removed, caps thinly sliced

1 cup frozen shelled edamame

TIP / *To amp up the protein level of this dish, add 2 cups shredded cooked chicken at the end and toss until warmed.*

Preheat the oven to 425 degrees. Line a baking sheet with parchment paper.

Spread out the rutabaga noodles on the prepared baking sheet and spray with cooking spray. Season with salt and black pepper and roast until softened, 20 to 25 minutes.

Meanwhile, in a small bowl, whisk together the garlic, ginger, vinegar, and soy sauce. Whisk in the arrowroot powder.

Heat the sesame oil in a large skillet over medium-high heat. When the oil is shimmering, add the scallions. Cook, stirring, until softened, about 2 minutes. Add the bell pepper, carrot, and mushrooms and cook, stirring, until softened, about 5 minutes. Add the soy sauce mixture, edamame, and rutabaga noodles and toss well for 2 minutes to let the rutabaga absorb the flavors.

Divide the noodles among four plates and serve.

ALSO WORKS WELL WITH
Kohlrabi / Zucchini
Parsnip / Butternut Squash

Spiralized / Saves Well
Gluten-Free
Dairy-Free (opt.)

NUTRITIONAL INFORMATION *Per serving*
Calories **415** / Fat **19g** / Sat Fat **6g** / Sodium **946mg**
Carbs **32g** / Fiber **6g** / Sugar **4g** / Protein **26g**

SPICY

BROCCOLI, QUINOA & SAUSAGE PASTA

/ *with* / PARMESAN

TIME TO PREPARE
15 minutes

TIME TO COOK
25 minutes

SERVES 2

For years, I wondered why my mother's sausage and peppers tasted so much more robust than mine. What I eventually found out was that she often oven-baked her sausage, whereas I just cooked mine in a skillet. I immediately tested it out and discovered a new truth: oven-baking your sausage is not only easier than cooking it on the stovetop, but it also really brings out the meat's flavor. With the pan juices from the sausage and the Parmesan cheese, this pasta dish (using broccoli noodles) is salty, savory, and just spicy enough to make you come back for seconds—and thirds.

2 sweet Italian sausage links

⅓ cup dry quinoa, rinsed

1 tablespoon extra-virgin olive oil

2 garlic cloves, minced

¼ teaspoon red pepper flakes, plus more to taste

3 cups broccoli florets (from 1 large head)

1 broccoli stem, peeled, spiralized with Blade D, noodles trimmed

½ cup low-sodium chicken broth, plus more as needed

Fine sea salt and pepper

¼ cup grated Parmesan cheese (optional)

Preheat the oven to 425 degrees.

Place the sausage in a small baking dish and bake until the sausage is browned and cooked through, 20 to 25 minutes. Slice the sausages on an angle into ½-inch-thick pieces.

Meanwhile, in a medium pot, combine the quinoa and 1 cup water and bring to a boil. Reduce the heat to medium-low, cover, and simmer until the quinoa is fluffy and tender, 15 to 20 minutes.

Heat the olive oil in a large skillet over medium-high heat. When the oil is shimmering, add the garlic, red pepper flakes, broccoli florets, broccoli noodles, and broth. Season with salt and black pepper. Toss and cook for 5 minutes, until the noodles are al dente. If the pan looks dry, add more broth as needed. Add the sausage and any juices from the baking dish and toss again. Remove the skillet from the heat and add the cooked quinoa and Parmesan, if desired. Toss well to coat.

Divide the pasta between two bowls and serve.

Not Spiralized /
Gluten-Free / Low-Cal

NUTRITIONAL INFORMATION *Per serving*
Calories **250** / Fat **14g** / Sat Fat **6g** / Sodium **1277mg**
Carbs **15g** / Fiber **5g** / Sugar **4g** / Protein **19g**

SHREDDED BRUSSELS SPROUTS CARBONARA

/ *with* / **PEAS & PANCETTA**

TIME TO PREPARE
15 minutes

TIME TO COOK
20 minutes

SERVES 4

Shredding Brussels sprouts thinly with a mandoline yields soft tendrils that can be treated just like cabbage as a pasta substitute. While a bit more of a stretch than most noodle alternatives, Brussels sprout pasta still does what an alternative needs to do: carry the sauce. This simple carbonara sauce with peas and pancetta is the star of the dish, and the sprouts give it a light texture and earthiness. Best part? Going for seconds without doubting the decision—after all, you're eating veggies!

4 ounces diced pancetta

1 pound Brussels sprouts, ends trimmed

2 large eggs

½ cup grated Parmesan cheese

Fine sea salt and pepper

2 garlic cloves, minced

¼ teaspoon red pepper flakes

¾ cup frozen green peas

Cook the pancetta in a large skillet over medium heat, stirring occasionally, until browned, about 7 minutes. Using a slotted spoon, transfer the pancetta to a paper towel–lined plate to drain. Set the skillet aside.

Meanwhile, using a mandoline, carefully shred the Brussels sprouts.

In a medium bowl, whisk together the eggs and Parmesan. Season with salt and black pepper.

Add the garlic and red pepper flakes to the skillet you used for the pancetta and cook, stirring, until fragrant, about 30 seconds. Add the Brussels sprouts and peas, season with salt and black pepper, and cook, stirring occasionally, until the sprouts are tender and browned at the edges, 7 to 10 minutes. Add the cooked pancetta.

Remove the skillet from the heat and slowly drizzle in the egg mixture. Stir continuously until the eggs form a creamy sauce, then return the skillet to the heat as needed to help the egg cook, but try to prevent them from scrambling.

Divide the carbonara among four plates and serve immediately.

TIP / *You can buy shredded Brussels sprouts instead of shaving them yourself—use 1 pound. The consistency and thinness won't be quite the same, but it's a great time-saver!*

Not Spiralized
Gluten-Free / Paleo
Dairy-Free / Low-Cal

NUTRITIONAL INFORMATION *Per serving*
Calories **256** / Fat **12g** / Sat Fat **4g** / Sodium **941mg**
Carbs **16g** / Fiber **3g** / Sugar **6g** / Protein **37g**

SPAGHETTI SQUASH FIDEOS
/ *with* / **SHRIMP & CHORIZO**

TIME TO PREPARE
20 minutes

TIME TO COOK
1 hour

SERVES 4

If I'm being totally honest, I used to think less of spaghetti squash pasta for not being as miraculous as spiralized pasta. It takes a bit more time to prepare and it's not as close in consistency to a noodle as a spiralized veggie is. However, spaghetti squash does carry its own nutritional benefits and has a buttery, tasty flavor that's not to be ignored, so I've come around to cooking with it. Spaghetti squash yields short, thin noodles, so it works perfectly as fideos, a kind of pasta similar to vermicelli that is most commonly used in soups. Fideos are of Spanish origin, so I created a smoky chorizo-and-shrimp dish. The extra pinch of smoked paprika is soaked up by the squash and creates a robust noodle dish that proves spaghetti squash is a major player in the pasta-substitute game.

1 tablespoon extra-virgin olive oil

2 (5-inch) Mexican chorizo links, casings removed, sliced into ¼-inch-thick rounds

½ cup chopped yellow onion

3 garlic cloves, minced

1 red bell pepper, diced

1 large cooked spaghetti squash (see page 17), scraped into noodles and squeezed of excess moisture

¼ teaspoon smoked paprika

¼ teaspoon cayenne

Fine sea salt and pepper

1 pound medium shrimp, peeled, tails left on, and deveined

½ teaspoon sweet paprika

¼ cup chopped fresh curly parsley, for garnish

Heat the olive oil in a large skillet over medium-high heat. When the oil is shimmering, add the chorizo and cook until browned, about 5 minutes. Using a slotted spoon, transfer to a plate. Add the onion, garlic, and bell pepper to the skillet and cook until softened, about 5 minutes. Add the spaghetti squash noodles, smoked paprika, and cayenne and season with salt and black pepper. Cook for 3 minutes, until the squash is warmed through. Return the chorizo to the skillet and toss well to combine.

Season the shrimp with salt, black pepper, and the sweet paprika. Nestle the seasoned shrimp into the skillet and cover. Cook until opaque, 3 to 4 minutes. Uncover the fideos and toss well.

Divide among four plates, garnish with the parsley, and serve.

NUTRITIONAL INFORMATION *Per serving*
Calories **349** / Fat **26g** / Sat Fat **4g** / Sodium **313mg**
Carbs **24g** / Fiber **11g** / Sugar **7g** / Protein **13g**

LEMON-GRILLED BABY ARTICHOKES

/ *with* / **ASPARAGUS NOODLES**

TIME TO PREPARE
20 minutes

TIME TO COOK
30 minutes

SERVES 2

◎ ◎ ◎

At almost every special occasion or holiday dinner, my family makes artichokes. It started with my grandfather—he'd so generously stuff them with garlic and fresh herbs, you could practically smell them cooking from the driveway. There were never any leftovers (because our family devoured them every time), but I always meant to save mine and slice the artichoke heart to use in pasta or a salad. Now I'm finally using them in this springtime pasta dish, incorporating shaved fresh asparagus to mimic pasta and pesto sauce for a creamy, salty flavor that coats these simple grilled baby artichokes.

1 lemon, halved, plus 1 tablespoon fresh lemon juice

4 baby artichokes

1 pound thick asparagus spears, ends trimmed

2 tablespoons extra-virgin olive oil

Fine sea salt and pepper

¼ cup prepared pesto sauce

TIP / *When shaving the asparagus, it can help to elevate the spears off the cutting board by setting them on top of two chopsticks pushed together.*

Squeeze half a lemon into a large bowl of water. Keep the other half close by.

Using a serrated knife, cut off the top third of the artichokes, including any sharp tips. Remove any dark green outer leaves until only the pale, tender inner leaves remain. Slice off most of the stem, leaving about 1 inch. Halve the artichokes lengthwise and squeeze lemon juice over them to prevent browning. Scoop out and discard the fuzzy choke in the center and transfer the prepared artichokes to the bowl of lemon water.

In a large pot fitted with a steamer basket, heat 1 inch of water over high heat. When the water comes to a boil, reduce the heat to medium-high and place the artichokes, cut-side down, in the steamer basket. Cover and steam for about 15 minutes, until you can pierce the hearts easily with a knife (the hearts are at the bottom of the artichoke, right above the stem).

While the artichokes cook, using a vegetable peeler, shave the asparagus stalks into ribbons. (Reserve the tips for another use.)

Heat a grill to high or heat a grill pan over high heat.

Brush the artichokes all over with 1 tablespoon of the olive oil. Season generously with salt and pepper. Place the artichokes cut-side down on the grill or grill pan. Grill, turning once, until the artichokes have grill marks, about 3 minutes per side. Transfer the artichokes to a plate and toss with the lemon juice.

Meanwhile, heat the remaining 1 tablespoon olive oil in a medium skillet over medium-high heat. When the oil is shimmering, add the asparagus noodles, season lightly with salt, and cook, tossing, until the asparagus no longer tastes raw, about 2 minutes. Remove the skillet from the heat, add the pesto, and toss to coat.

Divide the asparagus pasta between two plates, top with the artichokes, and serve.

NUTRITIONAL INFORMATION *Per serving*
Calories 176 / Fat 8g / Sat Fat 2g / Sodium 601mg
Carbs 15g / Fiber 4g / Sugar 9g / Protein 11g

FAJITA NIGHT PASTA
/ *with* / CHICKEN SAUSAGE

TIME TO PREPARE
15 minutes

TIME TO COOK
20 minutes

SERVES 4

Whenever I give spiralizing demos at events like cooking classes, I always make the same corny reference about "fajita night." Maybe you've even heard it? While rambling off all the different types of vegetables and fruits you can spiralize and explaining what they're best used for, I always get to bell peppers and onions and go, "Your Fajita Fridays have never been easier!" I say this because it's true—spiralizing bell peppers and onions is effortless compared to slicing them with a knife. The long pepper and onion noodles make a great pasta version of fajitas. Here the tomato paste, broth, herbs, and spices make a lightly creamy fajita sauce that glazes the chicken sausage as everything cooks together harmoniously. Try this on your next Fajita Friday—you'll get it!

For the fajita seasoning

¼ teaspoon cayenne pepper

1 teaspoon chili powder

¼ teaspoon garlic powder

½ teaspoon paprika

½ teaspoon smoked paprika

½ teaspoon onion powder

¼ teaspoon ground cumin

½ teaspoon salt

¼ teaspoon dried oregano

For the fajita pasta

1 tablespoon extra-virgin olive oil

¾ pound chicken sausage, casings removed

2 red bell peppers, spiralized with Blade A, noodles trimmed

1 green bell pepper, spiralized with Blade A, noodles trimmed

1 large white onion, peeled, spiralized with Blade A, noodles trimmed

2 medium zucchini, spiralized with Blade D, noodles trimmed

Fine sea salt and pepper

2 tablespoons tomato paste

½ cup low-sodium vegetable broth

Chopped fresh cilantro, for garnish

Make the fajita seasoning. In a small bowl, stir together the cayenne, chili powder, garlic powder, paprika, smoked paprika, onion powder, cumin, salt, and oregano. Set aside.

Make the fajita pasta. Heat the olive oil in a large skillet over medium-high heat. When the oil is shimmering, add the sausage and cook, breaking it up with a wooden spoon as it cooks, until browned, 5 to 7 minutes. Using a slotted spoon, transfer the sausage to a plate.

Add the bell peppers, onion, and zucchini to the skillet and cook until crisp-tender, 5 to 7 minutes. Return the sausage to the skillet, add the tomato paste, and cook, stirring continuously, until the tomato paste coats the vegetables. Add the fajita seasoning and toss to coat the vegetables. Add the broth and cook until the vegetables are softened and the mixture is slightly saucy, about 5 minutes more.

Divide the pasta among four plates and garnish with cilantro.

NUTRITIONAL INFORMATION *Per serving*
Calories **232** / Fat **11g** / Sat Fat **2g** / Sodium **502mg**
Carbs **16g** / Fiber **2g** / Sugar **3g** / Protein **15g**

LONG BEAN NOODLES
/ *with* / SCALLION-GINGER SAUCE & TOFU

TIME TO PREPARE
15 minutes

TIME TO COOK
45 minutes

SERVES 4

On Chinese New Year, long beans are eaten to symbolize a long and prosperous life. Thanks to their very long length, these beans, also known as "yardlong beans" or "Chinese long beans," can be used as a noodle substitute. Although the taste is similar to a green bean, the way you cook it can change that—these beans are best sautéed or fried, or else they taste super bland. Here we cook them in a quick scallion-ginger sauce and toss them with firm baked tofu for a fun spin on a noodle stir-fry. Cheers to a year of success with this dish!

1 (14-ounce) package extra-firm tofu, drained and cubed (see Tip, page 76)

¼ cup plus 1½ tablespoons low-sodium soy sauce (use coconut aminos or gluten-free tamari, if gluten-free)

Pepper

8 ounces Chinese long beans, ends trimmed

¾ cup thinly sliced scallions (green and light green parts only)

1 heaping tablespoon packed grated fresh ginger

2 tablespoons sesame oil

¼ cup low-sodium vegetable broth

1 teaspoon rice vinegar

1 teaspoon honey

Preheat the oven to 400 degrees. Line a baking sheet with parchment paper.

Place the tofu in a medium bowl with ¼ cup of the soy sauce and toss to coat. Season with pepper. Arrange on the prepared baking sheet and bake for 40 minutes, until browned and just crisp on the outside, shaking the pan halfway through and brushing with any soy sauce remaining in the bowl.

While tofu bakes, fill a large pot halfway with water and bring to a boil over high heat. Add the long beans and cook for 5 minutes, until fork-tender—they should have a slight crunch but be soft and noodlelike. Drain the beans in a colander.

In a small bowl, whisk together the scallions, ginger, sesame oil, broth, vinegar, and honey.

Heat a large skillet over medium-high heat. When the pan is hot, add the sauce and beans, and cook to heat through and develop the flavors, about 5 minutes. Add the cooked tofu and toss to combine.

Divide the mixture among four plates and serve.

ALSO WORKS WELL WITH
Zucchini / Jicama
Chayote

Spiralized / Gluten-Free

NUTRITIONAL INFORMATION *Per serving*
Calories **465** / Fat **24g** / Sat Fat **6g** / Sodium **447mg**
Carbs **36g** / Fiber **5g** / Sugar **10g** / Protein **32g**

MEXICAN
CORN & CHICKEN CHAYOTE PASTA

TIME TO PREPARE
15 minutes

TIME TO COOK
20 minutes

SERVES 2

When my mother and sister were throwing my baby shower, they asked if I had a theme in mind and, because of my love for everything cactus (I have a six-foot-and-growing cactus in my living room that I lovingly named Bart), I asked for a "fiesta" theme. Plus, who doesn't love tacos, chips, and guac? They had the shower catered by our favorite BBQ restaurant in Jersey City, Hamilton Pork, which also happens to have some great Mexican options, including tacos and the most amazing Mexican corn that comes shaved off the cob for easy eating. After the shower, we had plenty of leftovers. That evening, I tossed together zucchini noodles with leftover Mexican corn and shredded chicken. It was *muy bien*—and inspired this recipe.

2 tablespoons extra-virgin olive oil

1 boneless, skinless chicken breast, cut into ½-inch cubes

Kernels from 2 small ears raw corn

2 garlic cloves, minced

1 teaspoon chili powder

Fine sea salt and pepper

Juice of 1 lime

¼ cup nonfat plain Greek yogurt or mayonnaise

4 tablespoons grated cotija cheese

2 tablespoons minced fresh cilantro

2 chayote, spiralized with Blade D, noodles trimmed

TIP / *If you don't have access to fresh corn, substitute 1 cup canned or thawed frozen corn kernels.*

Heat 1 tablespoon of the olive oil in a medium skillet over medium-high heat. When the oil is shimmering, add the chicken, corn, garlic, and chili powder. Season with salt and pepper. Cook, stirring, until the chicken is no longer pink on the inside, about 10 minutes. Add the lime juice and stir to combine. Transfer the mixture to a large bowl and add the yogurt, 2 tablespoons of the cotija cheese, and 1 tablespoon of the cilantro. Stir well to combine and set aside.

In the same skillet, heat the remaining 1 tablespoon olive oil over medium-high heat. Add the chayote and season with salt and pepper. Cook until al dente, about 5 minutes. Add the chicken-corn mixture and toss well to combine.

Divide the chayote pasta between two bowls and garnish evenly with the remaining cotija cheese and cilantro.

NUTRITIONAL INFORMATION *Per serving*
Calories **328** / Fat **11g** / Sat Fat **2g** / Sodium **238mg**
Carbs **25g** / Fiber **4g** / Sugar **5g** / Protein **32g**

SPIRALIZED TUNA TATAKI BOWL

/ *with* / **GRILLED AVOCADO**

TIME TO PREPARE
10 minutes

TIME TO COOK
15 minutes

SERVES 4

One of the first meals I taught myself how to cook in college was a brown rice stir-fry bowl. I loved the way the fluffy, slightly chewy grains soaked up all the flavors of the sauces and all the vegetables gave the dish such great texture. In this more grown-up version of my classic college staple, I've kicked it up a notch with lightly seared tuna, veggies, avocado, and a perfectly spiced yogurt sauce that blends all the flavors together. And if you've never grilled avocado, you're in for a treat—it heats the avocado slightly and gives it a little extra flavor to complement the seared tuna.

½ cup nonfat plain Greek yogurt

2 tablespoons Sriracha

3 teaspoons toasted sesame oil

1 teaspoon rice vinegar

1 pound ahi tuna steak

Salt and pepper

1 avocado, pitted and peeled

1⅓ cups cooked brown rice

1 large carrot, peeled, spiralized with Blade D, noodles trimmed

1 seedless cucumber, spiralized with Blade D, noodles trimmed

1 tablespoon toasted sesame seeds

Heat a grill to medium-high or heat a grill pan over medium-high heat.

In a small bowl, whisk together the Greek yogurt, Sriracha, 1 teaspoon of the sesame oil, the vinegar, and 1 tablespoon water until smooth. Set aside.

Brush the tuna with the remaining 2 teaspoons sesame oil and season with salt and pepper. Grill the tuna and avocado, turning once, just until grill marks appear, 1 to 2 minutes per side. Transfer to a clean surface. Slice the tuna and avocado into ¼-inch-thick strips.

Divide the brown rice among four bowls and top evenly with the tuna, avocado, carrot, cucumber, and sesame seeds. Drizzle with the dressing and serve.

TIP / *If you want to go low-carb, omit the brown rice with or use spiralized daikon rice (see page 18) mixed with some fresh lime juice.*

ALSO WORKS WELL WITH
Broccoli / Turnip / Parsnip
Rutabaga

Spiralized / Vegan
Gluten-Free / Dairy-Free
Low-Cal

NUTRITIONAL INFORMATION *Per serving*
Calories 270 / Fat 9g / Sat Fat 1g / Sodium 521mg
Carbs 42g / Fiber 12g / Sugar 5g / Protein 10g

ROASTED GARLIC

CELERIAC PASTA PRIMAVERA

/ *with* / WHITE BEAN SAUCE

TIME TO PREPARE
15 minutes

TIME TO COOK
50 minutes

SERVES 4

Garlic lovers, rejoice! This dish is a cross between pasta primavera and fettuccine Alfredo and uses a whole head of roasted garlic to make a vegan cream sauce that's guaranteed to ward off vampires. All jokes aside, this creamy white sauce is so good, you may want to double the recipe and save some for future use. The tender veggies and tomatoes melt into the sauce, making this vegan springtime dish a must-make.

1 head of garlic

2 tablespoons plus
1 teaspoon extra-virgin olive oil

Fine sea salt and pepper

2 medium celeriac, peeled, spiralized with Blade C, noodles trimmed

Cooking spray

6 ounces snow peas, sliced lengthwise into thirds

2 cups chopped broccoli florets

1 cup cherry tomatoes, halved

1 small shallot, diced

1 tablespoon fresh thyme leaves

1 teaspoon fresh rosemary leaves

1 (15-ounce) can cannellini beans, undrained

¾ cup low-sodium vegetable broth, plus more as needed

Preheat the oven to 375 degrees. Line a baking sheet with parchment paper.

Cut the top ½ inch from the head of garlic to expose the cloves; discard the top. Place the garlic on a small piece of foil. Drizzle the sliced top with 1 teaspoon olive oil and season with salt and pepper. Wrap the garlic in the foil to completely enclose and set it directly on the oven rack. Roast until the cloves are tender, 35 to 45 minutes. Let cool and then squeeze the roasted cloves from their skins into a small bowl.

Meanwhile, arrange the celeriac noodles on the prepared baking sheet and spray with cooking spray. Season with salt and pepper and roast with the garlic for 20 minutes, until al dente, shaking the pan halfway through. Transfer the noodles to a large bowl.

While the garlic and celeriac cook, heat 1 tablespoon olive oil in a large skillet over medium-high heat. When the oil is shimmering, add the snow peas, broccoli, and tomatoes and season with salt and pepper. Cook, tossing, until the tomatoes start to release their juices, about 5 minutes. Remove the vegetables from the skillet and cover to keep warm.

Heat the remaining 1 tablespoon olive oil in the same skillet over medium-high heat. When the oil is shimmering, add the shallot and cook for 2 minutes, until softened. Add the thyme and rosemary and cook for 2 minutes more, until fragrant. Add the beans and roasted garlic. Season with salt and pepper and stir for 2 minutes to let the flavors to develop, then add the broth. Bring to a simmer, then reduce the heat to medium-low and cook for 5 minutes to allow the flavors to develop. Pour the mixture into a high-speed blender. Let cool until warm, then blend until smooth. Add more broth as needed, 1 tablespoon at a time, to thin out the sauce.

Add the sauce to the bowl with the celeriac noodles and toss to combine. Divide the pasta among four plates and top each with equal amounts of the cooked vegetables. Serve.

CASSEROLES

Not Spiralized / Saves Well
Gluten-Free / Paleo
Dairy-Free / Low-Cal

NUTRITIONAL INFORMATION *Per serving (3 rolls)*
Calories **79** / Fat **6g** / Sat Fat **1g** / Sodium **58mg**
Carbs **3g** / Fiber **1g** / Sugar **1g** / Protein **9g**

EGGPLANT ROLLS
/ *with* / CHICKEN SHAWARMA & TAHINI DRIZZLE

TIME TO PREPARE
20 minutes

TIME TO COOK
1 hour 25 minutes

SERVES 6

In New York City, there's no shortage of food carts on the streets. Whenever you walk past one, the fragrance of the seasoned meats draws you right in. In my early twenties, after a night out in the city, I couldn't resist ordering chicken shawarma in a flour wrap with yogurt-tahini sauce—probably not what my body needed at two a.m., but definitely what my belly wanted. With this lightened-up version, softened eggplant acts as the wrap to hold the chicken and also for extra vegetables, flavor, and texture. The tahini drizzle is a must and brings all the ingredients together—don't skip it!

3 tablespoons extra-virgin olive oil

2 garlic cloves, minced

1½ teaspoons ground cumin

1¼ teaspoons paprika

½ teaspoon ground turmeric

½ teaspoon garlic powder

⅛ teaspoon ground cinnamon

⅛ teaspoon cayenne pepper

Fine sea salt and pepper

1 pound boneless, skinless chicken breasts, sliced into ¼- to ½-inch strips

½ pound boneless, skinless chicken thighs (or additional breasts), sliced into ¼- to ½-inch strips

1 large Italian eggplant, ends trimmed, cut lengthwise into eighteen ¼-inch-thick slices

1 red onion, thinly sliced or spiralized with Blade A, noodles trimmed

2 tablespoons chopped fresh parsley, for garnish

1 tablespoon chopped fresh mint, for garnish

Tahini Drizzle (recipe follows)

In a medium bowl, stir together 2 tablespoons of the olive oil, the garlic, cumin, paprika, turmeric, garlic powder, cinnamon, and cayenne. Season with salt and black pepper. Add the chicken and toss well to coat. Cover with plastic wrap and refrigerate for at least 20 minutes or up to 24 hours to marinate.

Preheat the oven to 400 degrees. Line a baking sheet with parchment paper.

Arrange the eggplant slices on the prepared baking sheet. Bake until the eggplant is pliable but not cooked all the way through, about 10 minutes.

Meanwhile, heat the remaining 1 tablespoon olive oil in a large skillet over medium-high heat. When the oil is shimmering, add the onion, season with salt and black pepper, and cook until wilted, about 7 minutes. Remove the skillet from the heat.

Working on a clean surface, spread a thin layer of the cooked onion over each eggplant slice. Top with a layer of the marinated chicken (1 or 2 pieces of chicken). Starting at the shorter end, roll up the eggplant slice and then arrange it seam-side down on a large baking sheet. Repeat with the remaining onion, eggplant, and chicken. Bake the rolls until the chicken is cooked through, about 60 minutes.

In a small bowl, toss together the parsley and mint.

Place 3 rolls on each of six plates. Drizzle with the tahini sauce and garnish with the parsley and mint. Serve.

TIP / *This tahini sauce is my favorite for making quick grain bowls—serve a bowl of roasted veggies and quinoa with a drizzle of tahini for an easy, healthy meal. Bookmark this page or make extra tahini drizzle when you cook this recipe!*

TAHINI DRIZZLE

MAKES 1 CUP

⅓ cup tahini

2 tablespoons fresh lemon juice

2 to 3 tablespoons warm water

⅛ teaspoon garlic powder

Fine sea salt and pepper

In a large bowl, whisk together the tahini, lemon juice, water, and garlic powder. Season with salt and pepper. If the sauce is too thick, add more water 1 teaspoon at a time until it reaches a pourable texture. Taste and adjust the seasoning as desired. Store in the refrigerator in an airtight container for up to 1 week.

Spiralized / Gluten-Free
Saves Well / Vegetarian
Low-Cal

NUTRITIONAL INFORMATION *Per serving*

Calories **219** / Fat **13g** / Sat Fat **6g** / Sodium **207mg**
Carbs **15g** / Fiber **1g** / Sugar **1g** / Protein **12g**

RICOTTA & SPINACH

SPAGHETTI PIE

TIME TO PREPARE
15 minutes

TIME TO COOK
45 minutes

SERVES 6

Spaghetti pie is an effective use for leftover pasta (if you ever have any . . .). This spiralized version uses potato noodles instead of processed pasta to give you a bigger nutritional bang for your buck. The spinach sneaks in some dark-leafy-green calcium, and the ricotta gives the pie a fluffy, velvety texture and comfort-food flavor, making this dish a crowd-pleaser.

1 tablespoon extra-virgin olive oil

3 large russet potatoes, peeled, spiralized with Blade D

1 teaspoon garlic powder

Fine sea salt and pepper

6 cups packed spinach, chopped well

3 medium eggs, beaten

½ cup ricotta cheese (if desired, you can use part skim)

Preheat the oven to 400 degrees.

Heat the olive oil in a 12-inch oven-safe skillet over medium-high heat. When the oil is shimmering, add the potatoes and the garlic powder. Season with salt and pepper. Cook, tossing, until lightly browned, about 10 minutes, then transfer to a large bowl. Let cool for 5 minutes.

Immediately add the spinach to the same skillet and cook, stirring, until wilted, about 5 minutes. Transfer the spinach to the bowl with the potatoes and add the eggs and ricotta. Season with salt and pepper and toss well to combine.

In the same skillet, spread the mixture into an even layer. Transfer to the oven and bake for 15 to 20 minutes, until the noodles are set when pressed with the back of a spatula and the edges are just beginning to crisp.

Let rest 5 minutes before serving.

ALSO WORKS WELL WITH
Sweet Potato / Parsnip
Turnip / Rutabaga

Spiralized / Saves Well
Gluten-Free / Paleo
Dairy-Free

NUTRITIONAL INFORMATION *Per serving*
Calories **308** / Fat **8g** / Sat Fat **2g** / Sodium **195mg**
Carbs **34g** / Fiber **6g** / Sugar **9g** / Protein **29g**

SHEPHERD'S PIE
/ *with* / CELERIAC & BUTTERNUT SQUASH CRUST

TIME TO PREPARE
15 minutes

TIME TO COOK
40 minutes

SERVES 4

I first tasted shepherd's pie (also known as cottage pie) when I was studying in London. It is classic English comfort food at its finest, which is my favorite type to reinvent. Instead of the mashed potatoes topping the ground meat, I substitute slices of celeriac and butternut squash, which gives this pie a less starchy crust. Each serving still has a little bit of meat and a little bit of topping, true to the original—but with a better nutritional profile!

1 tablespoon extra-virgin olive oil

1 pound ground beef

Fine sea salt and pepper

1 medium onion, chopped

2 carrots, chopped

2 garlic cloves, minced

1 tablespoon tomato paste

¼ teaspoon dried thyme

½ cup frozen peas

¼ cup frozen corn kernels

1 tablespoon arrowroot powder

1 small celeriac, peeled

1 small butternut squash, peeled

Preheat the oven to 425 degrees.

Heat the olive oil in a large skillet over high heat. When the oil is shimmering, add the beef and season with salt and pepper. Cooking, breaking up the meat with a wooden spoon as it cooks, until browned, about 7 minutes. Add the onion and carrots and cook until the vegetables have softened, about 7 minutes more. Add the garlic and cook until fragrant, about 30 seconds. Add the tomato paste and cook for 1 minute more, until all the vegetables are coated. Add the thyme, peas, and corn and stir for 1 minute to warm through. Drain any liquid or oil from the beef mixture. Sprinkle the arrowroot powder over the beef and stir to coat. Season with salt and pepper.

Meanwhile, slice the celeriac and butternut squash halfway through lengthwise, being careful not to pierce through the center. Spiralize each vegetable using Blade A to yield chip-like slices. (You can also use a mandoline or sharp knife, if preferred.)

Transfer the beef mixture to a 2-quart baking dish and spread it evenly. Arrange the celeriac and butternut squash slices on top, alternating as you lay them down, to create a crisscross pattern. (You may end up with extra vegetable slices, which you can snack on or save for another use.) Cover with foil and bake for 25 minutes, until the top layer is fork-tender. Uncover and turn the broiler to high. Broil until the top begins to brown, 2 to 3 minutes more.

Slice and serve.

TIP / *For something even closer to the classic, try topping the meat with Cauliflower Mash (page 187) instead of this crust.*

Not Spiralized / Saves Well
Gluten-Free
Dairy-Free (opt.)

NUTRITIONAL INFORMATION *Per ½ stuffed eggplant without feta*
Calories **312** / Fat **11g** / Sat Fat **2g** / Sodium **93mg**
Carbs **28g** / Fiber **11g** / Sugar **16g** / Protein **31g**

INSIDE-OUT
MOUSSAKA

TIME TO PREPARE
15 minutes

TIME TO COOK
30 minutes

SERVES 4

Moussaka is a hearty casserole made with ground meat, eggplant, and potatoes; by using the whole eggplant to hold the ground meat, you eliminate the need for the potatoes and can enjoy a lighter version. I love stuffing vegetables with casserole fillings because it's much easier to serve, clean up, and save for leftovers. The chopped mint and parsley add a fresh hit of flavor at the end!

2 large eggplants, halved lengthwise

1 tablespoon plus 4 teaspoons extra-virgin olive oil

Fine sea salt and pepper

1 white onion, finely chopped

2 garlic cloves, minced

1 pound lean ground turkey, beef, or lamb

2 tablespoons tomato paste

1 (28-ounce) can no-salt-added diced tomatoes

2 teaspoons dried oregano

2 tablespoons chopped fresh mint

2 tablespoons chopped fresh parsley

⅓ cup crumbled feta cheese (optional)

TIP / *Make this dish vegetarian by replacing the meat with lentils or quinoa.*

Preheat the oven to 400 degrees. Line a baking sheet with parchment paper.

Place the eggplant halves cut-side up on the prepared baking sheet. Score the flesh in a crisscross pattern and brush each half with 1 teaspoon of the olive oil. Season with salt and pepper and bake until tender, 20 to 25 minutes.

Meanwhile, heat the remaining 1 tablespoon olive oil in a large skillet over medium-high heat. When the oil is shimmering, add the onion and cook until starting to soften, about 3 minutes. Add the garlic and cook until fragrant, about 30 seconds. Push the onion and garlic to the sides of the pan and add the ground meat to the center. Cook the meat, breaking it up with a wooden spoon as it cooks, until browned, about 7 minutes. Stir all the ingredients back together and add the tomato paste, stirring until the paste coats the onion and meat. Stir in the diced tomatoes and season with the oregano and salt and pepper to taste. Increase the heat to high and bring to a simmer, then reduce the heat to medium-low and cook until the liquid has completely reduced and the mixture is thickened, about 15 minutes. Taste and add more salt as needed. Stir in the mint and parsley.

Scoop out the flesh from the eggplants, leaving about ¼ inch attached to the eggplant skin, just enough to keep the skin intact. Stir the eggplant flesh into the meat mixture to combine well and warm through.

Stuff each eggplant shell with the filling. Top evenly with the feta, if desired, and serve.

Not Spiralized / Saves Well
Gluten-Free

NUTRITIONAL INFORMATION *Per serving*
Calories **383** / Fat **16g** / Sat Fat **9g** / Sodium **1163mg**
Carbs **35g** / Fiber **8g** / Sugar **8g** / Protein **25g**

CROQUE MONSIEUR
PARSNIP GRATIN

TIME TO PREPARE
15 minutes

TIME TO COOK
35 minutes

SERVES 4

If you've ever wondered the secret to the chic lives of French women, it's this: they eat very elegantly. Take the grilled cheese: French women have croque monsieurs and croque madames instead—and they're made with thin slices of salty ham and cheese. I think I ate my weight in croque madames both times I visited Paris. This gratin version is my attempt at bringing some of that elegance to Inspiralized—the only difference is that with thin slices of parsnip, ham, and cheese, this casserole is meant to be eaten with a fork. Berets optional!

Cooking spray

5 large parsnips

12 slices cooked ham

¼ cup Dijon mustard

6 slices Gruyère cheese

2 teaspoons fresh thyme leaves

Preheat the oven to 400 degrees. Grease a 9 × 13-inch baking dish with cooking spray.

Peel the parsnips and trim off ends thinner than 1 inch in diameter. Using a mandoline or sharp knife, slice the parsnips crosswise into ⅛-inch-thick slices.

Arrange an even layer of parsnip slices in the prepared baking dish, covering the bottom completely. Top with half the sliced ham, overlapping the slices as needed. Spread a very thin layer of mustard on top of the ham. Repeat the layers. Top with the remaining parsnip slices. Arrange the cheese over the top.

Cover with foil and bake until the parsnips are fork-tender and the cheese has melted, 25 to 35 minutes. Immediately garnish with the thyme.

Let rest for 5 minutes, then slice and serve.

TIP / *To make this dish spiralized, slice the parsnips halfway through lengthwise, being careful not to pierce through the center. Spiralize the parsnips using Blade A to yield chip-like slices.*

Not Spiralized / Saves Well
Vegetarian / Gluten-Free

NUTRITIONAL INFORMATION *Per serving*
Calories **316** / Fat **21g** / Sat Fat **10g** / Sodium **579mg**
Carbs **16g** / Fiber **2g** / Sugar **4g** / Protein **17g**

SPANAKOPITA BAKE

/ *with* / **POTATO CRUST**

TIME TO PREPARE
15 minutes

TIME TO COOK
55 minutes

SERVES 6

◎◎◎

Whenever I have late-afternoon meetings in New York City, I usually meet up with Lu afterward for dinner. I always try to pick a spot I've been meaning to check out or that a friend recommended, or maybe a place that just opened and has gotten fabulous reviews. On one of these occasions, we went to Periyali, Lu's business partner's favorite Greek restaurant in the city. It didn't disappoint. When the waiter rattled off the specials, all I heard was "spanakopita" and promptly ordered it. Spanakopita is typically made with phyllo dough baked on top of a spinach-and-feta mixture. It's my favorite Greek dish and I'm excited to be able to enjoy it more often with this wholesome version that uses russet potatoes in place of the phyllo dough.

Cooking spray

2 tablespoons extra-virgin olive oil

½ yellow onion, chopped

4 garlic cloves, minced

10 ounces baby spinach, coarsely chopped

Zest and juice of 1 lemon

1 tablespoon chopped fresh parsley

2 teaspoons fresh thyme

Fine sea salt and pepper

2 cups crumbled feta cheese

7 large eggs, lightly beaten

2 russet potatoes, peeled

Preheat the oven to 400 degrees. Grease a 9-inch pie pan with cooking spray.

Heat 1 tablespoon of the olive oil in a large saucepan over medium-high heat. When the oil is shimmering, add the onion and cook until softened, about 5 minutes. Add the garlic and cook for 30 seconds, until fragrant. Working in batches, add the spinach and cook, stirring, for 3 to 5 minutes per batch, until wilted down and very dark green and any liquid released has evaporated.

Transfer the cooked spinach mixture to a large bowl and add the lemon zest, lemon juice, parsley, and thyme. Season with salt and pepper and mix well. Add the feta and mix again. Let cool for 5 minutes, then stir in the eggs.

Using a mandoline or a very sharp knife, slice the potatoes crosswise into ⅛-inch-thick rounds.

Arrange the potato slices in an even layer in the pie pan, covering the entire bottom. Evenly spread the filling on top. Cover with the remaining potato slices and brush with the remaining 1 tablespoon olive oil. Season with salt and pepper and bake for 35 to 40 minutes, until the top is golden brown and crispy.

Slice into wedges and serve immediately.

TIP / *To make this dish spiralized, slice the potato halfway through lengthwise, being careful not to pierce through the center. Spiralize the potato using Blade A to yield chip-like slices.*

Not Spiralized / Saves Well
Vegetarian / Gluten-Free

NUTRITIONAL INFORMATION *Per serving (2 rolls)*
Calories **403** / Fat **27g** / Sat Fat **13g** / Sodium **566mg**
Carbs **16g** / Fiber **5g** / Sugar **5g** / Protein **27g**

COLLARD GREEN MANICOTTI

TIME TO PREPARE
15 minutes

TIME TO COOK
55 minutes

SERVES 6

Manicotti holds a special place in my heart because my grandfather always made it on Easter Sunday. My entire family looked forward to the dish, even though we knew how much food was still to come—we always saved room for this one. His flawless marinara sauce, the fluffy cheese stuffing inside those manicotti rolls, and the aromas that filled the kitchen made every Easter at his house magical. While my grandfather probably wouldn't approve of this collard green version, it's a way for me to enjoy a family tradition while also maintaining a healthy lifestyle. Besides, the best part is the sauce and the cheese—and there's plenty of that here!

12 large collard green leaves, stems trimmed

1 tablespoon extra-virgin olive oil

⅔ cup diced white onion

4 garlic cloves, minced

½ teaspoon red pepper flakes

1 (28-ounce) can crushed tomatoes

Fine sea salt and pepper

¼ cup very thinly sliced fresh basil leaves

1 cup grated Parmesan cheese

15 ounces ricotta cheese

1 cup plus ⅓ cup shredded mozzarella cheese

2 large eggs

Preheat the oven to 375 degrees.

Fill a large pot one-third of the way with water and bring to a boil. Add the collard green leaves and cook until tender and pliable, about 3 minutes. Transfer the leaves to a paper towel–lined plate to drain, then pat dry thoroughly with dry paper towels.

Meanwhile, heat the olive oil in a large skillet over medium-high heat. When the oil is shimmering, add the onion and cook until translucent, about 5 minutes. Add the garlic and red pepper flakes and cook, stirring, until fragrant, about 30 seconds. Add the tomatoes and season with salt and black pepper. Cook, stirring, until the tomatoes have thickened, about 15 minutes. Stir in the basil and remove the pan from the heat.

In a medium bowl, stir together the Parmesan, ricotta, 1 cup of the mozzarella, and the eggs. Season with salt and black pepper.

Spread half the tomato sauce over the bottom of a 9 × 13-inch baking dish.

Arrange 1 collard green leaf on a clean surface. Spread out about ⅓ cup of the cheese mixture on the leaf and roll it up like a burrito. Transfer the roll to the baking dish, seam-side down. Repeat with the remaining collard green leaves and filling. Pour the remaining sauce over the rolls and top evenly with the remaining ⅓ cup mozzarella.

Bake for 25 minutes, until the mozzarella on top begins to brown. Serve immediately.

Not Spiralized / Saves Well
Vegan / Gluten-Free
Dairy-Free / Low-Cal

NUTRITIONAL INFORMATION *Per 1 slice and ½ cup cauliflower mash*
Calories **284** / Fat **10g** / Sat Fat **1g** / Sodium **445mg**
Carbs **37g** / Fiber **13g** / Sugar **12g** / Protein **14g**

LENTIL MEAT LOAF
/ *with* / BBQ SAUCE & CAULIFLOWER MASH

TIME TO PREPARE
15 minutes

TIME TO COOK
45 minutes

SERVES 6

When I first graduated college and moved into my own apartment in Hoboken, New Jersey, my neighbors knocked on my door the day after I moved in and handed me a meat loaf. At twenty-two and on my own for the first time in my life, I welcomed the free meal and dug right in. It tasted exactly like I worried it would—too much meat, too little flavor. Fast-forward to the present day, when I was testing out a lentil meatball recipe that failed—it was all mush and I angrily squashed all the botched meatballs on the baking sheet. Hungry after a full hour of trying to prepare the meal, I tried the mashed mixture, I loved it, and a new recipe idea was born: a lentil loaf! Meatless and full of flavor.

½ cup dry green lentils

1 bay leaf

1 tablespoon extra-virgin olive oil

1 cup chopped white onion

1 carrot, chopped

1 celery stalk, chopped

Fine sea salt and pepper

2 garlic cloves, minced

3 tablespoons tomato paste

½ cup chopped walnuts

1 cup gluten-free old-fashioned oats

1 teaspoon dried basil

1 teaspoon dried oregano

1 teaspoon dried parsley

½ cup prepared gluten-free barbecue sauce

Cauliflower Mash (recipe follows), for serving

TIP / *If you prefer, use a marinara or tomato-basil sauce instead of the barbecue sauce.*

Preheat the oven to 375 degrees. Line a 9 × 5-inch loaf pan with parchment paper, leaving 1 to 2 inches overhanging the sides.

In a medium saucepan, combine the lentils, bay leaf, and 1½ cups water. Bring to a boil over high heat, then reduce the heat to medium-low and simmer until the lentils are tender but not mushy, 15 to 20 minutes.

Heat the olive oil in a large skillet over medium-high heat. When the oil is shimmering, add the onion, carrot, and celery and season with salt and pepper. Cook until softened, 5 to 7 minutes. Add the garlic and cook until fragrant, about 1 minute more. Add the tomato paste and stir until the vegetables are fully coated, about 30 seconds. Remove the skillet from the heat.

In a food processor or high-speed blender, combine the lentils, veggies, walnuts, oats, basil, oregano, parsley, ½ teaspoon salt, and a few grinds of pepper. Pulse until the mixture is just combined and sticky.

Transfer the mixture to the prepared loaf pan; flatten the top with a knife to create an even layer. Cover with foil and bake for 25 minutes, or until a toothpick inserted into the center of the loaf comes out clean. Uncover and bake for 5 minutes more, until lightly browned on the outside. Remove the loaf from the oven and let rest for 5 minutes.

Meanwhile, in a small saucepan, bring the barbecue sauce to a simmer over medium-high heat. Cook for 1 minute, or until warm. Pour the barbecue sauce over the lentil loaf. Use the parchment paper as handles to lift the loaf out of the pan.

Cut the lentil loaf into 6 slices, plate, and serve with Cauliflower Mash alongside.

CAULIFLOWER MASH

SERVES 4 TO 8

8 cups cauliflower florets (from 2 medium heads)

2 tablespoons nutritional yeast

¼ cup plus 2 tablespoons low-sodium vegetable broth, plus more as needed

2 teaspoons garlic powder

1 teaspoon onion powder

Fine sea salt and pepper

Fill a large pot halfway with water, cover, and bring to a boil over high heat. Add the cauliflower florets and cook until fork-tender, 5 to 7 minutes. Drain the cauliflower in a colander.

In a high-speed blender, combine the cauliflower, nutritional yeast, broth, garlic powder, onion powder, ½ teaspoon salt, and a few grinds of pepper. Blend until smooth with some texture remaining, being careful not to overmix. Taste and add more salt as needed. Store in an airtight container in the refrigerator for 3 to 5 days, or in the freezer for up to 3 months.

Not Spiralized / Saves Well
Vegetarian / Gluten-Free
Low-Cal

NUTRITIONAL INFORMATION *Per ½ cup serving*
Calories **247** / Fat **9g** / Sat Fat **4g** / Sodium **998mg**
Carbs **31g** / Fiber **9g** / Sugar **3g** / Protein **14g**

PUMPKIN-SAGE
"GNOCCHI" BAKE

TIME TO PREPARE
15 minutes

TIME TO COOK
25 minutes

SERVES 4 TO 6

This "gnocchi" bake uses thick butter beans in place of potato-based gnocchi. While they're not exactly the same, the beans have a dense, doughy interior that gives each bite a gnocchi-like consistency without the flour, cheese, or potatoes. The pumpkin-sage sauce will fill your kitchen with fall aromas. It makes a great side dish, so serve it at a Friendsgiving to impress all your guests!

1 tablespoon extra-virgin olive oil

5 fresh sage leaves

Pinch of red pepper flakes

¼ cup diced shallot (about 1 large)

2 garlic cloves, minced

1¼ cups pure pumpkin purée

¼ teaspoon ground nutmeg

½ teaspoon ground cinnamon

2 (15.5-ounce) cans butter beans, drained and rinsed

¼ teaspoon sea salt, plus more to taste

Pepper

⅔ cup low-sodium vegetable broth, plus more as needed

½ cup grated Parmesan cheese

½ cup shredded Gruyère cheese

Preheat the oven to 400 degrees.

Heat the olive oil in an 8-inch oven-safe skillet over medium-high heat. When the oil is shimmering, add the sage and fry until crispy, about 5 minutes. Remove with a slotted spoon and drain on a paper towel–lined plate.

Immediately add the red pepper flakes, shallot, and garlic to the skillet and cook, stirring continuously, until the shallot is translucent, about 2 minutes. Add the pumpkin purée, nutmeg, cinnamon, beans, and salt and season with pepper. Cook, stirring, for about 1 minute. Add the broth and stir well. Taste and adjust the seasoning with more salt, if needed. Turn off the heat and fold in the Parmesan.

Sprinkle the top evenly with the Gruyère. Transfer to the oven and bake until the cheese has melted, about 7 minutes.

Garnish with the fried sage leaves and serve.

Not Spiralized / Saves Well
Vegetarian / Gluten-Free
Low-Cal

NUTRITIONAL INFORMATION *Per serving (1 wrap)*
Calories **290** / Fat **18g** / Sat Fat **6g** / Sodium **614mg**
Carbs **22g** / Fiber **10g** / Sugar **6g** / Protein **10g**

CABBAGE-WRAPPED
VEGGIE ENCHILADAS

TIME TO PREPARE
20 minutes

TIME TO COOK
40 minutes

SERVES 8

I love enchiladas, but every vegetarian enchilada I've ever had has fallen apart as soon as I sliced into it. What's the point of the tortilla if it doesn't even hold everything together? So I replaced the tortillas with cabbage leaves. The best part of enchiladas is the sauce, anyway; it's typically started by whisking flour with oil, but this healthier version uses arrowroot powder instead. With melted cheese on top and plenty of well-seasoned veggies and beans, you'll be going for seconds!

Cooking spray

8 savoy cabbage leaves (see Tip)

1 tablespoon extra-virgin olive oil

1 small white onion, diced

3 garlic cloves, minced

1 red bell pepper, diced

1 green bell pepper, diced

1 carrot, diced

2 cups chopped broccoli florets

1 teaspoon dried oregano

Fine sea salt and pepper

1 (15-ounce) can black beans, drained, rinsed, and patted dry

1 cup canned no-salt-added corn kernels, drained

Enchilada sauce, store-bought or homemade (recipe follows)

1½ cups shredded Mexican cheese blend

Chopped fresh cilantro, for garnish

2 avocados, pitted, peeled, and chopped

Preheat the oven to 400 degrees. Grease a 9 × 13-inch baking dish with cooking spray.

Fill a large pot halfway with water and bring to a boil over high heat. Working in batches, add the cabbage leaves and cook for 2 to 3 minutes, until softened. Transfer the leaves to a paper towel–lined plate to drain, then pat dry with dry paper towels.

Heat the olive oil in a large skillet over medium-high heat. When the oil is shimmering, add the onion and cook until softened, about 5 minutes. Stir in the garlic, bell peppers, carrot, broccoli, and oregano. Season with salt and pepper. Cover and cook until the broccoli is bright green and the vegetables are soft, about 7 minutes. Transfer the vegetable mixture to a large bowl and add the beans, corn, and half the enchilada sauce.

Arrange 1 cooked cabbage leaf on a clean surface. Carefully cut out the tough stem from the bottom in a V shape. Fill the center with about ⅓ cup of the enchilada filling and roll the leaf up like a burrito. Place the roll seam-side down in the prepared baking dish. Repeat with remaining cabbage leaves and filling.

Pour the remaining enchilada sauce over the cabbage rolls and sprinkle evenly with the cheese. Bake until the cheese has melted, about 10 minutes.

Garnish with cilantro and the avocado and serve.

TIP / *Cabbage leaves can be tricky to separate. Slice off the bottom of the cabbage and pull off the leaves, being careful not to tear them. If you're having difficulty, try cutting around the core to better release the leaves. You only need 8 large leaves for this recipe; if you have fewer, you'll just end up with extra stuffing (save it for leftovers!). You can also use collard green leaves instead—just be sure to chop off the hard, crunchy stems.*

ENCHILADA SAUCE

MAKES 2 CUPS

2 tablespoons avocado oil
or extra-virgin olive oil

1 tablespoon arrowroot powder

1 (8-ounce) can tomato sauce

¾ cup low-sodium vegetable broth

¼ teaspoon ground cumin

1 tablespoon chili powder

¼ teaspoon garlic powder

Pinch of salt

Heat the oil in a medium pot over high heat. When the oil is shimmering, add the arrowroot powder. Reduce the heat to medium and whisk until combined, about 1 minute. Add the tomato sauce, broth, cumin, chili powder, garlic powder, and salt. Increase the heat to high to bring to a simmer, then reduce the heat to low and cook, stirring occasionally, for 15 to 20 minutes, until thickened. Store in an airtight container in the refrigerator for up to 1 week or in the freezer for up to 3 months.

Spiralized / Saves Well
Vegetarian / Gluten-Free

NUTRITIONAL INFORMATION *Per serving*
Calories **376** / Fat **23g** / Sat Fat **10g** / Sodium **520mg**
Carbs **25g** / Fiber **5g** / Sugar **10g** / Protein **19g**

RAINBOW LASAGNA

/ *with* / BEETS, SWEET POTATO & PESTO

TIME TO PREPARE
40 minutes

TIME TO COOK
1 hour 15 minutes

SERVES 6

Somewhere along the line, people started craving multicolored food. I blame Instagram and its proclivity toward instant eyeball gratification—"unicorn food" is everywhere! However, all of this multicolored food is full of artificial colors and high-sugar ingredients. Luckily, vegetables, and thus spiralizing, are colorful and naturally make rainbow food. Since lasagna, with all its layers, lends itself to this trend, I tried it with sweet potatoes, beets, and rutabaga—which feature three of nature's favorite colors. Talk about "tasting the rainbow"!

For the sweet potato filling

1 large sweet potato, peeled, spiralized with Blade D

Fine sea salt and pepper

½ teaspoon dried thyme

½ cup ricotta cheese

3 tablespoons grated Parmesan cheese

For the beet filling

4 medium beets, peeled, spiralized with Blade D

Cooking spray

½ teaspoon dried thyme

½ cup ricotta cheese

3 tablespoons grated Parmesan cheese

Fine sea salt and pepper

For the pesto filling

3 cups baby spinach

½ cup ricotta cheese

¼ cup prepared pesto sauce

Fine sea salt and pepper

To assemble

Cooking spray

1 large sweet potato, peeled

2 large beets, peeled

1 small rutabaga, peeled

1½ cups shredded mozzarella cheese

3 tablespoons chopped fresh parsley

Preheat the oven to 400 degrees.

Make the sweet potato filling. Arrange the sweet potato noodles on a baking sheet and spray with cooking spray. Sprinkle with the thyme and season with salt and pepper. Roast until very tender, 20 to 25 minutes. Transfer to a blender or food processor and add the ricotta and Parmesan. Season with salt and pepper and blend until smooth and evenly orange in color. Transfer to a small bowl. Clean out the blender jar or food processor bowl and blade.

Meanwhile, make the beet filling. Arrange the beet noodles on a baking sheet and spray with cooking spray and season with thyme. Roast until very tender, 15 to 20 minutes (you can roast them at the same time as the sweet potatoes). Transfer to the clean blender or food processor and add the ricotta and Parmesan. Season with salt and pepper and blend until smooth and evenly pink in color. Transfer to a separate small bowl. Clean out the blender jar or food processor bowl and blade.

/ recipe continues

Make the pesto filling. Heat a large skillet over medium-high heat. When water flicked onto the pan sizzles, add the spinach and cook until wilted, 3 to 5 minutes. Transfer to the clean blender or food processor and add the ricotta and pesto. Season with salt and pepper and blend until smooth and evenly green in color. Transfer to a separate small bowl.

Assemble the lasagna. Grease the bottom of an 11 × 7-inch baking dish with cooking spray.

Slice the sweet potato, beets, and rutabaga halfway through lengthwise, being careful not to pierce through the centers. Spiralize each vegetable using Blade A to yield chip-like slices. (You can also use a mandoline or sharp knife to cut the vegetables into ⅛-inch-thick slices, if preferred.)

Arrange a layer of the beet slices in the prepared baking dish, covering the bottom completely. Spread over the beet filling. Top with another layer of beet slices, then with a layer of sweet potato slices. Spread over the sweet potato filling. Top with another layer of sweet potato slices, then with a layer of rutabaga slices. Spread over the pesto filling. Top with a layer of rutabaga slices. Sprinkle evenly with the mozzarella and tent the dish with foil. (You will end up with extra vegetable slices once you assemble the lasagna, which you can snack on or save for another use.)

Bake the lasagna until a knife runs easily through the center of the lasagna, 30 to 40 minutes. Remove the foil and bake for 5 minutes more, until the cheese is golden brown.

Remove the lasagna from the oven, garnish with the parsley, and let cool for 5 minutes before slicing and serving.

ALSO WORKS WELL WITH
Sweet Potato / Kohlrabi
Golden Beet

Spiralized / One-Pot
Saves Well / Dairy-Free

NUTRITIONAL INFORMATION *Per 1 heaping cup*
Calories **375** / Fat **15g** / Sat Fat **2g** / Sodium **764mg**
Carbs **17g** / Fiber **5g** / Sugar **6g** / Protein **46g**

CHICKEN FRIED DAIKON RICE CASSEROLE

TIME TO PREPARE
20 minutes

TIME TO COOK
25 minutes

SERVES 6

When I first discovered how to make rice out of spiralized vegetables, the first dish I made was fried rice using sweet potato. I was immediately hooked! This casserole version has all the same umami flavors of a stir-fry, but it's baked in a casserole dish instead of stir-fried on the stovetop for a no-hassle meal—you can walk away from it instead of standing over the stove. Whether you're having a "takeout fakeout" night or nursing a hangover, this chicken fried rice won't disappoint—and will leave you with leftovers (trust me, you'll want them!).

Cooking spray

2 large daikon radishes (about 2 pounds total), peeled, spiralized with Blade D, then riced (see page 18)

2¼ pounds boneless, skinless chicken thighs, cut into ¼-inch strips

Salt and pepper

6 large eggs, beaten

2 garlic cloves, minced

2 tablespoons low-sodium soy sauce, plus more as needed

1½ tablespoons sesame oil

⅔ heaping cup diced white onion

1¼ cups frozen peas

1½ cups diced carrots

3 scallions, dark green and light green parts only, chopped

Sriracha, for garnish

Preheat the oven to 375 degrees. Grease a 9 × 13-inch baking dish with cooking spray.

Place the daikon rice in a clean kitchen towel and squeeze out the excess moisture over the sink. Place the drained rice in the prepared baking dish. Season the chicken with salt and pepper and nestle it into the rice.

In a large bowl, whisk together the eggs, garlic, soy sauce, sesame oil, onion, peas, and carrots. Pour the mixture over the rice and chicken. Bake for 25 minutes, stirring once after 15 minutes to help cook the eggs, until the chicken is cooked through and no longer pink inside.

Remove the casserole from the oven. Add the scallions and stir the rice mixture well. Taste and add another teaspoon of soy sauce, if desired.

Garnish with Sriracha and serve.

VEGETARIAN MAINS

Not Spiralized /
Gluten-Free / Vegetarian

NUTRITIONAL INFORMATION *Per serving*
Calories **364** / Fat **27g** / Sat Fat **13g** / Sodium **60mg**
Carbs **9g** / Fiber **2g** / Sugar **5g** / Protein **21g**

SAAG PANEER-STUFFED MUSHROOMS

TIME TO PREPARE
20 minutes

TIME TO COOK
25 minutes

SERVES 4

ⓢ ⓢ ⓢ

The resilient texture of the portobello mushroom makes it ideal for stuffing, topping, and generally being used as a vehicle for anything delicious, like this easy saag paneer. The Indian dish is similar in texture to creamed spinach, but more texturally appealing and flavorful, thanks to paneer, an Indian cheese, and all the inviting spices, such as garam masala, cumin, and chiles. Saag paneer is usually served with naan bread or over rice, but it's not missed here, thanks to the portobello, the perfect conduit.

2 tablespoons extra-virgin olive oil, plus more for brushing

1 teaspoon ground turmeric

½ teaspoon cayenne pepper

12 ounces paneer cheese

16 ounces frozen spinach, defrosted and warmed

4 large portobello mushrooms, stems removed and gills scooped out

Salt and pepper

1 white onion, finely chopped

3 garlic cloves, minced

1 tablespoon minced fresh ginger

1 large jalapeño or serrano chile, finely chopped

½ teaspoon garam masala

1 teaspoon ground cumin

¾ cup plain Greek yogurt

Preheat the oven to 400 degrees. Line a baking sheet with parchment paper.

In a medium bowl, whisk together 1 tablespoon of the olive oil, the turmeric, and the cayenne. Add the paneer and gently toss to coat.

Place the spinach in a food processor and process until smooth.

Brush the portobello caps all over with olive oil and season with salt and pepper. Arrange them on the prepared baking sheet, gill-side up. Bake for 10 to 15 minutes, until softened but still firm. Remove the mushrooms from the baking sheet and pat dry thoroughly.

Meanwhile, heat a large nonstick skillet over medium heat. When the pan is warm, pour in the marinated paneer and arrange the cheese in an even layer. Cook until browned on the bottom, 1 to 2 minutes. Using tongs, turn the paneer and brown it all over, 1 to 2 minutes per side. Remove the paneer from the skillet.

TIP / *If you can't find paneer cheese, you could substitute tofu or ricotta salata.*

Heat the remaining 1 tablespoon olive oil in the skillet over medium-high heat. When the oil is shimmering, add the onion, garlic, ginger, and jalapeño. Season with salt and pepper and cook, stirring frequently, until browned, about 8 minutes. If the vegetables are sticking or look dry, add water, 1 tablespoon at a time.

Add the garam masala and cumin. Cook, stirring often, until the spices are toasted, about 2 minutes. Add the spinach and stir well to incorporate. Stir in ½ cup water and cook until the liquid has reduced by half, about 2 minutes. Turn off the heat and slowly stir in the yogurt. When the yogurt is incorporated, add the paneer and stir well, adding water as needed, 1 tablespoon at a time, to loosen the mixture. Turn the heat to medium-low and cook until heated through, about 3 minutes.

Stuff the mushroom caps with the saag paneer and serve immediately.

Not Spiralized / Saves Well
Vegetarian / Dairy-Free

NUTRITIONAL INFORMATION *Per serving*
Calories **338** / Fat **11g** / Sat Fat **2g** / Sodium **601mg**
Carbs **51g** / Fiber **7g** / Sugar **11g** / Protein **15g**

PORTOBELLO MUSHROOM
BULGOGI BOWLS

TIME TO PREPARE
20 minutes

TIME TO COOK
15 minutes

SERVES 4

If you've never been to a restaurant that serves Korean barbecue, put it on your bucket list. Bulgogi, a popular Korean BBQ dish (and one of my favorites), is thin, marinated slices of beef or pork that are typically grilled. Thinly slicing the meat allows it to absorb the hot, sweet, and salty marinade quickly, so you don't have to wait hours to enjoy it. But we can enjoy these same flavors without the animal protein. This version uses thinly sliced portobello mushrooms in place of the meat. Just like in the original dish, the mushrooms absorb the marinade quickly for that sensational BBQ flavor.

½ cup low-sodium soy sauce (use coconut aminos or gluten-free tamari, if gluten-free)

2 tablespoons honey

2 tablespoons toasted sesame oil

3 garlic cloves, coarsely chopped

3 scallions, chopped, plus ¼ cup sliced scallion greens for garnish

1 teaspoon grated fresh ginger

3 large portobello mushrooms, stem removed, gills scooped out, and cap cut into ½-inch-long strips

1 white onion, thinly sliced

6 cups baby spinach

Cooking spray

4 large eggs

2 carrots, julienned

2 cups cooked brown rice

1 tablespoon toasted white sesame seeds, for garnish

In a food processor, combine the soy sauce, honey, sesame oil, garlic, chopped scallions, and ginger and process until well combined. Put the mushroom strips and onion in a medium bowl, pour over half the marinade, and toss to coat.

Heat a large, wide skillet over medium-high heat. When water flicked onto the skillet sizzles, using tongs, transfer the onion and mushrooms to the skillet, leaving the sauce behind, and cook, stirring occasionally, until the mushrooms are softened and the onion is browned, about 7 minutes. Stir in the spinach and cook until wilted, 1 to 2 minutes more. Divide the bulgogi among four bowls.

Heat a separate large nonstick skillet over medium-high heat and coat with cooking spray. When water flicked onto the skillet sizzles, crack in the eggs, working in batches as needed, and fry until the egg whites are set, 3 to 5 minutes.

Meanwhile, add the remaining marinade to the skillet you used to cook the vegetables and cook, stirring continuously, until thickened, about 2 minutes.

Add the carrots and rice to the bowls with the bulgogi, top with the eggs, and drizzle with the thickened marinade. Garnish with the scallion greens and sesame seeds before serving.

Not Spiralized / Saves Well
Vegan / Gluten-Free
Paleo / Dairy-Free (opt.)

NUTRITIONAL INFORMATION *Per serving*
Calories **413** / Fat **26g** / Sat Fat **7g** / Sodium **414mg**
Carbs **55g** / Fiber **14g** / Sugar **27g** / Protein **18g**

TAHINI-MARINATED SUNCHOKES
/ *with* / CAULIFLOWER COUSCOUS & TOMATO-CUCUMBER SALAD

TIME TO PREPARE
20 minutes

TIME TO COOK
25 minutes

SERVES 4

When I was invited by my alma mater, Wake Forest University, to speak on a panel with other female entrepreneur alumnae, I knew I wanted Lu to come—not only to see where I spent four years of my life but also to see more of North Carolina. After the event, we road-tripped to Chapel Hill so he could see the cute downtown and their gorgeous, sprawling campus. We spent hours walking around, then finally sat down at a Greek café and ordered the Mediterranean couscous platter. It came with tahini chicken, falafel, hummus, couscous, an Israeli cucumber salad, and veggies. We practically licked our plates clean before throwing ourselves into the car to head home. This dish is a re-creation of that platter using cauliflower rice and sunchokes in place of the couscous and chicken. Also known as Jerusalem artichokes, sunchokes have a hearty texture when roasted, and they work well with the accompanying flavors here.

¼ cup tahini

1 tablespoon chopped fresh parsley

3 garlic cloves, finely minced

Zest of ½ lemon

Juice of 1 lemon

1½ teaspoons ground cumin

1 teaspoon grated fresh ginger

¼ teaspoon red pepper flakes

1 pound sunchokes, scrubbed and chopped into 2-inch pieces

Fine sea salt and pepper

2 small heads cauliflower, cut into florets

1 tablespoon extra-virgin olive oil

¼ cup diced red onion

¼ cup finely chopped celery

½ cup finely chopped carrots

½ teaspoon dried oregano

For the tomato-cucumber salad

1½ cups chopped cherry tomatoes

1 seedless cucumber, diced

¼ cup diced red onion

2 tablespoons chopped fresh parsley

1 tablespoon chopped fresh mint

2 tablespoons extra-virgin olive oil

2 tablespoons fresh lemon juice

Fine sea salt and pepper

4 ounces feta cheese, cubed (optional)

Preheat the oven to 425 degrees. Line a baking sheet with parchment paper.

In a medium bowl, whisk together the tahini, parsley, ⅔ of the minced garlic, lemon zest, lemon juice, ½ teaspoon of the cumin, the ginger, and the red pepper flakes. Add the sunchokes and toss to coat. Season with salt and black pepper. Spread out the sunchokes on the prepared baking sheet. Bake until browned on the outside and tender within, 20 to 25 minutes.

Meanwhile, pulse the cauliflower in a food processor until rice-like, working in batches as needed.

Heat the olive oil in a large skillet over medium-high heat. When the oil is shimmering, add the onion, celery, and carrots and cook until softened, about 5 minutes. Add the remaining minced garlic and cook, stirring, for 1 minute, until fragrant. Add the cauliflower rice, remaining 1 teaspoon cumin, and the oregano and season with salt and black pepper. Stir well and cook until the cauliflower is warm and fragrant, 5 to 7 minutes. Divide among four bowls.

Make the salad. In a medium bowl, toss together the tomatoes, cucumber, red onion, parsley, mint, olive oil, and lemon juice and season with salt and pepper. Top with the feta (if using).

Divide the salad among the bowls on top of the cauliflower couscous. Top with the roasted sunchokes and serve.

Spiralized / Vegan
Gluten-Free / Dairy-Free

NUTRITIONAL INFORMATION *For each of 6 servings*
Calories **473** / Fat **16g** / Sat Fat **3g** / Sodium **1501mg**
Carbs **66g** / Fiber **13g** / Sugar **13g** / Protein **13g**

SOUTHWEST
BBQ JACKFRUIT BOWLS

TIME TO PREPARE
20 minutes

TIME TO COOK
20 minutes

SERVES 4 TO 6

Jackfruit is magical produce that easily transforms into something uncannily resembling pulled meat. Jackfruit has a mild taste and, with the proper seasonings, can take on almost any flavor. As it cooks, the jackfruit breaks down into strands like pulled chicken and pork do. Since I'm always craving Southwest flavors, I keep cans of jackfruit on hand so I can whip up these easy BBQ bowls whenever I want. Who knew you could pack in so many nutrients and colors from pantry items?

3 tablespoons extra-virgin olive oil

1 red onion, peeled, spiralized with Blade A, noodles trimmed

Fine sea salt and pepper

2 garlic cloves, minced

½ teaspoon sweet paprika

3 (14-ounce) cans jackfruit in water, drained and rinsed

1 cup low-sodium vegetable broth or water

1 cup gluten-free barbecue sauce

1 teaspoon liquid smoke (optional)

2 heads romaine lettuce, shredded

1 cup frozen corn kernels, thawed

1 (15-ounce) can pinto beans, drained and rinsed

1 large red bell pepper, seeded and chopped

½ teaspoon chili powder

1 ripe avocado, pitted, peeled, and sliced

¼ cup shelled roasted and salted pepitas (pumpkin seeds)

¼ cup chopped fresh cilantro, for garnish

1 lime, quartered

Heat 1 tablespoon of olive oil in a large skillet over medium-high heat. When the oil is shimmering, add the onion and season with salt and black pepper. Cook until the onion is mostly wilted, about 7 minutes. Add the garlic and paprika and stir to coat. Add the jackfruit and broth, and season again with salt and pepper. Cover and cook until the jackfruit softens and begins to pull apart, about 10 minutes. Using tongs or two forks, shred the jackfruit. Stir in the barbecue sauce and liquid smoke (if using). Cook until warmed through, 2 to 3 minutes.

Divide the lettuce among four bowls and top with the pulled jackfruit.

Carefully wipe the skillet clean and return to medium-high heat. Add the remaining 2 tablespoons olive oil, corn, beans, bell peppers, and chili powder and season with salt and black pepper. Cook until the bell peppers are softened, about 5 minutes.

Divide the corn mixture among the bowls and top with the avocado. Garnish with the pepitas and cilantro. Serve with the lime wedges.

TIP / *You can purchase canned jackfruit online if you can't find it in your grocery store.*

Not Spiralized / Saves Well
Vegan / Gluten-Free
Dairy-Free

NUTRITIONAL INFORMATION *Per serving with ½ cup corn succotash*
Calories **390** / Fat **23g** / Sat Fat **3g** / Sodium **694mg**
Carbs **38g** / Fiber **7g** / Sugar **16g** / Protein **9g**

CAULIFLOWER STEAKS & CHIMICHURRI
/ *with* / **CORN SUCCOTASH**

TIME TO PREPARE
35 minutes

TIME TO COOK
30 minutes

SERVES 4

I have made cauliflower steaks every way possible—Parmigiana, crispy-crusted, teriyaki, even as pizza. In this particular cauliflower experimentation, I decided to treat it like a true beef steak, with chimichurri on top and an irresistible corn succotash beneath. With all the different flavors and textures here, you won't miss the meat—and it might even inspire some cauliflower experiments of your own!

For the cauliflower steaks

2 medium heads cauliflower

1 tablespoon extra-virgin olive oil

Fine sea salt and pepper

For the chimichurri

1 cup packed fresh flat-leaf parsley leaves

1 teaspoon dried oregano

1 cup packed fresh cilantro

3 medium garlic cloves, chopped

1 serrano chile or jalapeño, seeded and diced

¼ cup diced white onion

3 tablespoons red wine vinegar

¼ cup extra-virgin olive oil

Fine sea salt and pepper

For the succotash

1 tablespoon extra-virgin olive oil

1 garlic clove, minced

1 medium white onion, diced

1 red bell pepper, diced

1 green bell pepper, diced

2 cups fresh corn kernels (from 2 medium ears corn)

1 pint cherry tomatoes, halved

1 teaspoon dried oregano

Fine sea salt and pepper

Make the cauliflower steaks. Preheat the oven to 400 degrees with a rack in the bottom position. Line a baking sheet with parchment paper.

Remove the leaves from the cauliflower heads. Using a large, sturdy knife, trim the rounded ends. Resting the cauliflower on one flat side, slice each head from the top through the stem into 2 thick steaks; repeat with the second head of cauliflower so you have 4 steaks total. Set the steaks on the prepared baking sheet. Brush both sides with the olive oil and season with salt and black pepper. Roast for 30 minutes, until fork-tender and browning on the edges.

Meanwhile, make the chimichurri. In a food processor, combine the parsley, oregano, cilantro, garlic, chile, onion, vinegar, and olive oil, season with salt and black pepper, and pulse until smooth but with some texture remaining. Set aside.

Make the succotash. Heat the olive oil in a large skillet over medium-high heat. When the oil is shimmering, add the garlic, onion, bell peppers, and corn. Cook until mostly soft, about 6 minutes. Add the tomatoes and oregano and season with salt and black pepper.

Divide the succotash among four plates and top each with a cauliflower steak, roasted side up. Spoon chimichurri over each steak and serve.

Not Spiralized / Saves Well
Vegan / Gluten-Free
Dairy-Free / Low-Cal

NUTRITIONAL INFORMATION *For each of 6 servings*
Calories **238** / Fat **11g** / Sat Fat **1g** / Sodium **45mg**
Carbs **26g** / Fiber **12g** / Sugar **5g** / Protein **11g**

VEGAN TACOS

/ *with* / JICAMA SHELLS

TIME TO PREPARE
20 minutes

TIME TO COOK
10 minutes

SERVES 4 TO 6

One of my fondest dinner memories from growing up is taco night. My mother would let us assemble our own tacos, and it was completely exhilarating—I wish I were that easily amused as an adult! We'd stuff crunchy fried tortilla shells with as much cheese, lettuce, salsa, and ground beef as we possibly could. I think it's time to bring back taco night—with a clean spin. This mushroom-walnut taco meat substitute tastes uncannily similar to beef, thanks to the texture and spices. The shells are slices of jicama that can be folded and stuffed, giving each taco that crisp, refreshing bite. If your jicama shells snap in half, have fun with it—just scoop up the filling with the pieces and keep going!

8 ounces button mushrooms, sliced

4 cups chopped cauliflower florets (from ½ medium head)

⅔ cup chopped raw walnuts

1 tablespoon extra-virgin olive oil

1 garlic clove, minced

2 teaspoons minced jalapeño

1 teaspoon chili powder

½ teaspoon ground cumin

½ teaspoon dried oregano

Fine sea salt and pepper

1 (15-ounce) can black beans, drained and rinsed

Fresh cilantro leaves, for garnish

1 small jicama, peeled and sliced into ⅛-inch-thick rounds

3 limes, quartered

Optional toppings: sliced black olives, shredded pepper Jack cheese, pico de gallo, mashed avocado

In a food processor, pulse the mushrooms until finely chopped, about 15 pulses. Transfer to a large bowl. Place the cauliflower in the food processor and pulse until crumbled, about 10 pulses; do not overpulse. Add to the bowl with the mushrooms. Place the walnuts in the food processor and pulse until ground but not powdered, about 7 pulses. Add to the bowl with the mushroom and cauliflower.

Heat the olive oil in a large, wide skillet over medium-high heat. When the oil is shimmering, add the garlic and jalapeño and cook until fragrant, about 30 seconds. Add the cauliflower mixture, chili powder, cumin, and oregano. Season with salt and pepper. Cook, stirring occasionally, until the mixture is no longer crunchy, about 5 minutes. Stir in the beans and cook for 2 minutes, until heated through. Taste and adjust the seasonings as needed.

Transfer the meat mixture to a serving bowl and top with the cilantro. Serve alongside the jicama shells, lime wedges, and optional toppings of your choosing for tableside assembly.

Not Spiralized / Saves Well
Vegetarian / Gluten-Free

NUTRITIONAL INFORMATION *Per serving*
Calories **332** / Fat **5g** / Sat Fat **1g** / Sodium **1601mg**
Carbs **65g** / Fiber **13g** / Sugar **24g** / Protein **12g**

HOISIN-PULLED HEARTS OF PALM

/ *with* / STUFFED SWEET POTATOES & GINGER-LIME SLAW

TIME TO PREPARE
20 minutes

TIME TO COOK
45 minutes

SERVES 4

I like to think of hoisin sauce as the Asian version of barbecue sauce—it's salty, sweet, thick, and meant to be slathered. Here, instead of a boring plate of coleslaw, potatoes, and BBQ-glazed meat in three piles, we're having baked sweet potatoes stuffed with a hoisin pulled "meat" made from hearts of palm and topped with a ginger-lime slaw to balance it all out. This is a fun way to sneak more veggies into your diet or to feed a vegetarian friend.

4 medium to large sweet potatoes

1 tablespoon extra-virgin olive oil

1 small red onion, thinly sliced

2 garlic cloves, minced

2 (14-ounce) cans or jars hearts of palm, drained, rinsed, and halved lengthwise

½ cup low-sodium vegetable broth, plus more as needed

Fine sea salt and pepper

½ cup hoisin sauce

¼ cup nonfat plain Greek yogurt

1 tablespoon fresh lime juice

1 teaspoon grated fresh ginger

1 teaspoon honey

1 cup shredded red cabbage

1 cup shredded green cabbage

1 cup matchstick carrots

Preheat the oven to 400 degrees. Line a baking sheet with parchment paper.

Pierce the sweet potatoes all over with a fork. Place them on the prepared baking sheet and bake until fork-tender, 45 minutes to 1 hour.

Fifteen minutes before the potatoes are done, heat the olive oil in a large skillet over medium heat. When the oil is shimmering, add the onion and cook for 3 minutes, until softened. Add the garlic and stir until fragrant, about 30 seconds. Add the hearts of palm and broth and season with salt and pepper. Cover and cook until the hearts of palm soften and can be pulled apart like shredded meat, about 10 minutes. If the pan looks dry, add more broth, 1 tablespoon at a time. Uncover and, using tongs or two forks, shred the hearts of palm. Add the hoisin sauce, stir, and cook until warmed through, 1 minute.

In a medium bowl, whisk together the yogurt, lime juice, ginger, and honey. Add water as needed, 1 teaspoon at a time, to loosen the dressing. Add the cabbages and carrots and toss to coat.

TIP / *For a shortcut, use a bag of premade coleslaw mix instead of the 2 cups cabbage.*

Halve each sweet potato lengthwise and mash the flesh lightly with a fork to make room for the toppings. Stuff each sweet potato with the hoisin-pulled hearts of palm. Top with the ginger-lime slaw or serve it alongside.

Not Spiralized / Saves Well
Vegan / Dairy-Free

NUTRITIONAL INFORMATION *Per serving*

Calories **372** / Fat **6g** / Sat Fat **1g** / Sodium **589mg**
Carbs **74g** / Fiber **5g** / Sugar **40g** / Protein **6g**

SWEET & SOUR

WHOLE ROASTED RADISH MEATBALLS

/ *with* / SESAME VEGETABLES

TIME TO PREPARE
20 minutes

TIME TO COOK
25 minutes

SERVES 4

ⓖ ⓖ ⓖ

When I was vegan for three years in my early twenties, I tried every single possible variation of the vegan meatball—quinoa, lentil, black bean, you name it. Now, as an omnivore, I still find myself looking for more vegetarian meatball ideas. One afternoon at the farmer's market, I spotted a bunch of perfectly rounded radishes and was inspired to try them out as meatballs. They didn't turn out as well as I'd hoped in my usual Italian-seasoned marinara sauce, but they did work brilliantly with an Asian glaze—the consistency was just right. Paired with some sesame vegetables and brown rice, these radish balls will satisfy your sweet-and-sour cravings in a plant-based way.

2 bunches radishes (about 20 radishes), trimmed and scrubbed

Cooking spray

⅔ cup pineapple juice

⅓ cup rice vinegar

⅓ cup coconut sugar or honey

3 tablespoons ketchup

1 tablespoon low-sodium soy sauce (use coconut aminos or gluten-free tamari, if gluten-free)

1 tablespoon toasted sesame oil

1 tablespoon arrowroot powder

1 small white onion, thinly sliced or spiralized with Blade A

Fine sea salt and pepper

2 cups broccoli florets

8 ounces snow peas, trimmed

2 cups cooked brown rice

1 tablespoon sesame seeds, for garnish

Preheat the oven to 400 degrees.

Arrange the radishes on a rimmed baking sheet. Spray with cooking spray. Roast for 25 to 30 minutes, shaking the pan halfway through, until fork-tender and browning at the edges.

Meanwhile, in a medium saucepan, combine the pineapple juice, vinegar, coconut sugar, ketchup, and soy sauce. Bring to a boil over medium heat.

In a small bowl, whisk together the arrowroot powder and 1 tablespoon water. When the sauce is boiling, add the arrowroot mixture and cook until thickened, 1 to 2 minutes. Remove the pan from the heat.

Heat the sesame oil in a deep 12-inch skillet over medium-high heat. When the oil is shimmering, add the onion, season with salt and pepper, and cook until softened, about 4 minutes. Toss in the broccoli. Add ¼ cup water, cover, and steam until the broccoli is crisp-tender, about 4 minutes, adding more water as needed if the pan looks dry. Remove the skillet from the heat and stir in the snow peas. Let stand for 2 minutes, stirring occasionally, until the snow peas are crisp-tender. Season with salt and pepper. Add the radish meatballs to the sauce and toss to coat.

Divide the radish meatballs, sesame vegetables, and rice among four plates. Drizzle with more sauce. Garnish everything with the sesame seeds and serve, passing any remaining sauce at the table.

Not Spiralized / Saves Well
Vegan / Gluten-Free
Dairy-Free / Low-Cal

NUTRITIONAL INFORMATION *Per serving*
Calories **286** / Fat **4g** / Sat Fat **1g** / Sodium **152mg**
Carbs **63g** / Fiber **18g** / Sugar **8g** / Protein **14g**

SPLIT PEA DAL
/ in / CURRY-ROASTED ACORN SQUASH CUPS

TIME TO PREPARE
15 minutes

TIME TO COOK
45 minutes

SERVES 4

One day I accidentally grabbed a bag of split peas at the grocery store instead of lentils, but it ended up being a blessing in disguise. I had never cooked with split peas before that, and now I eat them all the time. Like the lentil, the split pea is a legume that's high in protein and fiber. When cooked, they become creamy, perfect for making curries like this split pea dal. Instead of serving this Indian-spiced dish with naan bread and basmati rice, I stuffed it into a curry-roasted acorn squash for more flavor, more veggie, and more texture.

2 small to medium acorn squash

1 tablespoon extra-virgin olive oil, plus more for brushing

Fine sea salt and pepper

1 cup diced white onion

1 tablespoon minced fresh ginger

2 garlic cloves, minced

2 teaspoons ground coriander

2 teaspoons ground cumin

2 teaspoons ground turmeric

1 teaspoon chili powder

1 (14.5-ounce) can diced tomatoes

1 cup yellow split peas

3 cups low-sodium vegetable broth

¼ cup chopped fresh cilantro, for garnish

Preheat the oven to 375 degrees with a rack in the bottom position. Line a baking sheet with parchment paper.

Using a large, sturdy knife, halve the squash lengthwise and scoop out and discard the seeds. Brush the cut sides with olive oil and season with salt and pepper. Place cut-side down on the prepared baking sheet and roast until fork-tender, about 45 minutes.

Meanwhile, heat the olive oil in a large pot over medium heat. When the oil is shimmering, add the onion, season with salt and pepper, and cook until softened, 3 to 5 minutes. Add the ginger and garlic and cook until fragrant, about 30 seconds. Add the coriander, cumin, turmeric, and chili powder and cook until fragrant, about 30 seconds. Stir in the tomatoes. Add the split peas and broth, cover, increase the heat to high, and bring to a boil. Reduce the heat to medium and bring to a simmer. Uncover and cook, stirring occasionally, until the split peas are softened, 20 to 25 minutes. Season with salt and pepper.

Stuff each roasted squash half with the split pea dal and garnish with the cilantro before serving.

TIP / *This dish also works great with lentils instead of split peas.*

Not Spiralized / Saves Well
Vegetarian / Gluten-Free
Dairy-Free (opt.)

NUTRITIONAL INFORMATION *Per serving*
Calories **425** / Fat **14g** / Sat Fat **2g** / Sodium **702mg**
Carbs **62g** / Fiber **12g** / Sugar **20g** / Protein **21g**

SWEET CORN POLENTA

/ *with* / CAPONATA & FETA

TIME TO PREPARE
30 minutes

TIME TO COOK
45 minutes

SERVES 4

Polenta is a dish hailing from Northern Italy that's typically served as a warm porridge or cooled and baked as a savory cake. Although polenta is made from corn, the corn is harvested when the seeds are dry and thus considered a grain. If you're on a grain-free diet, luckily, I have a workaround: sweet corn polenta. Sweet corn is harvested before maturity and therefore considered a vegetable—and thus, this sweet corn polenta is just a big bowl of vegetables! It's thick like a true polenta and has a sweeter flavor, which is complemented by the crumbles of salty feta and the rich, chunky caponata.

For the caponata

1 large eggplant, chopped into ½-inch cubes

2 tablespoons extra-virgin olive oil

Fine sea salt and pepper

1 medium sweet onion, diced

2 celery stalks, diced

3 garlic cloves, minced

2 red bell peppers, diced

2 tablespoons tomato paste

1 (14.5-ounce) can crushed tomatoes

3 tablespoons capers

3 tablespoons chopped pitted green olives

3 tablespoons red wine vinegar

For the polenta

Kernels from 8 ears sweet corn

Fine sea salt

2 tablespoons grated Parmesan cheese

2 tablespoons very thinly sliced fresh basil leaves, plus additional leaves for garnish

Pepper

½ cup crumbled feta cheese, for serving (optional)

Make the caponata. Preheat the oven to 475 degrees.

On a rimmed baking sheet, toss the eggplant with 1 tablespoon of the olive oil. Season with salt and black pepper. Spread into an even layer and roast until browned and tender, about 15 minutes.

Heat the remaining 1 tablespoon olive oil in a large skillet over medium heat. When the oil is shimmering, add the onion and celery and cook until the onion is softened, about 5 minutes. Add the garlic and stir until fragrant, about 30 seconds. Add the bell peppers and season generously with salt and black pepper. Cook until the vegetables are almost tender, about 5 minutes. Add the roasted eggplant and stir for 3 to 5 minutes, until all the vegetables are tender. Add the tomato paste and stir to coat the vegetables. Add the tomatoes and cook until the liquid has thickened and the bottom of the skillet starts to brown, about 5 minutes. Add the capers, olives, and vinegar and scrape up any browned bits from the bottom of the skillet. Reduce the heat to medium-low and simmer for 15 to 20 minutes, until the flavors have melded. Taste and season with salt and black pepper as needed.

/ recipe continues

Meanwhile, make the polenta. Put the corn kernels in a medium saucepan and add water to cover. Stir in ½ teaspoon salt and cover. Bring the water to a boil over high heat, reduce the heat to low, and simmer, covered, for about 7 minutes to soften and cook the corn. Drain the corn in a colander and run under cold water to cool slightly, then shake off any excess liquid. Transfer the corn to a food processor and process until nearly smooth, stopping to scrape down the bowl as needed.

Return the corn to the saucepan and set it over low heat. Add the Parmesan and basil, and season with salt and pepper. Cook, stirring, until warmed through, about 1 minute.

Divide the polenta among four bowls. Top with the caponata, garnish with basil leaves, and sprinkle with feta, if desired. Serve.

Not Spiralized / Vegetarian
Gluten-Free / Low-Cal

NUTRITIONAL INFORMATION *Per serving with ½ cup sauce*
Calories **290** / Fat **6g** / Sat Fat **1g** / Sodium **1212mg**
Carbs **39g** / Fiber **8g** / Sugar **8g** / Protein **22g**

FALAFEL WAFFLE

/ *with* / CUMIN TZATZIKI

TIME TO PREPARE
30 minutes

TIME TO COOK
5 to 10 minutes

SERVES 2

The falafel from the Turkish restaurant down the street is one of Lu's and my guilty pleasures. It's crunchy, deep-fried, and absolutely delicious when dipped into tzatziki or hummus. While oven-baking is a way to make falafel healthier, the consistency isn't quite right, so I decided to think outside the traditional ball shape. Why not have fun with falafel? By making it in a waffle iron, the outside still crisps up. Plus, saying "falafel waffle" is super fun, too! Should we call them "faffles" for short?

For the falafel

1 (15-ounce) can chickpeas, drained, rinsed, and pat dry

3 tablespoons chopped fresh parsley

2 garlic cloves, minced

1½ teaspoons ground cumin

1 teaspoon ground coriander

¼ teaspoon chili powder

½ teaspoon fine sea salt

Pepper

1 large egg

For the tzatziki

1 cup plain nonfat Greek yogurt

1½ teaspoons lemon zest

1½ teaspoons fresh lemon juice

2 teaspoons chopped fresh parsley

½ teaspoon ground cumin

Fine sea salt and pepper

Make the falafel. Heat a waffle iron according to the manufacturer's instructions.

In a food processor, combine the chickpeas, parsley, garlic, cumin, coriander, chili powder, salt, and pepper to taste and pulse until smooth, stopping to scrape down the sides as you go. Transfer the mixture to a medium bowl. Season with pepper, add the egg, and mix well to combine. Spoon half the falafel mixture into the waffle iron and cook according to the manufacturer's instructions or until the waffle is set and the outer edges are firm and browned. Carefully transfer to a plate and repeat with the remaining falafel mixture.

Meanwhile, make the tzatziki. In a small bowl, whisk together the yogurt, lemon zest, lemon juice, parsley, and cumin. Season with salt and pepper.

Spread the tzatziki over the bottom of two plates using the back of a spoon. Top each with a falafel waffle and serve.

Not Spiralized / Saves Well
Vegan / Gluten-Free
Dairy-Free

NUTRITIONAL INFORMATION *Per serving*
Calories **414** / Fat **10g** / Sat Fat **1g** / Sodium **1154mg**
Carbs **70g** / Fiber **19g** / Sugar **17g** / Protein **19g**

VEGGIE QUINOA

CHILI-STUFFED 8-BALL ZUCCHINI

TIME TO PREPARE
20 minutes

TIME TO COOK
45 minutes

SERVES 6

There's always a vat of chunky vegetarian quinoa chili sitting in my freezer for easy weeknight meals. Usually, I include cubed zucchini, but here, I've stepped it up a notch. Instead, I scooped out the flesh of a round 8-Ball zucchini to use in the chili and stuffed the finished product into the empty shell. The consistency of the chili is thicker and it's more fun to eat it this way! Now when you spot this softball-shaped zucchini at the farmer's market, you'll know exactly what to use it for.

6 8-Ball zucchini, halved lengthwise

1 tablespoon extra-virgin olive oil

1 small red onion, diced

1 large carrot, diced

2 celery stalks, diced

1 green bell pepper, diced

1 red bell pepper, diced

1 jalapeño, diced

2 garlic cloves, minced

1 (15-ounce) can black beans, drained and rinsed

1 (15-ounce) can red kidney beans, drained and rinsed

1 cup dry quinoa, rinsed

1 (28-ounce) can no-salt-added diced tomatoes

2 (8-ounce) cans tomato sauce

1 tablespoon chili powder

1 tablespoon dried oregano

1 tablespoon ground cumin

Fine sea salt and pepper

Chopped fresh cilantro, for garnish (optional)

1 avocado, pitted, peeled, and thinly sliced

Preheat the oven to 375 degrees.

Using a spoon or melon baller, scoop out and discard the zucchini seeds. Scoop out most of the flesh, leaving ½ inch intact against the skin. Set the flesh aside in a bowl. Place the zucchini shells in a 9 × 5-inch baking dish and bake, uncovered, until fork-tender, 20 to 30 minutes.

Meanwhile, heat the olive oil in a large saucepan over medium-high heat. When the oil is shimmering, add the onion, carrot, celery, bell peppers, and jalapeño. Cook until softened, about 10 minutes. Add the garlic and cook until fragrant, 1 minute. Add the reserved zucchini flesh, the beans, quinoa, tomatoes, tomato sauce, oregano, chili powder, and cumin and season with salt and black pepper. Bring to a boil, then reduce the heat to medium-low and simmer until the chili thickens, about 30 minutes. Taste and adjust the seasonings as needed.

Divide the chili among the cooked zucchini shells. Garnish with cilantro, if desired, and avocado.

Spiralized / Vegetarian
Gluten-Free / Low-Cal

NUTRITIONAL INFORMATION *Per serving*

Calories **285** / Fat **18g** / Sat Fat **7g** / Sodium **274mg**
Carbs **18g** / Fiber **3g** / Sugar **1g** / Protein **16g**

SICILIAN BIANCA PIZZA
/ *with* / SHREDDED BROCCOLI & OLIVES

TIME TO PREPARE
30 minutes

TIME TO COOK
40 minutes

SERVES 4

The secret to a non-soggy spiralized pizza crust? Make it *bianca*—that is, leave off the traditional layer of tomato sauce before the cheese. If you love pizza but avoid ordering it because of the dough, you must try this recipe—and throw a Friday-night pizza party, because you're going to want to tell everyone about it!

2 tablespoons extra-virgin olive oil

2 large russet potatoes, peeled, spiralized with Blade D

Fine sea salt and pepper

½ teaspoon garlic powder

3 medium eggs, lightly beaten

¼ cup diced red onion

1 garlic clove, minced

1 cup finely chopped broccoli

4 to 5 ounces mozzarella cheese, shredded

¼ cup small pitted black olives, halved lengthwise

Grated Parmesan cheese, for garnish

Red pepper flakes, for garnish

Preheat the oven to 400 degrees.

Heat 1 tablespoon of the olive oil in a 10-inch oven-safe skillet over medium-high heat. When the oil is shimmering, add the potatoes and season with salt and pepper. Add the garlic powder and toss. Cook until softened and lightly browned, about 10 minutes, then transfer to a medium bowl. Let cool for 1 minute, then add the eggs and toss to coat.

Spread the noodles out in the skillet to form the pizza crust. Transfer the skillet to the oven and bake the pizza crust until the egg is cooked and the noodles are set when pressed down with the back of a spatula, about 10 minutes. The crust will start to brown and the edges will be slightly crispy.

While the crust cooks, heat the remaining 1 tablespoon olive oil in a medium skillet over medium-high heat. When the oil is shimmering, add the onion and cook for 2 to 3 minutes, until softened. Add the garlic and broccoli, season with salt and black pepper, and cook for 5 minutes, until the broccoli is bright green.

Remove the crust from the oven, keeping the oven on. Sprinkle with the mozzarella, leaving a ½-inch border all around. Spread the broccoli in an even layer over the mozzarella. Return to the oven and cook until the mozzarella has melted, 5 to 10 minutes more.

Garnish the pizza with the olives, Parmesan, red pepper flakes, and more black pepper. Transfer the pizza to a cutting board and let rest for 5 minutes before slicing. Serve warm.

Spiralized / Vegetarian
Gluten-Free / Dairy-Free

NUTRITIONAL INFORMATION *Per 2 fritters with*
2 tablespoons tzatziki and 1 cup salad
Calories **523** / Fat **45g** / Sat Fat **6g** / Sodium **232mg**
Carbs **26g** / Fiber **6g** / Sugar **6g** / Protein **13g**

ZUCCHINI FRITTERS
/ *with* / **SUNFLOWER TZATZIKI**

TIME TO PREPARE
20 minutes

TIME TO COOK
10 minutes

SERVES 4

Shredding zucchini for fritters can be monotonous and time-consuming—but spiralizing zucchini is fun and takes just seconds! If you haven't tried making fritters or latkes with spiralized vegetables yet, start here. Tried and true, these zucchini fritters are packed with fresh herbs and are even firm enough to be used as a sandwich bun! My favorite way to enjoy these is over a salad or in a grain bowl, with a drizzle of something salty, like this sunflower tzatziki. Puréeing sunflower seeds is a creative hack to get your dressings creamy without the cream.

For the fritters

1 medium zucchini, spiralized with Blade D, noodles trimmed into 1-inch pieces

2 large eggs, lightly beaten

1 onion, finely chopped

1 cup almond flour

2 tablespoons chopped fresh chives

1 tablespoon chopped fresh parsley

1½ teaspoons garlic powder

Fine sea salt and pepper

2 tablespoons extra-virgin olive oil

For the sunflower tzatziki

½ cup sunflower seeds

¼ cup fresh lemon juice

¼ cup extra-virgin olive oil

¼ teaspoon salt

2 tablespoons chopped fresh dill

½ seedless cucumber, diced

For the salad

2 tablespoons extra-virgin olive oil

1 tablespoon red wine vinegar

1 teaspoon Dijon mustard

Fine sea salt and pepper

4 cups packed mixed greens or arugula

1 cup cooked quinoa

1 cup cherry tomatoes, halved

Make the fritters. In a large bowl, toss together the zucchini, eggs, onion, almond flour, chives, parsley, and garlic powder. Season with ¼ teaspoon salt and ¼ teaspoon pepper.

Heat 1 tablespoon of the olive oil in a large skillet over medium-high heat. When the oil is shimmering, place four ¼-cup mounds of the zucchini mixture in the pan, spacing them apart evenly. Cook until set and browned on the bottom, 2 to 3 minutes. Flip and cook on the other side for 2 to 3 minutes more. Transfer to a plate and repeat with the remaining 1 tablespoon olive oil and zucchini mixture.

Make the sunflower tzatziki. In a food processor, combine the sunflower seeds, lemon juice, olive oil, salt, and dill and process until smooth, stopping to scrape down the sides as needed. Add the cucumber and pulse until incorporated and smooth. Set aside.

Make the salad. In a large bowl, whisk together the olive oil, vinegar, and mustard and season with salt and pepper. Add the greens, quinoa, and tomatoes and toss to combine.

Divide the salad among four bowls. Top each with 2 zucchini fritters and a dollop of the tzatziki before serving.

Not Spiralized / Saves Well
Vegetarian / Gluten-Free
Dairy-Free (opt.)

NUTRITIONAL INFORMATION *Per serving*
Calories **434** / Fat **19g** / Sat Fat **4g** / Sodium **1333mg**
Carbs **60g** / Fiber **18g** / Sugar **5g** / Protein **17g**

YUCCA TOSTADAS
/ *with* / **VEGGIES**

TIME TO PREPARE
35 minutes

TIME TO COOK
35 minutes

SERVES 4

Tostadas are simply tortillas that have been deep-fried or toasted until crispy—they're a tasty and resourceful way to use up tortillas that aren't fresh enough! The crisped tostadas are then topped with meats, veggies, cheeses, and anything else you like to create a kind of open-faced Mexican sandwich. When we go out, I usually order my tostadas over a salad instead of in the shell—it's healthier, but kind of underwhelming. With these tostadas made from fiber-full yucca, you still get that tortilla base, without the deep-frying or the flour or processed corn. Feel free to top these with some shredded chicken or the pulled BBQ jackfruit on page 204.

1 cup chopped peeled yucca

1 tablespoon sunflower oil or other neutral oil

⅛ teaspoon salt

1 teaspoon extra-virgin olive oil

1 garlic clove, minced

⅓ cup low-sodium vegetable broth

2 (15-ounce) cans black beans, drained and rinsed

For the guacamole

2 ripe avocados, pitted, peeled, and cubed

2 tablespoons minced fresh cilantro

1 small jalapeño, minced

Juice of 1 lime, plus more as needed

½ teaspoon fine sea salt, plus more as needed

For the pico de gallo

4 plum tomatoes, seeded and chopped

½ cup diced red onion

Juice of 2 limes

2 tablespoons minced fresh cilantro

Fine sea salt and pepper

⅓ cup crumbled queso fresco or cotija cheese, for serving (optional)

Preheat the oven to 350 degrees.

Fill a medium pot halfway with water and bring to a boil over high heat. Add the yucca and cook until fork-tender, about 15 minutes. Drain in a colander and transfer to a medium bowl. Add the sunflower oil and salt and, using a fork, mash until smooth (it will be very sticky). Refrigerate the yucca until cool, about 20 minutes.

Cut out nine 6-inch parchment paper squares. Divide the yucca evenly among 8 of the parchment paper squares, leaving 1 extra.

Place the extra piece of parchment paper on top of the yucca on 1 square and press down with your palm to flatten it like a tortilla. Use a rolling pin as needed to roll it as thinly as possible. Remove the top parchment paper and transfer the flattened tortilla, still on the bottom parchment piece, onto a baking sheet. Repeat with the remaining yucca to make 8 tortillas. (You may need to use two baking sheets.)

/ recipe continues

Bake the tortillas until lightly browned in spots but still pliable for soft tortillas, 12 to 15 minutes, or bake for 3 to 5 minutes more for crispier tortillas. Remove the tortillas from the oven and wrap them in a clean kitchen towel to keep warm.

Meanwhile, heat the olive oil in a medium skillet over medium-high heat. When the oil is shimmering, add the garlic and cook until fragrant, about 30 seconds. Add the broth and beans. Cook for 5 minutes, until the beans are warmed through. Remove the skillet from the heat and, using the back of a fork or a potato masher, mash the beans until smooth but with some texture remaining.

Make the guacamole. In a medium bowl, combine the avocado, cilantro, jalapeño, lime juice, and salt and mash with a fork until the desired consistency is achieved. Taste and adjust the seasonings with more salt or lime juice as needed.

Make the pico de gallo. In a medium bowl, use a spoon to toss together the tomatoes, onion, lime juice, and cilantro. Taste and season with salt and pepper.

Place a yucca tortilla in the center of a salad plate. Spread the black bean mash over the top. Top with the guacamole, pico de gallo, and cheese (if using). Repeat with remaining yucca tortillas and toppings. Serve.

ALSO WORKS WELL WITH
Sweet Potato / Parsnip

Spiralized / Vegetarian
Gluten-Free / Paleo
Dairy-Free

NUTRITIONAL INFORMATION *Per serving*
Calories **326** / Fat **26g** / Sat Fat **3g** / Sodium **83mg**
Carbs **35g** / Fiber **10g** / Sugar **12g** / Protein **8g**

WINTER HARVEST BOWLS

/ *with* / BUTTERNUT SQUASH & MAPLE-TAHINI DRESSING

TIME TO PREPARE
15 minutes

TIME TO COOK
30 minutes

SERVES 4

Lu thinks I'm crazy when fall and winter come around because I'm constantly buying candles. I just love making our home smell festive, and there's no better time to smell cozy and sweet than when it's chilly outside. I love the scent of cinnamon apples, spiced pecans, "Christmas cookies," pear spice, and pretty much any variety of those aromas. (In the summertime, my candles are usually coconut or fresh linen scented, to remind me of a beach house.) A natural way to get those aromas? Make this dish! You'll want to curl up on the couch after making this bowl, thanks to the spiced pecans, sweet butternut squash, and roasted Brussels sprouts—and it'll save you money on candles!

For the spiced pecans

1 tablespoon pure maple syrup

¼ teaspoon ground cinnamon

¼ teaspoon cayenne pepper

Fine sea salt

½ cup whole pecans

For the vegetables

1 pound Brussels sprouts, halved

1 tablespoon plus 2 teaspoons extra-virgin olive oil

1 tablespoon balsamic vinegar

Fine sea salt and pepper

1 medium butternut squash, peeled, spiralized with Blade C, noodles trimmed

For the dressing

3 tablespoons tahini

1 tablespoon apple cider vinegar

1 tablespoon pure maple syrup

1 tablespoon extra-virgin olive oil

Fine sea salt and pepper

½ cup pomegranate seeds, for serving

Make the pecans. Preheat the oven to 425 degrees. Line two baking sheets with parchment paper.

In a large bowl, whisk together the maple syrup, cinnamon, and cayenne to create a paste. Season lightly with salt. Add the pecans and stir to coat. Spread the pecans out on one of the prepared baking sheets and bake for 5 minutes, then flip the pecans and bake until fragrant and nearly dry to the touch, 5 minutes more. Transfer the parchment paper with the pecans to a clean surface and let cool. Keep the oven on.

Make the vegetables. Line the same baking sheet with clean parchment paper. Spread out the Brussels sprouts on the baking sheet, drizzle with 1 tablespoon of the olive oil and the balsamic vinegar, and toss well to coat. Season with salt and pepper. Bake until the leaves crisp up and the sprouts are crisp-tender, 25 to 30 minutes.

TIP / *The spiced pecans are great to have on hand for snacking or for appetizers for guests—and they always make your kitchen smell cozy.*

Arrange the butternut squash noodles on the other prepared baking sheet, drizzle with the remaining 2 teaspoons olive oil, and toss to coat. Season with salt and pepper. When the sprouts have 15 minutes left, add the pan with the squash to the oven and roast until tender, 10 to 15 minutes.

Meanwhile, make the dressing. In a small bowl, whisk together the tahini, apple cider vinegar, maple syrup, and olive oil and season with salt and pepper. Add water as needed, 1 tablespoon at a time, until the dressing is creamy enough to be drizzled.

Divide the Brussels sprouts and butternut squash noodles among four bowls and top evenly with the pomegranate seeds and pecans. Drizzle with the dressing and serve.

/ see photograph on next page

WINTER
HARVEST
BOWL

SUMMER
HARVEST
BOWL

ALSO WORKS WELL WITH
Zucchini

Spiralized / No-Cook
Vegetarian / Gluten-Free
Low-Cal

NUTRITIONAL INFORMATION *Per serving*
Calories **282** / Fat **24g** / Sat Fat **6g** / Sodium **87mg**
Carbs **12g** / Fiber **2g** / Sugar **10g** / Protein **7g**

SUMMER HARVEST BOWLS
/ *with* / GRILLED PEACH, BURRATA & CUCUMBER

TIME TO PREPARE
15 minutes

TIME TO COOK
5 minutes

SERVES 4

It's always hard to resist burrata when it's on the menu—it's a luxurious, pillowy cheese made from mozzarella and cream. My favorite way to have burrata is with peaches and pesto—the sweetness from the peaches and the fresh basil scream "summertime." Aside from a few pantry items like olive oil and red wine vinegar, all of these ingredients can be found at a farmer's market during the summer. Pick up a bottle of wine or some sparkling water on the way home and enjoy this easy, no-cook salad outside, savoring the warm weather.

For the dressing

1 ounce fresh basil

1 small garlic clove, chopped

¼ cup extra-virgin olive oil

2 tablespoons red wine vinegar

1 small shallot, chopped

Pinch of red pepper flakes

Fine sea salt

For the salad

4 ripe peaches, halved and pitted

2 teaspoons extra-virgin olive oil

2 cups packed baby arugula

1 seedless cucumber, spiralized with Blade D, noodles trimmed

1 ball (8 ounces) burrata cheese, quartered

Make the dressing. In a food processor, combine the basil, garlic, olive oil, vinegar, shallot, and red pepper flakes, season with salt, and pulse until smooth. Transfer to a medium bowl.

Make the salad. Heat a grill to medium-high or heat a grill pan over medium-high heat. Brush the cut sides of the peaches lightly with the olive oil. Place the peaches on the grill, cut-sides down, and cook until grill marks appear, 3 to 4 minutes. Halve the grilled peaches to yield 8 pieces total.

Add the arugula and cucumber noodles to the bowl with the dressing and toss to coat.

Divide the cucumber noodles among four bowls and top evenly with the grilled peaches and burrata.

Not Spiralized / Vegan
Gluten-Free / Dairy-Free
Low-Cal

NUTRITIONAL INFORMATION *Per ¼ slice of socca*
Calories **299** / Fat **16g** / Sat Fat **2g** / Sodium **359mg**
Carbs **33g** / Fiber **10g** / Sugar **3g** / Protein **11g**

SOCCA FLATBREAD

/ *with* / **WHITE BEAN SPREAD & CARAMELIZED LEEKS**

TIME TO PREPARE
15 minutes

TIME TO COOK
15 minutes

**SERVES 4 AS AN
APPETIZER OR 2 AS A
MAIN COURSE**

ⓢ ⓢ ⓢ

1 cup chickpea flour

1 cup lukewarm water

Fine sea salt and
pepper

4 tablespoons extra-
virgin olive oil

1 leek, thinly sliced and
rinsed well (see Tip)

1 (15-ounce) can white
beans, drained, rinsed,
and patted dry

1 medium garlic clove,
minced

½ teaspoon chopped
fresh rosemary

½ teaspoon chopped
fresh thyme

2 tablespoons low-
sodium vegetable
broth or water

Socca (also known as farinata) is like a thin pancake or crepe made of chickpea flour. Originally from the South of France, it's typically enjoyed as a flatbread seasoned with herbs such as rosemary. Some people slice up the socca and eat it like bread or pita chips. Either way, socca works well with a creamy spread on top, like this white bean one. To enjoy it as an appetizer, slice the socca into pieces and serve with the white bean spread as a dip, or for a protein-packed main course, top the socca with the spread and serve a bright green salad alongside. Note that chickpea flour is sometimes labeled garbanzo bean, besan, or gram flour.

Preheat the oven to 450 degrees. Place a 12-inch round nonstick baking pan or cast-iron skillet in the oven to preheat.

Place the chickpea flour in a medium bowl. While whisking, slowly pour in the lukewarm water, whisking to break up any lumps. Set aside for 30 minutes to let the flour completely absorb the water. Season with salt and pepper.

Carefully brush the bottom of the hot baking pan or skillet with 2 tablespoons of the olive oil. Pour in the batter. Bake for 10 to 15 minutes, until the socca is firm and the edges are set and beginning to lightly brown.

Meanwhile, heat 1 tablespoon of the olive oil in a large nonstick skillet over medium-high heat. When the oil is shimmering, add the leek and season with salt and pepper. Reduce the heat to medium and cook, stirring frequently, until well browned, about 7 minutes. If the pan seems too dry, add 1 tablespoon water and scrape up any browned bits from the bottom.

While leeks cook, in a food processor, combine the white beans, garlic, rosemary, thyme, broth, remaining 1 tablespoon olive oil, and a pinch each of salt and pepper. Pulse until smooth. Taste and adjust the seasonings as needed.

Carefully transfer the socca to a serving platter. Spread the white bean mixture over the socca, leaving a ½-inch border all around. Top with the caramelized leeks. Cut the socca into 4 wedges and serve.

TIP / *Leeks have lots of grit between their layers. To prepare them properly, slice off the dark green tops and about ½ inch of the bottom. Place them in a large bowl of cold water and swish them around to separate the layers. Let them sit for a few minutes, then scoop them out of the water to leave the dirt behind.*

NON-VEGETARIAN MAINS

Not Spiralized /
Gluten-Free / Low-Cal

NUTRITIONAL INFORMATION *Per serving*
Calories **280** / Fat **16g** / Sat Fat **9g** / Sodium **740mg**
Carbs **14g** / Fiber **5g** / Sugar **8g** / Protein **24g**

PEPPERONI PIZZA-STUFFED

HASSELBACK ZUCCHINI

TIME TO PREPARE
20 minutes

TIME TO COOK
25 minutes

SERVES 4

Ever since BuzzFeed started making its Tasty cooking videos, my Facebook feed hasn't been the same. I started seeing the craziest foods being made—some were creative and worth trying, while others were ridiculous (like a doughnut in the waffle iron). But a hasselback zucchini stuffed like a pizza by the geniuses at Delish, its health-focused site, popped up one day, and I immediately knew I had to see if it tasted as good as it looked. It definitely did—and with a few tweaks of my own, I have been blissfully enjoying this ingenious zucchini pizza ever since.

4 medium zucchini or yellow squash, ends trimmed

6 ounces mozzarella cheese, cut into 32 slices

32 slices turkey pepperoni, or more as needed (see Tip)

1 teaspoon Italian seasoning

¼ cup grated Parmesan cheese

1 cup prepared marinara sauce, for serving

Preheat the oven to 425 degrees. Line a baking sheet with parchment paper.

Place chopsticks on either side of the zucchini and, using a sharp knife, make 16 evenly spaced slits along the length of the zucchini (your knife should hit the chopsticks, preventing it from slicing all the way through the zucchini).

Place the zucchini on the prepared baking sheets and bake until softened, 15 to 20 minutes. Remove from the oven and let cool. Keep the oven on.

When the zucchini are cool enough to handle, stuff the slits with the mozzarella and pepperoni, alternating them as you go. Sprinkle each zucchini with ¼ teaspoon of the Italian seasoning and 1 tablespoon of the Parmesan. Return to the oven and bake until the cheese has melted and the pepperoni is crispy, about 8 minutes more.

Meanwhile, in a small saucepan, bring the marinara sauce to a simmer over medium-high heat. Reduce the heat to low to keep warm.

Serve the zucchini with the warmed marinara sauce for dipping.

TIP / *The thinner the hasselback slices, the more pepperoni will fit, so if you're serving this to meat lovers, keep that in mind.*

Spiralized / Gluten-Free
Paleo / Dairy-Free
Low-Cal

NUTRITIONAL INFORMATION *Per serving*
Calories **276** / Fat **9g** / Sat Fat **1g** / Sodium **272mg**
Carbs **11g** / Fiber **3g** / Sugar **7g** / Protein **38g**

BAKED HALIBUT
/ *with* / TOMATO-HERB BROTH
& SUMMER SQUASH NOODLES

TIME TO PREPARE
20 minutes

TIME TO COOK
25 minutes

SERVES 4

Halibut is naturally such a buttery, smooth fish that you don't need to cook it with much more than some olive oil, lemon, salt, and pepper. Anything else, like this tomato-herb broth, is just a bonus. The tomatoes' juices steam out and enrich the broth with their inherent sweetness. Pair this dish with a nice dry white wine or a seltzer with fresh lemon juice and enjoy summertime any time of year.

1 tablespoon extra-virgin olive oil, plus more for brushing

4 (6-ounce) halibut fillets

Fine sea salt and pepper

½ lemon

1 medium shallot, minced

2 garlic cloves, minced

½ teaspoon red pepper flakes

1 pint cherry tomatoes, halved

1 cup low-sodium chicken broth or vegetable broth

2 medium zucchini or yellow squash, spiralized with Blade A, noodles trimmed

1 tablespoon chopped fresh basil

1 tablespoon chopped fresh parsley

1 tablespoon chopped fresh thyme

Preheat the oven to 400 degrees. Brush the bottom of a casserole dish with olive oil.

Arrange the halibut fillets in the prepared baking dish in an even layer. Season generously with salt and black pepper and squeeze the lemon juice over the fish. Cover with foil and bake until the fish flakes easily with a fork, 12 to 15 minutes.

Meanwhile, heat the olive oil in a large wide skillet or medium saucepan over medium heat. When the oil is shimmering, add the shallot, garlic, and red pepper flakes and cook until the shallot is softened, about 3 minutes. Add the tomatoes, broth, and ¼ teaspoon salt and increase the heat to medium-high to bring the liquid to a simmer. Reduce the heat to medium-low and cook for 15 minutes, until the tomatoes break down and the sauce has thickened but still has moisture. Add the zucchini and cook for 3 to 5 minutes, until the zucchini noodles are al dente. Taste the broth and season with salt as needed. Remove the pan from the heat and stir in the basil, parsley, and thyme.

Pour the zucchini and broth over the fish and cover for 2 minutes to let the flavors develop. Uncover and serve.

TIP / *Try this dish with any other white flaky fish, such as cod or haddock.*

NUTRITIONAL INFORMATION *Per 2 fish cakes with 1½ cups broth mixture*
Calories **511** / Fat **34g** / Sat Fat **15g** / Sodium **883mg**
Carbs **19g** / Fiber **7g** / Sugar **6g** / Protein **32g**

THAI CHIA FISH CAKES
/ *with* / BOK CHOY & COCONUT-GINGER BROTH

TIME TO PREPARE
50 minutes

TIME TO COOK
20 minutes

SERVES 4

Chia seeds in a fish cake? Definitely. Chia seeds, thanks to their extremely high fiber content, can absorb up to twelve times their weight in water, making them gel up and, thus, work as a binding agent, eliminating the need for egg and bread crumbs in the fish cake. This trick works with meatballs and patties, too, to make them healthier foods with the benefits of the superfood chia seed—and any way we can creatively sneak in a superfood is a win! The ginger bok choy picks up the hints of grated ginger in the fish cakes, so be sure to save a little sauce for dipping.

For the fish cakes

1¼ pounds white-flesh fish, such as cod or haddock

3 garlic cloves, minced

1½ teaspoons grated fresh ginger

3 scallions, white parts only, finely chopped, plus 3 scallions, chopped, white and green parts kept separate

¼ cup fresh cilantro leaves, finely chopped

1 teaspoon fish sauce

1½ teaspoons low-sodium soy sauce (use coconut aminos or gluten-free tamari, if gluten-free)

2 teaspoons toasted sesame oil

2 tablespoons chia seeds

For the coconut-ginger broth

2 teaspoons coconut oil

3 scallions, diced, white and green parts separated

1 (2-inch) piece fresh ginger, peeled and minced

2 garlic cloves, minced

¼ teaspoon red pepper flakes

1 (14-ounce) can lite coconut milk, shaken

1 tablespoon low-sodium soy sauce (use coconut aminos or gluten-free tamari, if gluten-free)

Juice of ½ lime

5 to 6 cups chopped baby bok choy, bottom white stems trimmed off

¾ cup almond flour

Salt

1 large egg, lightly beaten

2 tablespoons sunflower oil or additional coconut oil

/ recipe continues

TIP / *Make this meal a little heartier by serving each portion with ¼ cup cooked brown rice, spiralized vegetable rice, or cauliflower rice.*

Make the fish cakes. Line a baking sheet with parchment paper.

Put the fish in a food processor and pulse until mostly smooth. Transfer to a medium bowl and add the garlic, ginger, scallions, cilantro, fish sauce, soy sauce, sesame oil, and chia seeds. Using your hands, mix thoroughly to combine. Form the mixture into 4 large or 8 small fish cakes and transfer to the prepared baking sheet. Cover and refrigerate for 30 minutes.

Meanwhile, make the coconut-ginger broth. Melt the coconut oil in a medium saucepan over medium-high heat. When the oil is shimmering, add the white parts of the scallions, the ginger, garlic, and red pepper flakes and cook until fragrant, about 1 minute. Add the coconut milk, soy sauce, and lime juice and stir well. Stir in the bok choy and cook until wilted, about 5 minutes. Stir in the green parts of the scallions. Reduce the heat to low and cover to keep warm until ready to serve.

Assemble the fish cakes. Place the almond flour and a pinch of salt in a shallow bowl or baking dish. Place the egg in a separate shallow bowl. Dip the chilled fish cakes in the beaten egg, letting any excess drip back into the bowl, then dredge both sides in the almond flour to coat. Repeat with the remaining fish cakes.

Heat 1 tablespoon of the sunflower oil in a large nonstick skillet over medium-high heat. When the oil is shimmering, working in batches as needed to avoid crowding the pan, add the fish cakes and cook until browned on the bottom, about 2 minutes. Flip and cook until browned on the other side, about 2 minutes more. Reduce the heat to medium-low and cook for about 2 minutes. Flip the cakes one more time and cook until just cooked through, about 2 minutes more. Transfer to a plate, heat the remaining 1 tablespoon sunflower oil, and cook the remaining fish cakes.

Using tongs, divide the bok choy among four bowls and ladle the coconut broth on top. Top each bowl with 1 or 2 fish cakes and serve.

PORK TENDERLOIN

/ *with* / SPIRALIZED MAPLE & THYME ROASTED CARROTS & PARSNIPS

TIME TO PREPARE
20 minutes

TIME TO COOK
35 minutes

SERVES 4

Everyone has certain family dishes that are favorites for life, those meals you request every time you're at your parents' house but never think to ask for the recipe. For me, that's my mother's roast chicken over vegetables. It's just bone-in chicken parts over veggies, but it's the best. When I finally got the recipe from my mother, I made it all winter long. After the fourth or fifth time, I wanted to create my own version that I could one day pass down, so I switched up the protein and used a pork tenderloin, the "other white meat." Pork tenderloin is lean like chicken, and just as easy to cook and flavor. With the spiralizer, this dish comes together in a pinch!

1¼ pounds pork tenderloin, trimmed and pat dry

4 tablespoons extra-virgin olive oil

Fine sea salt and pepper

¼ cup Dijon mustard

2 teaspoons pure maple syrup

2 teaspoons fresh thyme leaves

3 large carrots, peeled, spiralized with Blade D, noodles trimmed

3 large parsnips, peeled, spiralized with Blade D, noodles trimmed

Preheat the oven to 425 degrees.

Rub the pork tenderloin with 1 tablespoon of the olive oil and season with salt and pepper.

Heat 1 tablespoon of the olive oil in a large oven-safe skillet over medium heat. When the oil is shimmering, add the pork and cook, turning occasionally, until evenly browned all over, 10 to 12 minutes.

Brush the pork with the mustard, transfer the skillet to the oven, and roast until an instant-read thermometer inserted into the center registers 145 degrees, 10 to 15 minutes. Transfer the pork to a large plate, cover with foil, and let rest for 10 minutes. Keep the oven on.

Meanwhile, in a large bowl, whisk together the remaining 2 tablespoons olive oil, the maple syrup, and thyme and season with salt and pepper. Add the carrots and parsnips and toss well to coat and combine. Spread out the vegetables on a baking sheet and roast until al dente, about 20 minutes.

Cut the pork into 1-inch slices and serve the vegetables alongside.

Not Spiralized
Gluten-Free / Paleo
Dairy-Free

NUTRITIONAL INFORMATION *Per serving*
Calories **371** / Fat **13g** / Sat Fat **2g** / Sodium **1175mg**
Carbs **32g** / Fiber **6g** / Sugar **8g** / Protein **34g**

BRUSSELS SPROUT LATKES

/ *with* / SALMON & LEMON-DIJON SAUCE

TIME TO PREPARE
20 minutes

TIME TO COOK
20 minutes

SERVES 4

When I was growing up, my mother cooked most meals for our family by herself. As I got older, I started helping my mom as much as possible—not only on special occasions, but any time we all got together for dinner. One Christmas Eve in Florida, the warm breeze was coming through the kitchen windows and the wine was flowing freely. I was shredding Brussels sprouts for a salad and, thanks to the Sauvignon Blanc, I shredded *wayyyy* more than was needed. Long story short, I started bravely experimenting, mixing the sprouts with egg, flour, and seasonings, and these latkes were born. Smear a little Dijon on top and enjoy—with a nice glass of wine alongside!

For the latkes

1 large egg, beaten

2 egg whites

3 cups shredded Brussels sprouts

1 small onion, finely chopped

1 large garlic clove, minced

½ cup chickpea or almond flour, plus more as needed

1 teaspoon fresh thyme leaves

¼ teaspoon red pepper flakes

½ teaspoon fine sea salt

Pepper

2 tablespoons sunflower oil

For the salmon

4 (4-ounce) skinless salmon fillets

Fine sea salt and pepper

2 lemons, thinly sliced

Lemon-Dijon Sauce (recipe follows)

Preheat the oven to 425 degrees. Line a baking sheet with parchment paper.

Make the latkes. In a large bowl, mix the egg, egg whites, Brussels sprouts, onion, and garlic. Stir in the chickpea flour, thyme, red pepper flakes, salt, and black pepper to taste. Stir to combine until the mixture can be molded easily, adding more flour as needed, 1 tablespoon at a time, until the desired consistency is reached.

Heat 1 tablespoon of the sunflower oil in a large skillet over medium-high heat. When the oil is shimmering, add four heaping ¼-cup scoops of the Brussels sprout mixture to the skillet and flatten with a spatula. Cook, turning once, until browned, 3 to 4 minutes per side. Transfer to a paper towel–lined plate to drain. Repeat with the remaining 1 tablespoon sunflower oil and Brussels sprout mixture.

/ recipe continues

Meanwhile, make the salmon. Arrange the salmon fillets on the prepared baking sheet and season with salt and black pepper. Set 3 lemon slices on top of each fillet and bake until the salmon is opaque and flakes easily with a fork, 12 to 15 minutes for medium-well, depending on the thickness of the salmon.

Place 2 latkes on each of four plates, top each with a salmon fillet, and drizzle with the Lemon-Dijon Sauce. Serve.

TIP / *The Lemon-Dijon Sauce goes great on steak and chicken, too, so double it, save it, and use it again.*

LEMON-DIJON SAUCE

MAKES ABOUT 1½ CUPS

2 teaspoons extra-virgin olive oil

1½ tablespoons minced shallot

2 garlic cloves, minced

⅔ cup Dijon mustard

½ cup low-sodium vegetable broth or chicken broth

2 tablespoons fresh lemon juice

2 teaspoons honey

Heat the olive oil in a small saucepan over medium-high heat. When the oil is shimmering, add the shallot and garlic and cook until the shallot is translucent, about 1 minute. Whisk in the mustard, broth, lemon juice, and honey and bring to a boil. Reduce the heat to medium-low and simmer until the sauce has thickened, about 3 minutes. Store in an airtight container in the refrigerator for 1 to 2 days.

NUTRITIONAL INFORMATION *Per serving*
Calories **358** / Fat **27g** / Sat Fat **12g** / Sodium **817mg**
Carbs **7g** / Fiber **1g** / Sugar **3g** / Protein **22g**

SPICY CUMIN LAMB MEATBALLS & CUCUMBERS

/ *with* / HERBED TAHINI-YOGURT SAUCE

TIME TO PREPARE
20 minutes

TIME TO COOK
10 minutes

SERVES 4

From a piquant Mexican salsa to a fiery Italian fra diavolo sauce, I like it hot. My husband, however, doesn't feel the same way, so I've learned to balance out the flavors so both our palates and heat thresholds are satisfied. These meatballs are made with feisty red pepper flakes to give them a kick, but then the cool cucumber noodles and refreshing herbed tahini-yogurt sauce provide relief and equalize the spice. For those of you (like me) who want it on the spicier side, garnish with extra red pepper flakes. Everybody wins!

For the meatballs

½ cup chopped white onion

3 garlic cloves, chopped

2 tablespoons chopped fresh parsley

½ teaspoon dried oregano

1 teaspoon ground cumin

¾ teaspoon ground coriander

½ teaspoon red pepper flakes, plus more for serving if desired

1 teaspoon fine sea salt

1 pound ground lamb

For the yogurt sauce

½ cup nonfat plain Greek yogurt

2 tablespoons fresh lemon juice

1 tablespoon minced fresh cilantro

1 tablespoon minced fresh parsley

1 tablespoon minced fresh mint

¼ teaspoon fine sea salt

Cracked pepper

2 seedless cucumbers, spiralized with Blade A, noodles trimmed

Make the meatballs. Preheat the broiler with a rack set 3 inches below the heat source. Line a baking sheet with parchment paper.

In a food processor, combine the onion, garlic, and parsley and pulse until finely chopped. Transfer the mixture to a medium bowl and add the oregano, cumin, coriander, red pepper flakes, salt, and lamb. Mix together until fully combined. Using your hands, form about sixteen 1-inch meatballs and set them on the prepared baking sheet, spacing them ½ inch apart. Broil the meatballs for 8 to 10 minutes, until browned on top but still slightly pink inside.

Meanwhile, make the yogurt sauce. In a large bowl, whisk together the yogurt, lemon juice, cilantro, parsley, mint, salt, and black pepper to taste. Add the cucumbers and toss to coat.

Divide the cucumber noodles among four bowls and top each with 4 meatballs. Garnish with more red pepper flakes, if desired, and serve.

Spiralized / Saves Well
Gluten-Free / Paleo
Dairy-Free

NUTRITIONAL INFORMATION *Per serving*
Calories **416** / Fat **22g** / Sat Fat **6g** / Sodium **1439mg**
Carbs **29g** / Fiber **5g** / Sugar **8g** / Protein **27g**

ROAST CHICKEN & BUTTERNUT SQUASH PASTA

/ *with* / **WILTED GREENS & MUSHROOM GRAVY**

TIME TO PREPARE
15 minutes

TIME TO COOK
35 minutes

SERVES 4

For me, November is an excuse to eat Thanksgiving dinner for a whole month. Whether a Friendsgiving get-together, the real thing, or leftovers at home with Lu, I'm always in the holiday spirit for some roast turkey with gravy. But roast chicken is so much easier when you're preparing a weeknight dinner. This butternut squash pasta dresses up the shredded meat with a quick-and-easy mushroom gravy. Show how grateful you are for your friends or loved ones by making them a bowl of this seasonal pasta—in November, or any time of year!

2 tablespoons extra-virgin olive oil

1 white onion, chopped

2 garlic cloves, minced

8 ounces button mushrooms, sliced

Fine sea salt and pepper

2 tablespoons arrowroot powder

1 teaspoon dried thyme

2 cups low-sodium chicken broth

1 large butternut squash, peeled, spiralized with Blade C, noodles trimmed

Cooking spray

8 cups winter chard leaves, chopped

3 cups shredded rotisserie or other cooked chicken, warmed

Preheat the oven to 400 degrees. Line a baking sheet with parchment paper.

Heat 1 tablespoon of the olive oil in a small saucepan over medium-high heat. When the oil is shimmering, add the onion, garlic, and mushrooms and season with salt and pepper. Cook until the mushrooms shrink and release moisture, 5 to 7 minutes. Stir in the arrowroot powder and thyme. Add the broth and bring to a boil. Reduce the heat to medium-low and simmer until thickened like a gravy, 15 to 20 minutes.

Meanwhile, arrange the butternut squash noodles in an even layer on the prepared baking sheet. Spray with cooking spray and season with salt and pepper. Roast until al dente, 8 to 10 minutes.

Heat the remaining 1 tablespoon olive oil in a large skillet over medium-high heat. Add the chard and season generously with salt and pepper. Cook until very wilted, about 7 minutes.

Divide the squash noodles and chard among four plates. Using tongs, add the chicken. Drizzle each plate with gravy and serve.

ALSO WORKS WELL WITH
Broccoli / Turnip
Sweet Potato / Rutabaga

Spiralized / Gluten-Free
Paleo / Dairy-Free

NUTRITIONAL INFORMATION *Per serving*
Calories **519** / Fat **27g** / Sat Fat **3g** / Sodium **287mg**
Carbs **19g** / Fiber **6g** / Sugar **12g** / Protein **10g**

PORK MILANESE

/ with / BURST TOMATOES & ZUCCHINI NOODLES

TIME TO PREPARE
15 minutes

TIME TO COOK
20 minutes

SERVES 2

No matter what, there are four ingredients we always buy at the farmer's market in the summertime: garlic, basil, tomatoes, and zucchini. With just these, I feel like I can make anything, especially when the tomatoes are super ripe. I love to roast them until they burst, but when it's hot and I don't want to turn on my oven, I just pop the tomatoes into a covered skillet. This simple, bright dish will have you looking forward to your weekly trips to the farmer's market and excited to see what you can whip up with your spiralizer.

⅓ cup almond flour

½ teaspoon garlic powder

1 large egg, lightly beaten

2 pork cutlets (4 ounces each)

Fine sea salt and pepper

2 tablespoons extra-virgin olive oil

½ lemon

1 shallot, minced

2 garlic cloves, minced

1 pint heirloom cherry tomatoes, halved

½ cup low-sodium chicken broth

1 large zucchini (or 2 medium), spiralized with Blade C, noodles trimmed

¼ cup very thinly sliced fresh basil leaves

Place the almond flour and garlic powder in a shallow bowl or baking dish. Place the egg in a separate shallow bowl. Season the pork with salt and pepper. Working with one piece at a time, dip the pork cutlet in the egg, letting any excess drip back into the bowl, then dredge in the almond flour, flipping to coat all sides. Repeat with the second cutlet.

Heat 1 tablespoon of the olive oil in a large skillet over medium-high heat. When the oil is shimmering, add the pork and cook for 5 minutes, until bottom is cooked and opaque, then flip and cook until the pork is cooked through and the crust is golden brown, about 5 minutes more. Transfer the pork to a plate and squeeze the lemon over the top.

Meanwhile, heat the remaining 1 tablespoon olive oil in a separate large skillet over medium-high heat. When the oil is shimmering, add the shallot and garlic and cook until fragrant, about 1 minute. Add the cherry tomatoes and broth and season with salt and pepper. Cover and cook, shaking the pan occasionally, until the tomatoes burst, 5 to 7 minutes. Uncover, add the zucchini, and cook until the noodles are al dente, about 3 minutes. Stir in the basil.

Divide the zucchini noodle mixture between two plates and top each with a pork cutlet. Serve.

NUTRITIONAL INFORMATION *Per serving*
Calories **455** / Fat **26g** / Sat Fat **4g** / Sodium **371mg**
Carbs **38g** / Fiber **7g** / Sugar **19g** / Protein **23g**

FISH TACO BOWLS

TIME TO PREPARE
30 minutes

TIME TO COOK
10 minutes

SERVES 4

While running my first (and only) marathon in San Francisco in 2012, all I could think about during the last mile was Mexican food. Luckily, my spectator fan club (my parents and two friends) were on board. I still dream about the fish taco bowl I had at Tacolicious after the race. I've tried to replicate it here, with a creatively healthy twist. Instead of beer-battered-and-fried fish, I used quinoa to crust the cod, which gives it an extra boost of protein and an addicting crunchiness. The avocado cabbage slaw works as a sauce, adding creaminess to every bite, like a glob of guacamole. And yes, *this* fish taco bowl would also be worth the 26.2 miles!

For the slaw

1 ripe avocado, pitted and peeled

¼ cup plain nonfat Greek yogurt

Juice of 2 limes

2 tablespoons chopped fresh cilantro leaves

1 garlic clove, chopped

1 serrano chile or jalapeño, seeded and chopped

½ teaspoon salt, plus more if needed

3 cups shredded napa cabbage

For the fish

1 large egg, lightly beaten

1 cup cooked white quinoa

Salt

4 (4-ounce) cod fillets

2 tablespoons extra-virgin olive oil

3 tablespoons extra-virgin olive oil

Juice of 2 limes

1 tablespoon honey

3 tablespoons chopped fresh cilantro

Fine sea salt and pepper

4 cups shredded romaine lettuce

1 large ripe mango, pitted, peeled, and cut into strips

Preheat the oven to 375 degrees. Line a baking sheet with parchment paper.

Make the slaw. In a food processor, combine the avocado, yogurt, limes, cilantro, garlic, chile, and salt. Add ¼ cup water and purée until smooth. Add a little more water as needed, 1 tablespoon at a time, to loosen. Taste and adjust the seasoning as needed.

Pour half the dressing into a large bowl. Add the cabbage and toss to coat.

Make the fish. Place the egg in a shallow medium dish or large plate. Spread out the quinoa in a separate shallow medium dish and season with salt. Dip the fish in the egg, letting any excess drip back into the bowl, then roll it through the quinoa to coat. Repeat to coat the remaining fillets.

Heat the olive oil in a large skillet over medium-high heat. When the oil is shimmering, add the coated fish and cook until well browned on the bottom, 2 to 3 minutes. Flip the fish and cook until browned on the outside and cooked through, 2 to 3 minutes more. Transfer to a paper towel–lined plate to drain.

In a large bowl, whisk together the olive oil, lime juice, honey, and cilantro. Season with salt and pepper. Add the lettuce and toss to coat.

Divide the lettuce among four bowls and top each with a fish fillet, some mango, and some slaw. Serve, passing the remaining dressing at the table.

TIP / *You can use this quinoa crusting method on chicken, pork, and even other types of fish, in this dish or any other.*

ALSO WORKS WELL WITH
Butternut Squash /
Celeriac / Kohlrabi
Turnip / Rutabaga
Sweet Potato

Not Spiralized / Saves Well
Dairy-Free

NUTRITIONAL INFORMATION
1 spaghetti squash cake + ¼ of braised short rib
Calories **606** / Fat **28g** / Sat Fat **7g** / Sodium **1208mg**
Carbs **37g** / Fiber **4g** / Sugar **24g** / Protein **52g**

GINGERY BRAISED SHORT RIBS

/ *with* / SCALLION–SPAGHETTI SQUASH CAKES

TIME TO PREPARE
2 hours

TIME TO COOK
3 hours

SERVES 4

I've only ever made short ribs braised in a tomato sauce, because I always love how the tomatoes and their juices slow-cook the short rib so it falls right off the bone. In an attempt to branch out, I started experimenting with other flavors for the short ribs and tried a gingery Asian flavor. After all, if we're eating meat, we might as well sneak a superfood (ginger!) in there. Ginger is touted as an ancient Chinese cure-all—it reduces inflammation, improves digestion, zaps away colds, and helps with nausea, to name a few benefits. These gingery braised short ribs sit on scallion–spaghetti squash cakes that absorb the extra juices from the succulent ribs.

For the short ribs

2 pounds bone-in beef short ribs, trimmed and pat dry

4 garlic cloves, minced

1½ tablespoons minced fresh ginger

½ cup low-sodium soy sauce (use coconut aminos or gluten-free tamari, if gluten-free)

Juice of 1 lime

¼ cup honey

1 teaspoon toasted sesame oil

4 scallions, chopped

1 tablespoon extra-virgin olive oil

2 large carrots, chopped

For the squash cakes

1 tablespoon plus 4 teaspoons extra-virgin olive oil, plus more as needed

1 garlic clove, minced

¼ teaspoon red pepper flakes

1½ cups cooked spaghetti squash (see page 17), squeezed of excess moisture

1 large egg

¾ cup almond flour

1 teaspoon ground ginger

2 tablespoons chopped scallions (green parts)

¼ teaspoon fine sea salt

¼ teaspoon pepper

Preheat the oven to 300 degrees.

Make the short ribs. Place the short ribs in a sealable container or zip-top bag. In a medium bowl, whisk together the garlic, ginger, soy sauce, lime juice, honey, sesame oil, half the scallions, and ¼ cup water. Pour the marinade over the ribs and seal the container or bag. Marinate in the refrigerator for at least 20 minutes or up to 2 hours.

Heat the olive oil in a large Dutch oven over medium-high heat. Using tongs, add the short ribs, reserving the marinade, and cook until browned on all sides, 10 to 15 minutes total. Transfer the ribs and any pan juices to a plate.

Add the carrots to the Dutch oven and cook, stirring occasionally, until softened, about 10 minutes. Return the short ribs and any juices from the plate to the pot and add the reserved marinade and just enough water to cover the meat (about 2 cups). Stir, then cover the pot partially. Reduce the heat to low and cook for 1½ hours. Uncover, then cook until the meat is falling off the bone, 1½ hours more.

Make the squash cakes. When the short ribs are nearly done, heat 1 tablespoon of the olive oil in a medium skillet over medium-high heat. When the oil is shimmering, add the garlic and red pepper flakes and cook until fragrant, about 1 minute. Transfer to a large bowl. Add the squash, egg, almond flour, ginger, and scallions to the bowl and mix well. Season with the salt and black pepper.

Heat 1 teaspoon of the olive oil in the same skillet over medium-high heat. When the oil is shimmering, scoop a heaping ¼ cup of the squash mixture and, using your hands, form it into a cake and add it to the skillet. Cook, pressing on the squash cake to flatten it to ¼ to ½ inch thick, until browned on the bottom, 2 to 3 minutes. Flip and cook until the other side is browned, about 2 minutes more. Transfer the cooked squash cake to a plate. Repeat with the remaining squash mixture, using 1 teaspoon of the olive oil to cook each.

Meanwhile, remove the short ribs from the Dutch oven and, using two forks or tongs, pull the meat off the bones and shred into bite-size pieces. Transfer to a serving dish.

Serve the squash cakes alongside the short ribs and carrots, and spoon over ¼ cup of the sauce from the Dutch oven.

NUTRITIONAL INFORMATION *Per serving*
Calories **276** / Fat **11g** / Sat Fat **4g** / Sodium **1511mg**
Carbs **21g** / Fiber **4g** / Sugar **14g** / Protein **34g**

SESAME SHRIMP & GREEN BEANS
/ *with* / SCALLION KOHLRABI RICE

TIME TO PREPARE
20 minutes

TIME TO COOK
15 minutes

SERVES 4

It's easy to overthink dinner. With easy access to the Internet and shelves of cookbooks, the options and flavors are limitless. When I want a healthy, filling, and flavorful dinner but don't want to spend hours crafting a creative meal, I turn to a classic stir-fry. Keeping quick-cooking proteins like shrimp in the freezer and key oils and seasonings in the pantry helps me throw together dishes like this one without having to scroll the Web for hours.

12 ounces green beans, trimmed

½ cup low-sodium soy sauce (use coconut aminos or gluten-free tamari, if gluten-free)

2 tablespoons rice vinegar

1 tablespoon grated fresh ginger

2 garlic cloves, minced

2 tablespoons toasted sesame oil

1 tablespoon honey

⅓ cup fresh orange juice (from about 2 oranges)

2 teaspoons Sriracha, or a pinch of red pepper flakes

1 pound medium shrimp, peeled, tails left on, and deveined

2 kohlrabi, peeled, spiralized with Blade D

1 tablespoon toasted sesame oil

Fine sea salt and pepper

⅓ cup chopped scallions (green parts only)

Sesame seeds, for serving (optional)

TIP / *Give this dish a sweet Hawaiian flair by adding pineapple with the scallions and stirring until the fruit heats through.*

Fill a large bowl halfway with ice. Fill a large pot halfway with water and bring to a boil over high heat. Add the green beans and cook for 5 minutes, until fork-tender. Drain the beans in a colander and set the colander over the ice to cool the beans.

In a medium bowl, whisk together the soy sauce, vinegar, ginger, garlic, sesame oil, honey, orange juice, and Sriracha. Add the shrimp to the marinade. Pat the beans dry and add them to the bowl. Toss to coat.

In a food processor, pulse the kohlrabi noodles until rice-like. Melt the coconut oil in a skillet over medium-high heat until shimmering; add the kohlrabi rice and season with salt and pepper. Cook until the kohlrabi softens, about 5 minutes. Stir in the scallions and cook for 1 minute more. Transfer to a large bowl and cover to keep warm.

Wipe the skillet clean and set it over medium-high heat. Using tongs, add the shrimp and green beans to the pan, arranging the shrimp in a single layer. Cook for 3 minutes, then flip the shrimp and cook until opaque, about 2 minutes. Transfer the shrimp to a clean bowl. Cook the green beans, tossing, until crunchy-tender, about 2 minutes longer. Transfer to the bowl with the shrimp.

Divide the rice among four bowls and top evenly with the shrimp and green beans. Sprinkle with sesame seeds, if desired, and serve.

ALSO WORKS WELL WITH
Kohlrabi

Spiralized / Gluten-Free
Dairy-Free

NUTRITIONAL INFORMATION *Per serving*
Calories **414** / Fat **17g** / Sat Fat **3g** / Sodium **410mg**
Carbs **38g** / Fiber **14g** / Sugar **9g** / Protein **33g**

TURKEY BURRITO BOWLS
/ *with* / AVOCADO JICAMA RICE

TIME TO PREPARE
20 minutes

TIME TO COOK
15 minutes

SERVES 4

For my thirtieth birthday, I flew down to my parents' home in Florida with three of my best friends, Lu, my sister, and her then fiancé (now husband). We were celebrating more than just the end of my twenties—it was also the weekend we revealed the gender of our first baby! With good vibes flowing all around, we went for a late birthday lunch at the sadly now-closed restaurant Nick & Johnnie's in Palm Beach, where I had an avocado rice bowl. Since food always summons the strongest memories for me, I'll now forever associate that joyous trip with that rice bowl—the rice mixed with smashed avocado and lime juice in every bite. Obviously, I had to spiralize it as soon as I got home. Here it is, and it is celebration-worthy indeed!

For the turkey

1 tablespoon extra-virgin olive oil

2 garlic cloves, minced

1 small jalapeño, seeded and minced

1 pound lean ground turkey

1 teaspoon ground cumin

1 teaspoon dried oregano

Fine sea salt and pepper

¾ cup frozen corn kernels, thawed

¾ cup canned black beans, drained and rinsed

For the tomato-jalapeño salad

1 medium red onion, diced

6 plum tomatoes, diced

⅓ cup chopped fresh cilantro

Juice of 1 lime

1 medium jalapeño, seeded and minced

¼ teaspoon salt

For the rice

2 small jicamas, peeled, spiralized with Blade D

Juice of 2 limes

Fine sea salt and pepper

2 ripe avocados, pitted, peeled, and smashed

Make the turkey. Heat the olive oil in a large skillet over medium-high heat. When the oil is shimmering, add the garlic and jalapeño and cook until fragrant, about 1 minute. Add the ground turkey, cumin, and oregano and season with salt and pepper. Cook, breaking up the meat with a wooden spoon as it cooks, until browned, about 7 minutes. Stir in the corn and black beans and cook until warmed through, about 2 minutes. Remove the skillet from the heat.

Meanwhile, make the tomato-jalapeño salad. In a medium bowl, combine the onion, tomatoes, cilantro, lime juice, jalapeño, and salt. Set aside.

Make the rice. Place the jicama noodles into a food processor and pulse until rice-like. Put the rice in a clean kitchen towel and gather the sides. Squeeze out excess moisture over the sink. Transfer the rice to a large bowl.

Add the lime juice and season with salt and pepper. Add the avocado and stir to combine. Taste and add more salt, if needed.

Divide the rice among four bowls and top with the turkey and tomato-jalapeño salad. Serve.

ALSO WORKS WELL WITH
Sweet Potato

Spiralized / Saves Well
Dairy-Free

NUTRITIONAL INFORMATION *Per serving*
Calories **469** / Fat **28g** / Sat Fat **7g** / Sodium **657mg**
Carbs **21g** / Fiber **5g** / Sugar **11g** / Protein **42g**

THAI CHICKEN SKEWERS
/ *with* / ZUCCHINI NOODLES IN PEANUT SAUCE

TIME TO PREPARE
25 minutes

TIME TO COOK
15 minutes

SERVES 4

Peanut sauce is a classic, and a favorite in Asian cuisine. When it coats noodles, you probably shovel them into your mouth because they have some sort of addicting flavor: that's sugar. Not only can peanut butter contain added sugars, but so can the sauce itself, making this seemingly healthy menu choice actually rather unhealthy. Thanks to some thoughtful swapping, we can have this classic combo with all the flavor and none of the processed ingredients—leaving a little extra room for dessert!

For the chicken

⅓ cup coconut cream (see Tip)

2 tablespoons chopped fresh cilantro, plus more for garnish

1 teaspoon Thai red curry paste

1 teaspoon grated fresh ginger

1 tablespoon fresh lime juice

Fine sea salt and pepper

1¼ pounds boneless, skinless chicken breasts, chopped into ¾-inch cubes

For the peanut noodles

1 teaspoon grated fresh ginger

1 garlic clove, mashed to a paste

½ cup creamy natural peanut butter

1½ tablespoons fresh lime juice

2 tablespoons low-sodium soy sauce (use coconut aminos or gluten-free tamari, if gluten-free)

1 teaspoon honey

3 medium zucchini, spiralized with Blade D, noodles trimmed

⅓ cup chopped roasted peanuts, for garnish

Make the chicken. In a medium bowl, whisk together the coconut cream, cilantro, curry paste, ginger, and lime juice. Season with salt and pepper and add the chicken. Toss to coat. Cover and marinate in the refrigerator for at least 20 minutes and up to 2 hours.

Meanwhile, make the peanut noodles. In a large bowl, whisk together the ginger, garlic, peanut butter, lime juice, soy sauce, and honey. Add the zucchini noodles and toss to coat.

Heat a grill to medium-high or heat a grill pan over medium-high heat.

Thread the chicken onto 4 skewers, dividing it evenly. Cook for 10 to 12 minutes, turning every 3 to 4 minutes, until the chicken is charred all over and no longer pink inside.

Divide the peanut noodles among four plates. Top each with a chicken skewer, garnish with extra cilantro and the peanuts, and serve.

TIP / *To get coconut cream, refrigerate a can of full-fat coconut milk overnight. Open it and scrape the solids off the top into a bowl. Discard the liquid remaining in the can. You can also just purchase canned coconut cream.*

ALSO WORKS WELL WITH
Butternut Squash /
Sweet Potato / Parsnip
Rutabaga / Zucchini

Spiralized / Gluten-Free
Paleo / Dairy-Free (opt.)

NUTRITIONAL INFORMATION *Per serving*
Calories **389** / Fat **24g** / Sat Fat **4g** / Sodium **738mg**
Carbs **22g** / Fiber **4g** / Sugar **1g** / Protein **30g**

CHICKEN SALTIMBOCCA SKILLET

/ *with* / SPINACH & ROSEMARY POTATOES

TIME TO PREPARE
15 minutes

TIME TO COOK
25 minutes

SERVES 2

Saltimbocca is an Italian dish of chicken or veal wrapped with prosciutto and sage or basil. Unless you have the time to visit a quality butcher, it can be tough to get a tender enough piece of veal, so replacing it with chicken here is easier. The salty and slightly sweet prosciutto cooks with the juices of the chicken while the rosemary-flavored potato noodles soak it all up. Served right from the skillet, this meal is perfect for an intimate date-night in.

1 boneless, skinless chicken breast, butterflied and thinly pounded

Fine sea salt and pepper

2 fresh sage leaves

2 slices prosciutto

1½ tablespoons almond flour

2 tablespoons extra-virgin olive oil

2 medium red potatoes, spiralized with Blade D, noodles trimmed

1 teaspoon fresh rosemary

½ teaspoon garlic powder

4 cups baby spinach

Grated Parmesan cheese, for garnish (optional)

Season the chicken with salt and pepper. Place a sage leaf on each piece of chicken. Place 1 slice of prosciutto on top of each chicken breast and wrap the prosciutto around the chicken, tucking it underneath the breast and pressing down to adhere. Sprinkle the top and bottom lightly with the almond flour.

Heat 1 tablespoon of the olive oil in a large skillet over medium heat. When the oil is shimmering, add the chicken and cook, turning once, until cooked through and no longer pink, about 3 minutes per side. Transfer the chicken to a plate.

Heat the remaining 1 tablespoon olive oil in the same skillet over medium-high heat. When the oil is shimmering, add the potatoes, rosemary, and garlic powder and season with salt and pepper. Cover and cook, tossing occasionally, until softened, about 10 minutes. Uncover and stir in the spinach. Create 2 wells in the noodles and nestle the chicken with juices in the wells. Cover and cook until the spinach wilts, about 2 minutes.

Uncover and serve, garnished with grated Parmesan cheese, if desired.

TIP / *If you're having trouble wrapping the chicken with the prosciutto, simply top the chicken with the prosciutto once you return it to the skillet with the cooked potato noodles.*

DESSERTS

Not Spiralized / No-Cook
Saves Well / One-Pot
Vegan / Gluten-Free
Paleo / Dairy-Free

NUTRITIONAL INFORMATION *Per serving*
Calories **304** / Fat **17g** / Sat Fat **11g** / Sodium **81mg**
Carbs **30g** / Fiber **10g** / Sugar **19g** / Protein **7g**

VEGAN
EGGNOG CHIA PUDDING

TIME TO PREPARE
10 minutes
plus 4 hours chilling

SERVES 6

You either love eggnog or you hate it—there's rarely a middle ground. I remember my mother allowing me to have the smallest pour of eggnog when I was a little girl, a true treat. It made me want it even more, but once I was older and realized what was in it (raw eggs, sugar, whole milk, and cream), I was less interested. This vegan chia pudding version has that familiar nutmeg kick, but with much cleaner ingredients. You can enjoy a whole serving and still feel nourished and festive.

1 (14-ounce) can full-fat coconut milk

2 cups unsweetened almond milk

¾ cup chia seeds

½ cup pure maple syrup

½ teaspoon vanilla extract

Pinch of salt

½ teaspoon freshly grated nutmeg, plus more for serving

In a large bowl, whisk together the coconut milk, almond milk, chia seeds, maple syrup, vanilla, salt, and nutmeg. Pour or ladle into six small serving bowls or glass jars and refrigerate for at least 4 hours or up to overnight, until set.

Garnish each with a little more grated nutmeg before serving.

TIP / *This pudding can double as a sweet breakfast. Make the recipe in the evening and let the pudding sit overnight—you'll wake up and it'll be like Christmas morning!*

Not Spiralized / No-Cook
Saves Well / Vegan
Dairy-Free / Low-Cal

NUTRITIONAL INFORMATION *Per pop*
Calories **264** / Fat **22g** / Sat Fat **4g** / Sodium **75mg**
Carbs **11g** / Fiber **2g** / Sugar **7g** / Protein **7g**

CAKE BATTER POPS

TIME TO PREPARE
15 minutes,
plus 5 hours to freeze

MAKES 4 POPS

Whenever I go out for frozen yogurt with Lu, we always get the cake batter flavors and add little balls of cookie dough on top. This healthier ice pop version uses pure ingredients to healthfully mimic our favorite frozen yogurt flavor. And the couple that eats healthy together stays together, right?

¼ cup natural cashew butter or almond butter

¼ cup roasted coconut butter

1 tablespoon pure maple syrup

½ teaspoon vanilla extract

Pinch of salt

1 cup coconut yogurt (or vanilla Greek yogurt, if not vegan)

In a medium bowl, mix together the cashew butter, coconut butter, maple syrup, vanilla, and salt. Add the coconut yogurt and stir to combine. Divide the mixture evenly among four ½-cup ice pop molds. Insert sticks into the molds.

Freeze the ice pops for at least 5 hours.

When ready to serve, run the molds under warm water to help release the pops. Serve immediately.

TIP / *There are lots of ice pop molds out there—some have the sticks attached (which is what I use), some have slots for the sticks, and some don't! If your sticks don't stand up immediately after pouring the batter into the molds, let the pops freeze for about 1 hour before inserting the sticks.*

Not Spiralized / Vegan
Gluten-Free / Paleo
Dairy-Free

NUTRITIONAL INFORMATION *Per shake*
Calories **331** / Fat **9g** / Sat Fat **5g** / Sodium **113mg**
Carbs **64g** / Fiber **11g** / Sugar **46g** / Protein **5g**

RED VELVET BEET SHAKE
/ *with* / CACAO NIBS

TIME TO PREPARE
10 minutes

SERVES 2

Red velvet is my favorite flavor in baked goods—cupcakes, cakes, cookies, brownies—and now in this dessert shake! A cross between a smoothie bowl and a milk shake, this treat will satisfy your sweet tooth while nourishing your body. Blended with real, healthy ingredients, it has a beautiful red color and a just-sweet-enough flavor. The cacao nibs make for a crunchy, semi-sweet topping. Serve this in a glass and drink it, or serve it in a bowl with a spoon!

1 cup unsweetened almond milk

1 large frozen banana

1 cup ice cubes

1 small beet, cubed

½ cup frozen raspberries

4 dates, pitted

3 tablespoons cacao nibs

In a blender, combine the almond milk, banana, ice, beet, raspberries, dates, and 2 tablespoons of the cacao nibs. Purée until smooth.

Divide the shake between two glasses or bowls. Sprinkle evenly with the remaining 1 tablespoon cocoa nibs before serving.

TIP / *For an added crunch, top with crumbled pecan halves.*

Not Spiralized / Vegetarian
Gluten-Free / Paleo
Dairy-Free / No-Cook
Low-Cal

NUTRITIONAL INFORMATION *Per serving*
Calories **212** / Fat **4g** / Sat Fat **3g** / Sodium **9mg**
Carbs **46g** / Fiber **3g** / Sugar **39g** / Protein **3g**

WATERMELON DESSERT PIZZA

TIME TO PREPARE
15 minutes

SERVES 8

When I first saw my friend Gina from the popular food blog *Skinnytaste* make savory watermelon "pizzas" with feta cheese and balsamic vinegar, I thought it was so creative and brilliant. What this dish has in common with traditional pizza is just that it's meant to be eaten in slices, topped with whatever you desire. I went in the opposite direction from Gina and made it into a dessert, topped with whipped coconut cream and berries. When it's the middle of the summer and you want to serve something refreshing and sweet, this is it!

1 small watermelon

Coconut cream from 1 (14.5-ounce) can full-fat coconut milk (see Tip, page 255)

Zest of 1 lime

Pinch of salt

1½ to 2 cups seasonal berries, sliced if large, for topping

¼ cup honey

⅓ cup torn fresh mint or basil leaves

Slice two 1-inch-thick rounds out of the center of the watermelon. Reserve the rest of the melon for another use.

In a medium bowl using a handheld mixer, beat the coconut cream, lime zest, and salt until fluffy and spreadable. Spread the cream over the watermelon rounds, leaving a 1-inch border all around.

Arrange the berries on top in a pretty pattern and drizzle with the honey. Scatter over the mint or basil leaves. Slice each watermelon round into 4 wedges and serve.

TIP / *If pressed for time, use vanilla-flavored Greek yogurt instead of preparing the coconut cream.*

Not Spiralized / Saves Well
Vegetarian / Gluten-Free
Low-Cal

NUTRITIONAL INFORMATION *Per serving*
Calories **124** / Fat **5g** / Sat Fat **3g** / Sodium **229mg**
Carbs **20g** / Fiber **4g** / Sugar **9g** / Protein **5g**

MEXICAN HOT CHOCOLATE BROWNIES

TIME TO PREPARE
15 minutes

TIME TO COOK
35 minutes

SERVES 12

Mexican hot chocolate is a twist on your classic hot chocolate drink. It's prepared with a variety of spices (like cayenne pepper) for a more robust flavor and spicy kick with every sip. With these brownies, you get that same kick in every *bite*. These brownies taste even better with some cold, sweet ice cream, like the Avocado Ice Cream on page 269, to balance the subtle spice from the cayenne. Consider yourself warned: the sweet-and-spicy combination is super addictive!

1 (15-ounce) can black beans, drained and rinsed

3 large eggs

1 ripe banana, mashed

1 tablespoon coconut oil, melted and cooled to room temperature

½ cup raw cacao powder

¼ teaspoon ground cinnamon

¼ teaspoon cayenne pepper

½ teaspoon baking powder

¼ teaspoon baking soda

¼ teaspoon salt

1 teaspoon vanilla extract

⅓ cup pure maple syrup

⅓ cup vegan chocolate chips (I like Enjoy Life brand)

Ice cream, for serving (optional)

Preheat the oven to 350 degrees. Line an 8-inch square baking pan with parchment paper.

In a high-speed blender or food processor, combine the black beans, eggs, banana, coconut oil, cacao powder, cinnamon, cayenne, baking powder, baking soda, salt, vanilla, and maple syrup and blend until smooth. Add the chocolate chips and pulse just to incorporate. Transfer the brownie batter to the prepared pan and spread it evenly.

Bake for 25 to 35 minutes, until a toothpick inserted into the center comes out clean. Transfer the pan to a wire rack to cool for at least 15 minutes.

Cut the brownies into 12 squares. Top with ice cream before serving, if desired.

TIP / *If you're not going to serve these with ice cream, try topping with a dollop of coconut cream, or melt ½ cup vegan chocolate chips and drizzle the chocolate over the finished brownies in the baking pan for extra moisture before cutting and serving.*

NUTRITIONAL INFORMATION *Per serving*
Calories **340** / Fat **25g** / Sat Fat **3g** / Sodium **183mg**
Carbs **27g** / Fiber **3g** / Sugar **17g** / Protein **8g**

GRAIN-FREE

ORANGE-OLIVE OIL CAKE

TIME TO PREPARE
15 minutes

TIME TO COOK
25 minutes

MAKES ONE 9-INCH CAKE (SERVES 6)

As much as I love chocolate, my heart is with yellow cakes. A slice of pound cake or olive oil cake is my favorite. Chocolate and frosting can taste too sweet, especially if you're regularly eating less-processed foods. You start to appreciate the sweet notes in vegetables, and really enjoy fruit for its natural sugars. This olive oil cake has a beautiful balance of sweet and savory, thanks to the citrus, honey, and almond extract.

Baking spray

1½ cups almond flour

⅓ cup tapioca starch

1 teaspoon baking powder

¼ teaspoon baking soda

¼ teaspoon salt

Zest of 1 orange

⅓ cup honey, plus more for serving

¼ cup extra-virgin olive oil, plus more for greasing

2 large eggs

½ teaspoon pure almond extract

Sliced oranges, for serving

Preheat the oven to 325 degrees with a rack in the center position. Spray an 8-inch round cake pan with cooking spray and line the bottom with parchment paper cut to fit. Spray the paper with baking spray.

In a large bowl, whisk together the almond flour, tapioca starch, baking powder, baking soda, salt, and orange zest.

In a small bowl, whisk together the honey, olive oil, eggs, and almond extract. Stir the wet ingredients into the dry ingredients. Scrape the batter into the prepared pan and smooth the top.

Bake the cake, rotating the pan halfway through, for 25 to 30 minutes, until a toothpick inserted into the center of the cake comes out clean. Let cool in the pan for 10 minutes. Invert the cake onto a wire rack and peel off the parchment paper. Let cool completely.

Drizzle the cake with honey before cutting. Serve with slices of orange.

Not Spiralized / No-Cook
Saves Well / Vegan
Dairy-Free / Gluten-Free
Paleo / Low-Cal

NUTRITIONAL INFORMATION *Per serving (about 2 small scoops)*
Calories **172** / Fat **13g** / Sat Fat **7g** / Sodium **9mg**
Carbs **13g** / Fiber **3g** / Sugar **9g** / Protein **1g**

MINT CHOCOLATE CHIP
AVOCADO ICE CREAM

TIME TO PREPARE
5 hours

TIME TO COOK
35 minutes

SERVES 12

When my mother first discovered spiralizing, she was trying out raw veganism to help manage her blood sugar levels, as she's a type 1 diabetic. As part of that diet, she stumbled upon mint chocolate chip avocado ice cream and made it for me on several occasions when I visited her. I was always blown away by how creamy, minty, and subtly sweet it was. Thanks to my mother again for discovering another game-changing food. Moms really do know best!

Coconut cream from 2 (14.5-ounce) cans full-fat coconut milk (see Tip, page 255)

4 ripe avocados, pitted and peeled

½ cup pure maple syrup

2 tablespoons coconut oil

1 teaspoon pure mint extract

½ cup cacao nibs

12 fresh mint leaves, for garnish (optional)

TIP / *For extra decadence, melt ½ cup vegan chocolate chips and drizzle the chocolate over the ice cream.*

Line a 9 × 5-inch loaf pan with parchment paper.

In a high-speed blender, combine the coconut cream, avocado, maple syrup, coconut oil, and mint extract. Blend until smooth and creamy. Stir in the cacao nibs.

Pour the ice cream mixture into the prepared pan and freeze for at least 5 hours.

Place 2 or 3 scoops of ice cream in each bowl. Garnish with fresh mint, if desired, and serve.

Not Spiralized / Saves Well
Gluten-Free / Vegetarian

NUTRITIONAL INFORMATION *Per serving*
Calories **387** / Fat **27g** / Sat Fat **20g** / Sodium **135mg**
Carbs **32g** / Fiber **4g** / Sugar **25g** / Protein **6g**

CHOCOLATE AQUAFABA MOUSSE

TIME TO PREPARE
20 minutes

TIME TO COOK
35 minutes

SERVES 12

〰 〰 〰

Every Valentine's Day, I like to make a dessert for Lu and me to come home to after dinner out. The dessert has to be something that can be prepared ahead, something that's not too heavy that will leave us belly-up on the couch. That's not very romantic! One year, after learning about aquafaba, the liquid in a can of chickpeas, I used it for a chocolate mousse! This dessert is meant to be savored and enjoyed—whether it's your Valentine's Day date or you just want to indulge after a long day in your PJs!

For the cake

Cooking spray

8 ounces vegan semisweet chocolate chips

¾ cup melted coconut oil

½ cup raw cacao powder

½ teaspoon sea salt

2 teaspoons vanilla extract

½ cup pure maple syrup

6 large eggs

For the mousse

6 ounces vegan semisweet chocolate chips

Aquafaba from 2 (15-ounce) cans chickpeas (see Tip)

5 tablespoons pure maple syrup

2½ teaspoons vanilla extract

Pinch of sea salt

Preheat the oven to 325 degrees. Grease a 9-inch springform pan or a cake pan with baking spray.

Make the cake. Melt the chocolate and coconut oil together in a medium saucepan over low heat, stirring continuously until melted and combined. Remove from the heat and whisk in the cacao powder, salt, vanilla, and maple syrup until the cacao has dissolved and the mixture is thickened. Scrape the mixture into a medium bowl and let cool for 5 minutes.

In a small bowl, beat the eggs. Gradually pour the eggs into the chocolate mixture, whisking well to form a thick batter.

Pour the batter into the prepared pan and smooth the top. Bake for 35 to 40 minutes, until a toothpick inserted into the center of the cake comes out nearly clean and the edges are firm. The cake might rise unevenly in the oven, but don't worry, it will fall so it's more even afterward. Transfer the cake to a rack and let cool to room temperature.

Prepare the mousse. While the cake bakes, melt the chocolate in a small saucepan over low heat, stirring continuously until melted. Remove from the heat and let cool.

In the bowl of a stand mixer fitted with the whisk attachment, whip the aquafaba on medium-high speed for 12 to 15 minutes, until it holds medium-stiff peaks. (Alternatively, whip the aquafaba in a medium bowl using a handheld mixer, although this won't work as effectively as a stand mixer.) With the machine running, add the maple syrup, vanilla, and salt, whipping until combined. Gently fold in the melted chocolate and stir to combine well.

Spread the mousse over the cooled cake while still in the pan. Refrigerate for 3 to 4 hours to set. (If refrigerated for more than 4 hours, let the cake sit out for 10 to 15 minutes to soften before serving.)

When ready to serve, carefully release the cake from the pan onto a serving platter or cake stand, slice, and serve.

Not Spiralized / No-Cook
Saves Well / Vegan
Gluten-Free / Paleo
Dairy-Free

NUTRITIONAL INFORMATION *Per serving*
Calories **365** / Fat **23g** / Sat Fat **10g** / Sodium **60mg**
Carbs **36g** / Fiber **4g** / Sugar **26g** / Protein **7g**

NO-BAKE VEGAN CHEESECAKE

/ *with* / **POMEGRANATE**

TIME TO PREPARE
30 minutes
plus 6 hours soaking
and 3 hours chilling

**MAKES ONE 8-INCH
CAKE (SERVES 12)**

ⓐ ⓐ ⓐ

A cheesecake without cream cheese? You will be amazed. With a beautiful warm pink pomegranate layer on top, an impeccably sweetened cashew-based cheesecake layer in the middle, and a sweet, dark, walnut-chocolate crust, this dessert is one you'll want to display at a party on one of those adorable cake stands. This well-balanced cheesecake is meant to be shared and admired for its elegant presentation and, thus, excessively Instagrammed.

For the crust

1½ cups walnuts

10 dates, pitted

¼ cup raw cacao powder

¼ teaspoon salt

For the filling

3 cups raw cashews, soaked for at least 6 hours, drained, and rinsed

½ cup coconut cream (see Tip, page 255)

½ cup pure maple syrup

½ cup fresh lemon juice (from about 3 lemons)

¼ cup coconut oil, melted

For the topping

½ cup coconut cream (see Tip, page 255)

¼ cup pomegranate juice, no sugar added

¼ cup frozen raspberries

1 tablespoon chia seeds

1 teaspoon pure maple syrup

Pomegranate seeds, for serving

Make the crust. In a food processor, combine the walnuts, dates, cacao powder, and salt and pulse until a dough forms. Press the dough into the bottom of an 8-inch springform pan or round cake pan and refrigerate while you make the filling.

Make the filling. In a high-speed blender or food processor, combine the soaked cashews, coconut cream, maple syrup, lemon juice, and coconut oil and blend until very smooth, stopping to scrape down the sides as needed. Pour the filling into the chilled crust and smooth the top. Freeze for 30 minutes, until chilled. Clean out the blender jar or food processor bowl and blade.

Make the topping. In the blender or food processor, combine the coconut cream, pomegranate juice, raspberries, chia seeds, and maple syrup and blend until smooth. Pour the topping over the cheesecake and freeze until the cheesecake is firm, about 1 hour.

Unlatch the springform ring to see if it pulls away from the sides of the cake. (If it doesn't, freeze the cake for 30 minutes more and test again.) Relatch the ring and refrigerate the cake until it's easy to cut, at least 2 hours or up to 3 days.

Sprinkle the cheesecake with pomegranate seeds, then slice and serve.

ACKNOWLEDGMENTS

I feel like I'm still in the honeymoon phase, and I don't mean that about my marriage (although that's true, too!)—I mean that about Inspiralized. I'm often asked, "How do you have so much energy to do everything you do?" My honest answer? The energy comes from gratitude: I truly love what I do—I love getting to build recipes to make healthy eating more approachable, accessible, and less overwhelming for thousands of people. I'm humbled to be able to share my journey with these people every day. I'm absolutely uplifted by such an amazing community, and without them, books number 1, 2, and now 3 would never have happened. So thank you to each and every one of my Inspiralized readers—you're just as much a part of this as I am!

I have a lot of other people to thank for this gorgeous book you're holding:

To the CLARKSON POTTER TEAM for continuing to believe in me and Inspiralized. Without your vision and dedication to growing my brand, this cookbook would never be in the hands of so many inspired cooks. Doris, thank you for giving me yet another chance at Inspiralizing the world. Jana, Natasha, and Carly, thank you for giving this book the opportunity to reach more and more people. And to everyone supporting me backstage (Stephanie, Mia, Laura, Mark, Alex, Nick, and Heather), I couldn't have done it without your expertise and guidance.

Special thanks are in order for my editor, AMANDA ENGLANDER. Thank you for broadening my horizons with the theme of this cookbook and for taking me out of my comfort zone to create something truly special. You challenge me and push me to my creative limits, while respecting my vision, and I'm so happy we found our groove. No one works under pressure like we do, and I'm grateful to have you along for that journey!

ALYSSA REUBEN, you are a real Inspiralized pioneer! Each project is better and better having you in my corner. I sleep easier knowing I can always come to you. I'm excited to see where this new direction with Inspiralized & Beyond brings me!

To the PHOTOGRAPHY TEAM—when I didn't think I could be any more impressed after two stunning cookbooks, you've blown me away. Evan Sung, thank you for once again running the show and putting everyone at ease on set. I looked forward to every day of the shoot, knowing my recipes would come to life thanks to your brilliant way of capturing food. Carla Gonzalez-Hart, you hustled even while seven months pregnant and proved that artists work from a place of passion and true talent. Andrea Greco, it was a blast having you on set. Kate Schmidt, from every sprinkle of kosher salt to each tweezer removal of wilted herbs, you made the food look better than I could ever imagine it could. Thank you for all the little tweaks that added beauty to every shot—and congrats on the marriage!

KRISTIN DONNELLY, thank you for racing with me to the very finish! All of your suggestions, modifications, and responses to my frantic text messages made this book sing! I couldn't be happier with how all of the recipes turned out.

LAURA ARNOLD, thank you again for your help testing the spiralized recipes in this cookbook.

MEAGHAN, I mean it when I say you're a lifesaver. Whether we're Gchatting all day long or you're sitting next to me in the office, I feel like the Inspiralized team is strong and we are growing this brand into a true household name together! Work is more fun with you there. Thank you for believing in Inspiralized even "off the clock" and always managing to get everything done—I don't know how we do it, but I love our little two-woman show!

GRAMS, the past year has been the toughest our family has ever had to face with the loss of Poppy. As devastating as it has been to go through, we've gone through it together, as we always do. You and Pops will always inspire me, and whenever I think of you two together, I'm filled with nothing but happiness and love. I know Pops is looking down now and overjoyed to see you as a great-grandmother! I love you, Grams.

FELICIA, by the time this book is published, you'll be a married woman! Although Ben may not love vegetables as much as you and I do, he's always been such a supporter of Inspiralized, and for that he's a keeper. I love you so much and am so proud of you—as a friend, a sister, a daughter, and Aunt Feef! Cheers to having fun together while keeping healthy, always.

DAD, you've graduated to a grandpa! I couldn't be more excited for my baby boy to get to know his "Poppy." I've loved seeing you enjoy spiralized veggies and healthy food more and more each year, and I know Mom will be cooking you plenty of the recipes from this book to totally convert you into a health nut! Thank you for continuing to support me at every stage of life. I love you.

MOM, I'll always have to give you credit for discovering spiralizing and introducing me to it, but this time around, I want to thank you for inspiring me to go *beyond* Inspiralized. You always encourage my creativity, support me with all of my ideas, and fight for me when I need that extra support. I love the corny quotes you text me, and I'll never stop counting down the "sleeps" to our visits! I couldn't have survived the photo shoot without you; I loved having you there to take care of Luca—he loves you so much! I hope to be the type of mother to our baby boy as you were to me: the best! I love you more.

LU, you win husband of the year every year we're married. Thank you for everything. Thank you for doing the dishes (almost) every night. Thank you for making me laugh constantly and making even the most mundane of days exciting. Thank you for inspiring me to be a better friend, daughter, sister, wife, and person. Thank you for encouraging me to push myself as an entrepreneur and being such an inspirational one yourself (a shout-out to the New Tradition team for crushing it!). Thank you for bragging to every person you meet about Inspiralized—I'm finally convinced you're my #1 fan (sorry, Mom!). But above all else, thank you for giving me the greatest gift of all: our baby boy, Luca.

APPENDIX A:
RECIPES BY CATEGORY

	SPIRALIZED	NOT SPIRALIZED	VEGAN	VEGETARIAN	GLUTEN-FREE	PALEO	DAIRY-FREE	DAIRY-FREE (OPT.)	LOW-CAL	NO-COOK	SAVES WELL	ONE-POT
Spiralized Cantaloupe & Blackberry Greek Yogurt Bowl with Goji Berry Granola	●			●	●							
No-Bake Greek Yogurt Tart with Date-Pecan Crust		●		●	●					●	●	
Apple Pie Smoothie Bowl		●		●	●	●	●			●		
Carrot Cake Breakfast Cookies		●		●	●	●	●				●	
Baked PB&J Oatmeal with Chia Raspberry Jam		●	●	●	●						●	
Apple French Toast with Cinnamon Streusel		●	●	●	●		●					
Autumn Brussels Sprout Quiche with Sweet Potato Crust		●		●	●			●	●		●	
Flourless Breakfast Crêpes with Peaches & Sunflower Butter		●		●	●		●		●			
Cinnamon-Raisin Sweet Potato Bagels with Maple Cashew Cream Cheese	●			●	●	●	●		●		●	
Huevos Rancheros with Blender Plantain Tortillas		●		●	●			●				
Breakfast Blender Plantain Tortillas		●		●	●	●	●		●			
Zucchini Crust Breakfast Pizza with Arugula & Sweet Peppers		●		●	●							
Delicata Squash Egg Cup Bake with Lentils & Feta		●		●	●							
Vegetarian Breakfast Quesadilla		●		●								
Cheesy Squashbrown Skillet with Bacon & Eggs		●		●					●			
Sheet Pan Omelet with Spiralized Bell Peppers, Onions & Ham	●				●	●	●		●			
Eggs Benedict with Avocado Hollandaise & Parsnip Cakes	●			●	●		●					
Sesame Bagel Yucca with Scrambled Eggs & Garlicky Chard		●		●	●	●	●					

	SPIRALIZED	NOT SPIRALIZED	VEGAN	VEGETARIAN	GLUTEN-FREE	PALEO	DAIRY-FREE	DAIRY-FREE (OPT.)	LOW-CAL	NO-COOK	SAVES WELL	ONE-POT
Parsnip Eggs-in-a-Hole	●			●	●	●	●					
Three-Ingredient Matcha Pancakes with Toasted Coconut		●		●	●	●	●		●			
Margherita-style Charred Broccoli Slabs		●		●	●				●		●	●
Salt & Vinegar Spiralized Potatoes	●		●		●	●	●		●		●	
Artichoke & Olive Sausages with Hummus		●		●			●		●			
Any-Veggie Tots		●		●	●				●		●	
Smoky, Savory Brussels Sprouts Mini Sliders with Tofu		●	●				●		●			
Sweet Potato Skin Nachos		●		●	●							
Lime-Jicama Chips with Cashew Dip		●	●	●		●	●		●	●		
Whole Roasted Smashed Kohlrabi with Thyme & Garlic		●		●	●			●	●			
Soy-Glazed Roasted Cabbage Steaks with Edamame Purée		●	●				●					
Cucumber Summer Rolls with Avocado Mash		●	●		●	●	●			●		
Tomato Tartare with Garlic-Rosemary Flaxseed Crackers		●	●		●	●	●		●			
Pistachio & Cranberry Vegan Cheese Ball with Endive Chips		●	●		●	●	●		●	●	●	
Ricotta & Fig Golden Beet Crostini with Honey		●			●				●	●		
Cauliflower Pretzel Rings with Mustard		●		●	●	●						
Cheesy Cauliflower Biscuits		●		●	●				●		●	
Mini Wedge Salads with Tofu Bacon Bits & Hearts of Palm Dressing		●	●				●		●			
Zucchini Pork Dumplings		●							●		●	
Tuscan White Bean & Chard Soup with Celeriac Rice	●			●	●			●			●	
Chorizo & Chickpea Stew with Kohlrabi	●				●		●				●	
Stracciatella Soup with Broccoli Noodles	●			●	●				●			●
Chicken Chili Stew with Jicama Noodles	●				●		●				●	●
Hearts of Palm Ceviche		●	●		●	●	●		●	●	●	●

	SPIRALIZED	NOT SPIRALIZED	VEGAN	VEGETARIAN	GLUTEN-FREE	PALEO	DAIRY-FREE	DAIRY-FREE (OPT.)	LOW-CAL	NO-COOK	SAVES WELL	ONE-POT
Beef Pho with Zucchini Noodles	•				•	•	•		•			
Buffalo Cauliflower Salad with Avocado & Vegan Ranch		•	•		•	•	•					
French Onion Soup with Rutabaga		•			•							
Mediterranean Zucchini Pasta Salad	•			•	•		•			•		•
Cacio e Pepe Kale with Fried Egg		•		•	•							
Corn Chowder Salad with Bacon & Potatoes	•				•		•				•	
Spicy Pork Coconut Curry Soup with Daikon Noodles	•				•	•	•					
Beet Poké Bowl with Seaweed		•	•				•		•			
Thai Cashew Chopped Salad with Sesame-Garlic Dressing	•			•			•				•	
Chickpea "Tuna" Salad with Avocado & Sunflower Seeds		•	•		•		•		•	•		
Kielbasa & Sauerkraut Sandwiches on Potato "Buns"	•				•	•	•		•			
Open-Faced Roasted Veggie & Havarti Rutabaga Melts		•		•	•				•			
Vegetarian Meatball Sub in Zucchini		•		•	•				•			
Sweet Potato Waffle Grilled Cheese	•			•	•				•			
Open-Faced Red Cabbage Reuben	•			•	•				•			
BLT Sweet Potato Sliders with Cilantro Lime Avocado Mayo		•			•	•	•		•			
Philly Cheesesteaks in Bell Pepper Cups	•				•						•	
Teriyaki Eggplant Nori Burrito Roll		•		•			•		•			
Collard Green Fajita Wraps with Black Bean–Avo Mash	•		•		•		•		•			
Mushroom-Walnut Larb in Lettuce Cups		•	•			•	•				•	
Potato Toast with Green Pea–Avocado Mash, Shaved Egg & Radishes		•		•	•		•		•			
Spaghetti al Tonno with Celeriac Noodles	•				•	•	•					
Spicy Shrimp Cabbage Pad Thai	•						•					

	SPIRALIZED	NOT SPIRALIZED	VEGAN	VEGETARIAN	GLUTEN-FREE	PALEO	DAIRY-FREE	DAIRY-FREE (OPT.)	LOW-CAL	NO-COOK	SAVES WELL	ONE-POT
Crab Fra Diavolo with Fennel Noodles		●			●	●	●		●			
Rutabaga Noodle Vegetable Stir-Fry	●						●		●		●	
Spicy Broccoli, Quinoa & Sausage Pasta with Parmesan	●				●			●			●	
Shredded Brussels Sprouts Carbonara with Peas & Pancetta		●			●				●			
Spaghetti Squash Fideos with Shrimp & Chorizo		●			●	●	●		●			
Lemon-Grilled Baby Artichokes with Asparagus Noodles		●		●								
Fajita Night Pasta with Chicken Sausage	●				●	●	●				●	
Long Bean Noodles with Scallion-Ginger Sauce & Tofu		●		●			●		●			
Mexican Corn & Chicken Chayote Pasta	●				●							
Spiralized Tuna Tataki Bowl with Grilled Avocado	●				●							
Roasted Garlic Celeriac Pasta Primavera with White Bean Sauce	●		●		●				●			
Eggplant Rolls with Chicken Shawarma & Tahini Drizzle		●				●	●		●		●	
Ricotta & Spinach Spaghetti Pie	●			●	●						●	
Shepherd's Pie with Celeriac & Butternut Squash Crust	●				●	●	●				●	
Inside-Out Moussaka		●			●			●			●	
Croque Monsieur Parsnip Gratin		●			●						●	
Spanakopita Bake with Potato Crust		●		●	●						●	
Collard Green Manicotti		●		●	●						●	
Lentil Meat Loaf with BBQ Sauce & Cauliflower Mash		●	●		●		●		●		●	
Pumpkin-Sage "Gnocchi" Bake		●		●	●				●		●	
Cabbage-Wrapped Veggie Enchiladas		●		●	●				●		●	
Rainbow Lasagna with Beets, Sweet Potato & Pesto	●			●	●						●	
Chicken Fried Daikon Rice Casserole	●						●				●	●

	SPIRALIZED	NOT SPIRALIZED	VEGAN	VEGETARIAN	GLUTEN-FREE	PALEO	DAIRY-FREE	DAIRY-FREE (OPT.)	LOW-CAL	NO-COOK	SAVES WELL	ONE-POT
Saag Paneer–Stuffed Mushrooms		●		●	●							
Portobello Mushroom Bulgogi Bowls		●		●			●				●	
Tahini-Marinated Sunchokes with Cauliflower Couscous & Tomato-Cucumber Salad		●	●		●	●	●				●	
Southwest BBQ Jackfruit Bowls	●		●		●		●					
Cauliflower Steaks & Chimichurri with Corn Succotash		●	●		●		●				●	
Vegan Tacos with Jicama Shells		●	●		●		●			●	●	
Hoisin Pulled Hearts of Palm with Stuffed Sweet Potatoes & Ginger-Lime Slaw		●		●			●				●	
Sweet & Sour Whole Roasted Radish Meatballs with Sesame Vegetables		●	●				●					
Split Pea Dal in Curry-Roasted Acorn Squash Cups		●	●		●						●	
Sweet Corn Polenta with Caponata & Feta		●		●	●						●	
Falafel Waffle with Cumin Tzatziki		●		●	●						●	
Veggie Quinoa–Chili Stuffed 8-Ball Zucchini		●	●		●						●	
Sicilian Bianca Pizza with Shredded Broccoli & Olives	●			●	●						●	
Winter Harvest Bowl with Butternut Squash & Maple-Tahini Dressing	●			●	●	●	●					
Summer Harvest Bowls with Grilled Peach, Burrata & Cucumber	●			●	●				●	●		
Zucchini Fritters with Sunflower Tzatziki	●			●	●		●					
Yucca Tostadas with Veggies	●			●	●			●			●	
Socca Flatbread with White Bean Spread & Caramelized Leeks		●	●		●				●			
Pepperoni Pizza–Stuffed Hasselback Zucchini		●			●				●			
Baked Halibut with Tomato Herb Broth and Summer Squash Noodles	●				●		●		●			
Thai Chia Fish Cakes with Bok Choy & Coconut-Ginger Broth		●					●					
Pork Tenderloin with Spiralized Maple & Thyme Roasted Carrots & Parsnips	●				●	●	●				●	

	SPIRALIZED	NOT SPIRALIZED	VEGAN	VEGETARIAN	GLUTEN-FREE	PALEO	DAIRY-FREE	DAIRY-FREE (OPT.)	LOW-CAL	NO-COOK	SAVES WELL	ONE-POT
Brussels Sprouts Latkes with Salmon & Lemon-Dijon Sauce		•			•	•	•					
Spicy Cumin Lamb Meatballs & Cucumber with Herbed Tahini-Yogurt Sauce	•				•							
Roast Chicken & Butternut Squash Pasta with Wilted Greens & Mushroom Gravy	•				•	•	•				•	
Pork Milanese with Burst Tomatoes & Zucchini Noodles	•				•	•	•					
Fish Taco Bowls		•			•							
Gingery Braised Short Ribs with Scallion–Spaghetti Squash Cakes		•					•				•	
Sesame Shrimp & Green Beans with Scallion Kohlrabi Rice	•						•		•			
Turkey Burrito Bowls with Avocado Jicama Rice	•				•		•					
Thai Chicken Skewers with Zucchini Noodles in Peanut Sauce	•						•				•	
Chicken Saltimbocca Skillet with Spinach & Rosemary Potatoes	•				•	•		•				
Vegan Eggnog Chia Pudding		•	•		•	•	•			•	•	•
Cake Batter Pops		•	•				•		•	•	•	
Red Velvet Beet Shake with Cacao Nibs		•	•		•	•	•					
Watermelon Dessert Pizza		•		•	•	•	•		•	•		
Mexican Hot Chocolate Brownies		•		•	•				•		•	
Grain-Free Orange–Olive Oil Cake		•		•			•				•	
Mint Chocolate Chip Avocado Ice Cream		•	•		•		•		•	•	•	
Chocolate Aquafaba Mousse Flourless Cake		•		•	•						•	
No-Bake Vegan Cheesecake with Pomegranate		•	•		•	•	•			•	•	

APPENDIX B:
BEST FRUITS & VEGETABLES
FOR SPIRALIZING

There are 25 to 30 different fruits and veggies you can spiralize. The most common are:

APPLE

BEET

BELL PEPPER

BROCCOLI

BUTTERNUT SQUASH

CABBAGE

CARROT

CELERIAC

CHAYOTE

CUCUMBER

JICAMA

KOHLRABI

ONION

PARSNIP

PEAR

RADISH

RUTABAGA

SWEET POTATO

TURNIP

WHITE POTATO

ZUCCHINI AND
SUMMER SQUASH

There are certain vegetables and fruits that can be spiralized, but aren't used as noodle alternatives—they're spiralized as a beautiful garnish or a more fun shape. Some of these include:

CANTALOUPE—spiralize cantaloupe to add a twist to a salad

LEMONS, LIMES, AND ORANGES—spiralize a citrus fruit to infuse water or use as a garnish in a cocktail

PINEAPPLE—spiralize a pineapple to yield thin slices to use as a snack or dessert

INDEX